An Undevotional

An Undevotional

Jesus is Still Speaking Through the Gospel of Luke

JIMMY R. WATSON

WIPF & STOCK · Eugene, Oregon

AN UNDEVOTIONAL
Jesus is Still Speaking Through the Gospel of Luke

Copyright © 2019 Jimmy R. Watson. All rights reserved. Except for brief quotations in critical publications or reviews, no part of this book may be reproduced in any manner without prior written permission from the publisher. Write: Permissions, Wipf and Stock Publishers, 199 W. 8th Ave., Suite 3, Eugene, OR 97401.

Wipf & Stock
An Imprint of Wipf and Stock Publishers
199 W. 8th Ave., Suite 3
Eugene, OR 97401

www.wipfandstock.com

PAPERBACK ISBN: 978-1-5326-7358-0
HARDCOVER ISBN: 978-1-5326-7359-7
EBOOK ISBN: 978-1-5326-7360-3

Manufactured in the U.S.A.   MARCH 7, 2019

I dedicate this book to my late father, Louis, who didn't have a devotional bone in his body, and yet became our family's peacemaker.

Contents

Introduction | ix

Luke 1:26–35 | 1
Luke 1:39–44 | 10
Luke 2:4–11 | 14
Luke 2:25–27 | 27
Luke 2:41–51 | 32
Luke 3:2b–6 | 37
Luke 3:21–22 | 41
Luke 4:1–13 | 45
Luke 4:16–30 | 49
Luke 5:1–11 | 63
Luke 6:20–26 | 67
Luke 6:27–38 | 74
Luke 7:36–50 | 79
Luke 8:26–29 | 86
Luke 9:28–36 | 90
Luke 9:57–62 | 94
Luke 10:1–4 | 102
Luke 10:9b | 104
Luke 10:25–37 | 108
Luke 10:38–42 | 116
Luke 11:1–13 | 123

LUKE 12:13–31 | 131
LUKE 12:32–34 | 143
LUKE 13:1–9 | 146
LUKE 13:10–17 | 153
LUKE 13:31–35 | 164
LUKE 14:1–14 | 171
LUKE 14:25–33 | 176
LUKE 15:1–10 | 180
LUKE 15:11–32 | 184
LUKE 16:1–13 | 193
LUKE 16:19–31 | 196
LUKE 17:5–10 | 199
LUKE 17:11–19 | 201
LUKE 18:1–8 | 210
LUKE 18:9–14 | 215
LUKE 19:1–10 | 223
LUKE 19:29–40 | 227
LUKE 20:27–38 | 236
LUKE 21:25–36 | 241
LUKE 23:33–43 | 252
LUKE 24:13–35 | 256
LUKE 24:36–48 | 265

Bibliography | 271

Introduction

Luke was one of those writers who was fortunate enough to have his story of Jesus published in the New Testament, or Christian Bible. I'm not sure which publisher or literary agent he used. I assume Mark and Matthew gave him a good reference. Nevertheless, Luke was *not* fortunate enough to get any royalty money from his efforts, which is a shame because an awful lot of people have read his work. The following pages are my reaction to Luke's portrayal of Jesus. I have focused primarily on the words Luke or Luke's redactors put into Jesus' mouth. Some of these words, of course, were never spoken by Jesus, and yet I'm not really concerned about that.

If you read my previous book, *Big Jesus,* you probably realize that I am not a Jesus professional. Yes, I get paid to be a clergyperson, and yes, I have a PhD in religion, blah, blah, blah. I'm not an academic, and therefore I prefer to put myself in the *semi-professional* category. I played a little semi-pro fast-pitch softball back in the day, so I know a thing or two about this category of expertise. It basically means someone is good enough to be on the field *but ain't nobody payin' to watch you.* Now, please don't get me wrong. I would prefer that you pay for this book. Don't pull some kind of Abbie Hoffman and steal it. Stealing books is a crime against the Ten Commandments and nobody—I mean nobody—wants to anger the God who wrote the Ten Commandments. So just *act* like I'm a Jesus professional and buy this book.

Of course, I'm dodging the question about why I'm not terribly concerned whether Jesus spoke every word Luke says he spoke. Here's my semi-pro answer: I'm not concerned because at this point in time there really isn't much proof one way or another. We can give educated guesses and such. (By "such" I mean guesses based less on education and more on ignorance.) The Jesus Seminar and previous attempts to discover the historical Jesus have given us a lot to chew on. At the end of the day, however, we may have chewed on a lot of stuff that shouldn't actually be swallowed. Therefore, my approach to this book is less about commenting on what Jesus actually said and more about commenting on Luke's *portrayal* of Jesus.

INTRODUCTION

This book devoted to Luke's portrayal of Jesus is less of a devotional and more of an *undevotional*. I don't mean to say that I'm not devoted to Jesus. I am. I dare anyone to be more devoted to Jesus than I am because the only way to be more devoted to Jesus than I am is to nail yourself to a tree and have someone pierce your side to make sure you're dead. Short of that, don't try to one-up me here.

By "undevotional" I'm harkening back to the days when (m)ad men in business suits used to call 7-Up the "Un-Cola." By calling 7-Up the "Un-Cola" they were not saying that 7-Up was less tasty than the dark colas; they were saying that 7-Up just didn't quite look like the other colas. Well, this book is not going to look exactly like a devotional based on the Gospel of Luke. Nevertheless, it will taste just as good and, in fact, is better for you if you have an upset stomach.

The other point I want to make is that this book is more a work of art than anything else. It's not a Picasso, however, because that would entail bad spelling, grammar, misused capital letters, and well, just a bunch of goofy remarks that have no place in the Jesus genre. Still, let's not kid ourselves here. Religion per se is an art form. My wife is an artist and therefore I'm an expert on art. Okay, I'm not even a semi-expert on art, and yet as a semi-professional religionist I feel semi-qualified to explain myself:

I think we can all agree that art is a very subjective thing. In terms of the fine arts, which is the creation of something visual, the artist is employing at least three things other than his or her utensils: imagination, aesthetic sensitivities, and intelligence. Some artists are more skilled in these areas than others, and yet determining one's skill level is not a simple task. Most of the people in the world who have an inherent ability to draw, paint, sculpt, etc. are not household names. Few people know their work. (Isn't that right, aunt Glenda?) Personally, I have never contributed to the fine arts, unless it was something I did in grade school. Nevertheless, I suppose that with a little training and encouragement I could make *something*. Everyone can be an artist, although most of us would never produce anything worth showing to the public.

In a very real and existential way, the observance and practice of religion is something that each one of us fashions for ourselves much like an artist produces something that only they can produce. We somehow find a way to apply meaning to what we do, whether we are praying before a statue or chewing on a piece of gluten-free bread that has been declared "the body of Christ." Religion is an art, we are the individual artists, and many of us belong to colonies of other religious artists. All the elements of the arts are there: the aesthetics, the music, the poetry, and the intelligence (along with a good supply of ignorance). What some people fail to grasp is that religion also makes great use of the human imagination.

The Bible itself is an art collection. It is a product of all things artful, especially the imaginations of those who contributed to its contents over a period of about fifteen hundred years. Furthermore, those souls who have adhered to and practiced within the boundaries of the various religious traditions throughout history have utilized their artful imaginations in ways—often subtle—that contribute to nothing less than a masterpiece. The congregation that I currently serve—and the congregations I have served in the past—are all masterpieces in the sense that they are the products of many skilled (and unskilled) artists through the decades of their existence. The aesthetic sensitivities, the intelligence, the imagination—all have been there, and continue to be the tools we use to improve the product. The church is a canvas, the people are the artists, and the words, music, visuals, etc. are artistic expressions beyond parallel in the secular world.

As I said, some religious artists are more skilled than others. Religionists who fit the description of "fundamentalists"—and I am being blunt on purpose—have about as much skill as a grade school child drawing stick figures in black and white. While their beliefs and practices often seem extraordinarily complex, in reality they have no taste for nuanced interpretations. There is very little color scheme, flexibility, or variety in fundamentalism.

I have no way of determining which religious group—Christian or otherwise—is most skilled as religious artists. Perhaps the agnostic seekers or the postmodern deconstructionists are the better skilled precisely because they keep the rest of us uneasy within our contentment—unless one is a fundamentalist and not open to the questions and struggles of a cutting-edge approach to religion. As someone who has been honing my religious skills for over three decades I can easily fall into the temptation of believing that I have arrived as a religious artist, and then I awake the next morning wishing to grab a brush and paint new strokes on my canvas. My canvas never seems to get full enough to want to show my work to the public, although I have learned that there is nothing wrong with showing an unfinished piece. *Big Jesus* is proof of that.

The following is my undevoted artistic response to a fellow who goes by the name of "Luke," one of my favorite ancient religious artists, and his portrait of Jesus of Nazareth. By the way, the Catholic Church considers St. Luke to be the patron saint of artists. So, there's that. Also, my sense of artfulness is admittedly more playful and sarcastic than his. Sometimes my imagination takes over and persuades me to draw a picture of Jesus beyond Luke's imagination. Nevertheless, Luke portrayed the life of Jesus in a way that is pleasing to our senses. He has painted a portrait of a man in a manner that compels us to stop what we are doing, give serious reflection to his literary masterpiece, and try our best to derive meaning from it. We may leave his art gallery in as bewildered a state as when we arrived, or we may be inspired to pick up our paintbrushes and add a few more strokes.

Full disclosure: A few years ago, I wrote a series of devotionals for my denomination, the United Church of Christ. They were published on the UCC's website under the heading, "Still Speaking Devotionals." Most of the devotions are penned by the "Still Speaking Writer's Group," a collection of mostly East or West Coast UCC pastors and professors. As someone who lives in a flyover state, I was trying to work my way into this group of esteemed writers. My devotionals were published about once a month until, finally, nothing. I kept writing and submitting, but still, nothing. I decided to write to the one who took care of the Still Speaking Devotionals and was told I would never be part of this group because I don't fit the right demographic. In other words, being male, pale, stale, and straight is somewhat of a handicap these days, one that I proudly embrace so that those groups who have been historically underrepresented can have their turn. Nevertheless, this experience led me to think that if I don't fit any of the preferred contemporary demographics for devotional writers—or am simply not good enough—then at least I can write an *undevotional*. So here it is.

LUKE 1:26–35[1]

In the sixth month the angel Gabriel was sent by God to a town in Galilee called Nazareth, to a virgin engaged to a man whose name was Joseph, of the house of David. The virgin's name was Mary. And he came to her and said, "Greetings, favored one! The Lord is with you." But she was much perplexed by his words and pondered what sort of greeting this might be. The angel said to her, "Do not be afraid, Mary, for you have found favor with God. And now, you will conceive in your womb and bear a son, and you will name him Jesus. He will be great, and will be called the Son of the Most High, and the Lord God will give to him the throne of his ancestor David. He will reign over the house of Jacob forever, and of his kingdom there will be no end." Mary said to the angel, "How can this be, since I am a virgin?" The angel said to her, "The Holy Spirit will come upon you, and the power of the Most High will overshadow you; therefore the child to be born will be holy; he will be called Son of God."

NO END IN SIGHT

FOR MOST PEOPLE, THE announcement of a new baby is good news. That's probably not true for the young couple I eyed walking into a local Walmart one day with a baby in a carriage and three preschool children in tow, the young woman pregnant and in tattered clothing, and the young male who looked so famished that he swaggered into the trashy chain store like he was about to enter a three-star restaurant. For the most part, however, babies are

---

1. All Scripture quotations are from the New Revised Standard Version.

a grand event. Unless the baby arrives unexpectedly or in unusual—if not unwanted circumstances—most babies are welcomed into this world with open arms.

The announcement that a peasant couple named Joseph and Mary were going to have a baby would have been an insignificant event if it weren't for the way it is reported in Luke's Gospel. You know your baby might be important someday if an angel shows up to give the birth announcement. I'll take that over a store-bought card every time. Although angels are mythological creatures that serve the purpose of bridging the gap between religion and fantasy (not that this gap is very wide), this is probably the best use of an angel's time because the word "angel" in one of those ancient languages that no one speaks any longer literally means "messenger." The angel even has a name—Gabriel—and in his announcement of the new baby he doesn't mince words: "He will be great, and will be called the Son of the Most High, and the Lord God will give to him the throne of his ancestor David. He will reign over the house of Jacob forever, and of his kingdom *there will be no end*." Welcome to the world, Jesus. No pressure.

Gabriel is announcing the birth of the long-awaited Jewish messiah. That was really good news. Their understanding of the role of the messiah, however, was different than ours, mainly because our understanding of the messiah had to be reinterpreted by the New Testament's spin-masters after Jesus died an untimely death. Because he was such a cool, handsome man who could work up a crowd, they believed he would be a literal king and would reestablish the throne of David, the most popular king in Israel's history. He would not be like King Herod, who was nothing more than a puppet king, a butt-kissing vassal to the Roman Empire. The messiah would be a real king with a real kingdom. After Jesus died, however, the Gospel writers made a wonderful attempt to spiritualize his kingdom. Jesus' kingdom could no longer be considered a political and geographical entity. His kingdom morphed from one that rules land to a kingdom that rules lives.

Hyperbolically, Gabriel claims that of Jesus' kingdom there will be no end. How do we wrap our minds around that? What could that possibly mean? There are two ways a kingdom can conceivably exist without an end, which has never happened, of course. The first way to exist without end is to be economically and militarily superior, to build an empire, and to be the world's superpower. Even that isn't good enough, however. History is littered with examples of empires that ruled over a great deal of land and people. At the height of the British Empire in the early twentieth century, for example, 22 percent of the earth's land was under British rule. Even more remarkable, at the height of the Persian Empire in the fifth century BCE, 44.5 percent of the earth's people were under Persian rule. Both the British and the Persians (who are roughly equivalent to modern-day Iranians) continue to exist, but they are no longer the economic and military superpowers of the world. That would be the US.

Unfortunately (or fortunately, if you are tired of American nationalism and knuckle-dragging rednecks), the United States of America, the world's superpower since World War II, may be on a downward trajectory. Our status could be fading away because superpowers always inevitably lose their superpower status. They all have their kryptonite. Our kryptonite is probably a foreign policy that makes decisions based on "American interests" and an ever-growing theocratic approach to social issues. This makes Gabriel's claim of an unending kingdom all the more intriguing. Are we really supposed to believe that? In what way could that possibly be true?

Perhaps the main reason superpowers always have an end is because they are propped up by violence. Violence is competitive in nature and therefore there will always be someone seeking to destroy you. Let me use a sports analogy. The National Football League (NFL) team that wins the Super Bowl the previous year becomes the target for every other NFL team to beat the following year. The opposing teams circle the date they will play the defending Super Bowl champions. Everyone wants to defeat them. For that and other reasons that have to do with injuries, aging players, and too much money spent on particular superstars, the superpower will eventually, if not immediately, be knocked off of their throne—unless you're the New England Patriots.

Likewise, because the United States of America is the reigning superpower of the world, there are a lot of people out there wanting to bring us down. Because terrorism is the only method (other than Russian meddling) that can work against a vastly superior military power, people will use terrorist tactics. Terrorism per se can never be defeated because the killing and imprisonment of those who resort to terrorist tactics stirs up even more young men and women who are ideologically driven to join the fight.

Whether those who resort to terrorist tactics are eventually victorious or not, someone will knock off the superpower, sooner or later. A nation that is propped up by violence will eventually be destroyed by violence. Or just as likely, the collapse of the superpower could be only indirectly related to the loss of military power. It could be more directly related to the excessive spending that leads to such power in the first place. The bottom line is that all superpowers fall . . . eventually. Such is, or will be, the fate of all political and geographical kingdoms, empires, or superpowers, including us.

The second way a kingdom or superpower could conceivably have no end is if it is propped up by peace rather than violence. The superpower of God—what Jesus calls the kingdom of God—is authentic only when it is propped up by peace. Peace is the primary characteristic of the biblical notion of the kingdom of God. Biblical scholars refer to the "Peaceable Kingdom," which is inferred from the books of Isaiah and Micah and Jesus' Sermon on the Mount. The words found in Isaiah 11:6–9 serve as a great example:

> The wolf shall live with the lamb, the leopard shall lie down with the kid, the calf and the lion and the fatling together, and a little child shall lead them. The cow and the bear shall graze, their young shall lie down together; and the lion shall eat straw like the ox. The nursing child shall play over the hold of the asp, and the weaned child shall put its hand on the adder's den. They will not hurt or destroy on all my holy mountain; for the earth will be full of the knowledge of the LORD as the waters cover the sea.

In contrast to violence, peace is non-competitive in nature. "The wolf shall live with the lamb" (an event that will never happen unless evolution takes an interesting turn) is an image of non-competitive peace. No one in Isaiah's imagined scenario is trying to hurt or destroy anything. If the biblical view of the Peaceable Kingdom has any merit, then peace will be the only thing left standing after violence has run its course in human history. Like cockroaches after a nuclear war, peace will never be eradicated. It is a kingdom of which there will be no end.

This is the kind of kingdom the angel Gabriel is linking with his birth announcement. In the Christian imagination, Jesus becomes a messiah of peace, not violence (after his death). He is not the only messiah of peace in the history of humanity; and the religion that bears his name, Christianity, has not always brought peace to the world, yet the Jesus tradition has made a very important contribution to the human vision of a peaceful world. The followers that bear his name do not always live up to the promise of the baby whose birth announcement suggests a lasting peace, but to be fair that's not his fault.

Two thousand years after Jesus, however, isn't the world more violent today than ever before? Hasn't the biblical vision of a Peaceable Kingdom failed? The answer may be "no." Harvard psychology professor, Steven Pinker, in his book, *The Better Angels of our Nature: Why Violence has Declined*,[2] argues that we are probably living in the most peaceful moment in human history. Really? I was skeptical at first, but then I read on. As evidence for this he notes that in sixteenth-century Paris, a popular form of entertainment was cat-burning—a cat was hoisted in a sling on a stage

---

2. Pinker, *Better Angels of our Nature*, xxi.

and slowly lowered into a fire. According to the historian Norman Davis, the spectators, including educated elites and royalty, laughed as the animals, howling with pain, were singed, roasted, and basically cremated. Dr. Pinker concludes that such sadistic behavior would be unthinkable in most of the world today.

There are many things people used to do that were acceptable in the past and yet are no longer acceptable to most people. Pinker lists cruelty as entertainment, human sacrifice to indulge superstition, slavery as a labor-saving device, conquest as the mission statement of a government, genocide as a means of acquiring real estate, torture and mutilation as routine punishment, the death penalty for misdemeanors and differences of opinion, assassination as the mechanism of political succession, rape as the spoils of war, pogroms as outlets for frustration, and homicide as the major form of conflict resolution. Today these kinds of activities are rare to nonexistent. We are becoming more peaceful and less violent. The reason why so many of us think we are more violent than ever before is because television and social media make us more aware when bad things happen. Seemingly every violent event in the world today, from beheadings of journalists in the Middle East to police shootings of unarmed black men in middle America, are brought immediately to the public's awareness.

The truth is that the percentage of people who die a violent death has been diminishing for a long time, even during the bloody twentieth century. Pinker claims that if the wars of the twentieth century had killed the same proportion of the population that die in the wars of a typical tribal society, there would have been two billion deaths, not one hundred million.[3] I could go on and on with the evidence he presents, yet assuming he is right, that we are less violent and more peaceful today than ever before, how do we explain it? Pinker gives four answers. I will add a fifth.

First, we are less violent today because of laws and the ability to enforce laws. Despite the unnecessary violence sometimes created by militaries and police forces, they act overall as a deterrent to violence. Remember the Wild West in American lore? Violence was a big problem until the arrival of the peace officers.

Second, we are less violent today because modern medical technology has given us longer life spans and thus we place a higher value on life.

Third, we are less violent today because the global economy has created a scenario where we want to cooperate with others rather than fight with them.

---

3. Pinker, *Better Nature of Our Angels*, 47–56.

Fourth, we are less violent today because modern communication technology like television and social media has created more empathy in us. We know more about other people and cultures, and when you put a human face on others you are less likely to want to kill them.

To these reasons, I would add a fifth: We are less violent today because of the birth of Jesus. Yes, that's a hyperbolic statement, but consider this: More people are literate and have access to information than ever before. Therefore, logical thinking suggests that there is more awareness of Jesus and the biblical vision of a Peaceable Kingdom than ever before, a vision Jesus shared with the prophetic tradition of his faith. This awareness began with the accessibility of the Bible through the invention of the printing press, increased through literacy and education, and continues to grow exponentially today because of the internet. In addition to the reasons Dr. Pinker gave, the Jesus tradition continues to help chip away at the human lust for violence. Those of us who are steeped in the Jesus tradition, at least those who adhere to a more progressive understanding and practice of Christianity, seek peace today like never before. Our hope is that a lasting peace might be our future. And in some ways that future is linked with a moment in humanity's distant past when a winged mythological creature named Gabriel announced the birth of a baby whose kingdom would endure for a long, long time.

CAVEAT: THE WAR ON NOTHING

The progressive-minded Jesus may be the ultimate symbol for peace, yet some of his more conservative followers prefer conflict, particularly around his fabricated birthday celebration called "Christmas." I opened my newspaper to the "funnies" one morning before Christmas and scanned a cartoon depicting a little boy in school sitting in the corner with a bar of soap in his mouth. Another little boy asks if he was being punished for rap lyrics, and a girl answered, "No, he said 'Merry Christmas.'"

Are people really trying to take Christ out of Christmas, as is so often claimed these days? Is there a war on Christmas in our society? It is easy to have that impression, especially when a brief book search reveals John Gibson's *The War on Christmas*. Don't get me started about the giant windbag, Bill O'Reilly, formerly of FOX News, who regularly asserts that the anti-Christmas forces are gathering troops at the border for an invasion. O'Reilly is just one big tool.

Still, the perception is out there that Christians are in some kind of otherworldly battle against anti-Christmas forces. The primary claim is that our government and other "atheists" are trying to take Christ out of Christmas. The most popular reason people give to prove that there is an effort to do this is the ubiquitous "Xmas" signs. When I was a young adult I wanted to put "Merry Christmas" on my front glass door with white shoe polish but the word "Christmas" wouldn't fit, so I wrote "Xmas" instead. My grandmother gave me the dickens (pun intended) for doing that until I told her that the "X" is really the Greek letter *Chi*, which is the first letter in the Greek word for Christ *(Christos)*. Therefore, when I or others replace the word "Christ" with *Chi* (X) we are not taking Christ out of Christmas; we are simply showing off our knowledge of biblical Greek. Perhaps a way to be clever about this is to say that Jesus is the "X-factor."

So, if the Xmas crowd hasn't declared war on Christmas, then who has? What about all those people who insist we shouldn't say "Merry Christmas" or refer to a "Christmas" tree? For instance, one time years ago, Walmart informed their employees that they have to say "Happy Holidays" rather than "Merry Christmas." That same year, evangelical Christians boycotted Macy's for changing their window signs to read the same (although oddly they didn't boycott the cheap products sold in Walmart). Christmas trees are often called "holiday trees," "community trees," or my favorite, "trees of illumination." Christmas celebrations occasionally receive new names such as "Holly-dazzle." By the way, why do people get upset about changing the name for Christmas but not Halloween? No one seems to get angry when we blandly rename Halloween carnivals "fall festivals." This happened years ago in my West Texas hometown so I declared a war on fall festivals. My weapon of choice: toilet paper in the trees.[4]

Again, who are these modern-day Scrooges who want to take Christ out of Christmas? It seems to me that there are at least four types of these Christmas Scrooges lurking behind extravagantly decorated holiday bushes and drinking spiked eggnog. First, just as we suspect, there are those who are genuinely hostile to Christianity in general and Christmas in particular. These are the people who would slap a lawsuit on you for saying "Merry Christmas" to them in a heartbeat. They are just mad that there are Christians running around who want to celebrate the birth of Christ at all. Personally, I have never met anyone who feels that strongly against Christmas, and yet if there are people like that, and if their agenda is simply to eradicate any hint of Christmas and Christianity from the public square, then they can rightly be called bigots. Nevertheless, one might be hard-pressed to find such a Scrooge-like character in our midst.

---

4. When you think about it, littering trees with toilet paper, which are made from trees, is sort of like anointing oily skin with olive oil.

Second, there are those in our society who are simply trying to be politically correct. The politically correct are not as much hostile to Christmas as they are sensitive to those of other minority faiths or of no faith at all. We usually find the politically correct in government institutions like schools or courthouses trying their best to implement the wall of separation between church and state, a wall that is very difficult and confusing to discern. It's often a fuzzy wall. We also find the politically correct among business executives who opt for generic slogans like "Happy Holidays" rather than "Merry Christmas." These business execs are in the unenviable position of trying to keep their Christian customers happy while at the same time trying not to offend their non-Christian customers, or worse, receive lawsuits. What should be our attitude about this? I think we should be critical of political correctness when it goes too far and actually becomes discriminatory against Christianity, yet we should also pay attention so that we do not become oppressive with our majority status. At the very least we can learn tolerance from the politically correct crowd.

A third type of Christmas Scrooge claims that Christmas has been ruined by commercialism, so we ought to leave the innocent Christ child out of it. These people believe that Christmas has been sold out, commercialized, co-opted, and corrupted by Madison Avenue. You may be surprised to learn, however, that Christmas and the celebrations that came before it (e.g. Zagmuk, Saturnalia, and Yule) have long been a time of overindulgence, excess, and generosity. Gift-giving and revelry have always been a main component of the season. For those who think Santa Claus is a recent invention created by Madison Avenue to boost fourth-quarter sales figures, remember that St. Nicholas has been leaving gifts for children since the twelfth century.

The fourth type of Christmas Scrooge claims that Christ was never really in Christmas to begin with. Jesus was not born on December 25 in 0 or 1 CE and there is no command in the Bible to celebrate Jesus' birthday. The early church didn't observe the day at all since it smacked of the observance of the feast days of the pagan gods, such as Saturnalia. In fact, Jesus' birth was assigned to December 25 by Bishop Julius 1 of Rome in the fourth century because the Romans refused to stop celebrating Saturnalia. Julius ordered the celebration to be in Christ's honor and he also ordered a "mass" to go with it, hence the word Christ*mas*.

Later, the Mithrans also had a holiday on December 25, the birth of Mithras. According to their mythology, Mithras was created by Ahura-Mazda, the god of Zoroastrianism (a Persian religion) to save the world. He was born to a virgin, and died after a last supper with his followers. Then he ascended to heaven. His followers were baptized in the blood of a bull, ate bread and wine to represent Mithras's body and blood, and held

Sunday sacred. Mithraism became popular in the Roman Empire and so the conversion of the Mithrans would have been a high priority of the Christian church at that time. The point is, even if Christ is in Christmas today, historically he had a lot of company. Perhaps there were people in that day claiming there was a "war against Mithraism" as they were shouting, "Let's keep Mithras in Mithraism!" No doubt Bill O'Reilly's ancestors had something to do with that.

Is there really a war against Christmas? Are there people trying to take Christ out of Christmas? Yes, but we shouldn't give a rat's ass. If people want to say "Happy Holidays" rather than "Merry Christmas," that's their right. If people want to light up their "holiday tree" rather than a "Christmas tree," so be it. This is a free country. No one is going all jihad on us and beheading anyone for not agreeing with them (at least not in our country). Have we forgotten that? Walmart can make their employees say whatever they want and the president of the United States can call his tree anything he wants to call it. Even if a higher-up at Burger King, Inc. comes along and tells the Burger King down the street that they have to get rid of the manger scene next to the cash register, they have the right to do so. The First Amendment guarantees religious freedom (at least in the private sector). As far as I know, no one wants to get rid of the First Amendment.

The only thing that matters is how you and I choose to celebrate Christmas. And it should only matter to us. No one needs to declare a war about anything. I've put a manger scene above my mantel on occasion and until now there have been no government agents busting down my door before Santa Claus gets a chance to eat his soggy cookies. Here's a thought: Maybe one of the reasons why there seems to be a war against Christmas in the first place is because we Christians haven't always celebrated Christmas as we should. We play into the hands of the Christmas Scrooges when we practice our own brand of bigotry, when we ridicule other's beliefs and try to impose our religion on everyone else, and, yes, when we overindulge in the commercialization of Christmas. In other words, Christians haven't done a very good job of "keeping Christ in Christmas" either, so why should we expect non-Christians to do any better? Let's admit to ourselves that the baby born as a symbol of everlasting peace will never get his kingdom off the ground as long as those who use his name in our liturgical gatherings continue to contradict everything he grew up to become.

Luke 1:39–44

In those days Mary set out and went with haste to a Judean town in the hill country, where she entered the house of Zechariah and greeted Elizabeth. When Elizabeth heard Mary's greeting, the child leaped in her womb. And Elizabeth was filled with the Holy Spirit and exclaimed with a loud cry, "Blessed are you among women, and blessed is the fruit of your womb. And why has this happened to me, that the mother of my Lord comes to me? For as soon as I heard the sound of your greeting, the child in my womb leaped for joy."

JUMPING JOHN

THE NEWS CAME OUT one day that fully 86 percent of all Americans believe in Santa Claus when they are children, and that the average age of a child learning the truth about Santa is eight years old. Do you remember the time you first discovered the truth about Santa? I do. I was playing in my backyard in San Angelo, Texas when an older girl, probably about ten years old, walked up to the fence and said, "Hey, little boy, do you know that Santa Claus isn't real? He doesn't exist." (Apparently, older children love to tell younger children about Santa. It makes them feel big and important, just like people today use Facebook to inform their "friends" about every truth they have discovered in their remarkable lives.) Terribly upset, I ran into the house and confronted my mother about it. She reluctantly gave me the cold hard facts about Santa. Hold on, I wasn't quite through with her. I figured there were other things these grownups weren't telling me, like why my mother's belly was getting huge. I had not yet received a straight answer about that. Fortunately, my mother was in a revealing mood. I then learned the PG-13 facts about childbirth as well, a few short weeks before my little brother was born.

Not too long ago I read another article about how children figure out the Santa Claus myth all on their own, even if no one tells them. Usually, the author claimed, when a parent finally sits down with their child to give them the lowdown about Santa the child's response is, "I already knew." The same is true, I suspect, about how babies are born. We may not understand all the biology, yet our minds are able to distinguish between mythology and reality at a fairly young age. We laugh about the Santa and stork myths, understanding that only a child would be naïve enough to believe them, and yet doesn't our religion continue to hang on to some rather unusual birth stories, stories that were born—excuse the pun—in the myth-producing frenzy of the ancient world?

You have to admit that some of the birth stories we read about in the Bible are fairly hard to swallow. For example, there is the story of Abraham and Sarah having a child at an extremely advanced age, well past Sarah's childbearing years. The book of Genesis concludes that they lived to an age that few people live to today, much less in the ancient world when life spans were much shorter. There is the story of Hannah giving birth to Samuel, although her womb had previously been barren. Of course, there is the virgin birth story of Mary and Jesus, a story that blatantly defies our understanding of human reproduction.

Obviously we tend to be more skeptical of these stories than our ancient brothers and sisters because we live in a modern scientific world. It is much more difficult for us to believe something that defies the laws of science as we understand them. If people in the ancient world did accept these mythological birth stories as literally true, then we can chalk it up to the fact that they had less knowledge about pregnancy and childbirth than we do today. Nevertheless, they knew enough to realize that women who are old, have barren wombs, or are virgins, are just not supposed to be pregnant.

The story of Elizabeth's pregnancy is one that is rarely mentioned in the same breath as the other "miraculous" pregnancies or birth stories of the Bible. Perhaps it should be however. Luke gives us a brief account of a meeting that took place between two pregnant women, Elizabeth and Mary, the latter being the soon-to-be-mother of Jesus. Elizabeth was the wife of a priest named Zechariah. Unfortunately the couple was getting on in years and Elizabeth, like Sarah and Hannah before her, had a barren womb. We assume that Elizabeth was barren in the sense of not being able to have children even when she was younger, because in a time before reliable birth control any woman who was able would have had children, probably many children. Either that, or Zechariah stayed a little too busy at the temple or, just as likely, suffered from erectile dysfunction.

One day while Zechariah was performing his priestly duties in the temple, a familiar-sounding event occurred. Luke writes that the angel Gabriel appeared before Zechariah and said to him, "Do not be afraid, Zechariah, for your prayer has been heard. Your wife Elizabeth will bear you a son, and you will name him John." Gabriel is sort of the New Testament version of a stork, which is appropriate because angels have wings. This would be a great place to mention the energy drink, Red Bull, but I won't.

Gabriel goes on to say how John will prepare people "for the Lord." John later became known as John the baptizer or Baptist. No, not the kind of Baptist you are thinking. John didn't have slicked-back hair and a floppy Bible.

Now, if all we knew about Elizabeth's pregnancy is that she conceived while she was old and barren we would think to ourselves, "That's nice, but we've heard it all before." And yet there is one more element to this familiar-sounding pregnancy. After Mary discovers she is pregnant, Gabriel tells her about Elizabeth's pregnancy. Gabriel was a gossip. Luke describes Mary and Elizabeth as cousins, therefore Mary would have known about Elizabeth's age and inability to have children. Naturally curious to see if the news is true, Mary "went with haste to a Judean town in the hill country" where Zechariah and Elizabeth resided. She wants to check on her relative, Elizabeth, to see if the news is true.

Luke tells us that when Mary greets Elizabeth, now in her sixth month of pregnancy, the baby "leaped in her womb." I refer to this as "prenatal calisthenics." I assume Luke means that the unborn child moves or kicks in Elizabeth's womb. I don't recall ever hearing a pregnant woman claiming her fetus "leaped," but if one did I would assume this is an exaggerated way of saying it kicked really hard. Why did the baby in Elizabeth's womb leap? Did he sense his mother's excitement and respond instinctively? No one knows for sure, yet I would assume that a mother's emotions can affect an unborn child. Although a physician, Luke probably knew less about the science of pregnancies than I do and so he felt quite comfortable implying to his readers that the unborn baby leaped because it sensed the presence of the Lord in Mary's womb.

Impossible, you say? Not any more impossible than a pregnant old woman who was barren throughout her child-bearing years, much less a pregnant virgin. One could make the argument that one of the most important themes in both the Old and New Testaments is uncommon, extraordinary, miraculous pregnancies and births, which, by the way, was about as common in the ancient world as corncobs in Indiana.

So what is Luke trying to say with this interesting little account of a baby leaping in his mother's womb? I believe the answer is found in the following verse. Elizabeth says to Mary, "For as soon as I heard the sound of your greeting, the child in my womb leaped *for joy.*" The message Luke wants to give his readers is not that John the Fetus leaped, but that John the Fetus leaped for joy. In a typically exaggerated manner, Luke is telling us that even before Jesus was born he had brought a level of joy to the world that caused prenatal fetuses to jump around like a child on a playground. Excusing the hyperbole, that might sound obvious. Of course Jesus brought joy to the world. That's a given, but it misses the point. When Jesus came into the world there was very little joy to be had.

Most of us today can find a measure of joy in our lives. Compared to the unfortunate souls who existed in the ancient world, we have more leisure time, more technological advantages, and more freedom than any other society in the history of humanity. We can find joy in any number of things on a daily basis: a good book, our favorite television program, music we love, recreational activities, good food, and just the comfort and quietness of home. Unless we are going through a difficult situation—and yet even then, relatively speaking—joy is not hard to find in twenty-first century America. We even have pills that help those who are suffering from anxiety and depression experience joy. In first-century Palestine, however, the mostly poor and illiterate people had very little to be joyful about. They certainly didn't have any happy pills. They were hungry, dirty, sick, crippled, and tired. Most of their spare time was spent trying to survive (not playing video games or cooking their favorite recipes), so they really didn't have any spare time. They were controlled, oppressed, and over-taxed by the Roman government. Their religion was exclusive, judgmental, dogmatic, and harsh. You and I can't even imagine what life was like in first-century Palestine. I mean, if you had erectile dysfunction, well, tough.

Therefore, to have a writer, namely Luke, looking back a few decades after Jesus' death to claim that Jesus brought so much joy to the world that even an unborn baby leaped in his mother's womb at the mere sight of Jesus' mother, ought to give us pause for reflection. Something was going on in this small, emerging group of people known as "the Way" or followers of Jesus of Nazareth. During the last two thousand years Christianity has been a lot of things to a lot of people. To some people it has brought immense suffering and heartache. Christianity has often been a force for evil more than a force for good. And yet what if we began each day with the mindset that the primary purpose of this religion is to bring joy to the world?

Jesus didn't exit his mother's womb in order to bring judgment, misery, crankiness, negativity, or scowls to our faces. He came in order to bring joy to people who simply had very little joy. Even John the Fetus figured that one out.

Luke 2:4–11

Joseph . . . went from the town of Nazareth in Galilee to Judea, to the city of David called Bethlehem, because he was descended from the house and family of David. He went to be registered with Mary, to whom he was engaged and who was expecting a child. While they were there, the time came for her to deliver her child. And she gave birth to her firstborn son and wrapped him in bands of cloth, and laid him in a manger, because there was no place for them in the inn. In that region there were shepherds living in the fields, keeping watch over their flock by night. Then an angel of the Lord stood before them, and the glory of the Lord shone around them, and they were terrified. But the angel said to them, "Do not be afraid; for see—I am bringing you good news of great joy for all the people: to you is born this day in the city of David a Savior, who is the Messiah, the Lord."

THE BOTTOM OF THE BARREL

WHAT IS THE PLOT of the Christmas story? On the surface, it seems very clear. Joseph and Mary go to Bethlehem to register for a census (which likely never happened by the way, but we'll overlook that minor inconvenience for now). Mary is with child and goes into labor while in Bethlehem. They seek lodging, yet all the cheap motel rooms are taken. They presumably find shelter in a stable. After the baby is born Mary lays him down in a manger, a trough to hold food and water for cattle and other domestic animals. They either found someone to let them use their stable or they are trespassing on someone's property (which adds an interesting nuance to the inclusion of the word "trespasses" in the Lord's Prayer). Then the plot thickens when we learn that an angel, presumably the very busy and underpaid Gabriel, appears to a group of shepherds tending their flocks that evening. After getting over their initial fright at seeing such a strange phenomenon—and not realizing that angels may have been extraterrestrial creatures who forgot the Prime Directive[1]—they are encouraged to go to Bethlehem to check out this baby which Luke refers to as "Savior," "Messiah" or "Christ," and "Lord." They head into Bethlehem, find the child lying in the manger, and, because gossip was the only thing that kept their lives interesting, they begin telling everyone about their experience.

This is a familiar story line, one that you and I have heard multiple times at Christmas Eve midnight services. It is a nostalgic story that warms our hearts in the midst of holiday festivities of family gatherings, gift-giving, and home-cooked feasts. Unfortunately, we have heard it so many times that we are no longer surprised by what it is saying to us. And yet I would like to point out something in the plotline that really should surprise us, particularly in our bacterially sensitive world: Mary laid her newborn son in a manger, a trough.

Although I don't know what troughs looked like in first-century Palestine, I do know what they look like in my native West Texas. They ain't pretty. They're not anything I would want to play around in because, well, animals eat and drink out of them. They probably pee and poop nearby if not directly on them. Troughs are long, narrow open containers that hold food and water for domestic beasts. They're gross. Because of this, I believe the manger or trough serves as a perfect symbol for both the Christmas story and the good news that is propagated in this story. The good news is this: *God scrapes the bottom of the barrel.* The reason this is good news is because I'm pretty sure most of us see ourselves as bottom of the barrel people from time to time.

The biblical narrative is full of bottom of the barrel people. The peasant girl, Mary, the "mother of God," comes to mind. The notion that Jesus came from the womb of a young girl who was likely either promiscuous (i.e. sexually active before marriage) or was raped by a Roman soldier makes for a good narrative. This explains why Joseph, a character that is only spoken about early in the story, is not the father and yet he decides to marry Mary in order to cover up what really happened to her. (Like "marrying Mary," I

---

1. The Prime Directive is explained in the *Star Trek* television and movie series as the command not to interfere with intelligent creatures on planets that have yet to discover life elsewhere in the universe. We should probably apply the same protocol in American foreign policy in terms of not interfering with the evolution of other cultures—except for the fact that other cultures are very much aware of our presence in the world today. So never mind.

once jimmied open the door of a GMC Jimmy . . . and my name is Jimmy. Try to beat that.) Personally, I don't think the paternity of Jesus is all that important. He can still be the "Son of God" without being the product of a case of divine adultery. The point of the story is not who sired Jesus; the point is that God scrapes the bottom of the barrel, which is good news for the rest of us. If the Savior or Messiah is an illegitimate child, all the better I say.

I also think it would be better to instill a little reality into the birth narrative. The baby is born in a trough, surrounded by urine and stench, rats and cockroaches. The mother doesn't enjoy the dulling effect of an anesthetic so she screams in pain, no doubt startling the surrounding animals. There is blood, womb goo, and an umbilical cord. The second verse of "O Little Town of Bethlehem" does not ring true: "How silently, how silently, the wondrous gift is given." No, she's screaming at the top of her lungs, cursing whatever man did this to her . . . or the one holding her hand.

MARY HAD A LITTLE SHEPHERD

Speaking of the bottom of the barrel, I think we can safely say that if any group of people in the ancient Middle East needed a bath and a dose of social graces, the shepherds come readily to mind. According to the Gospel of Luke, when Jesus' life began, sheep, or more precisely their guardian shepherds, were a prominent part of the story. Including the shepherds in the birth story of Jesus doesn't seem all that out of place because shepherding sheep was one of the most common occupations in that place and time. Shepherds were about as common then as fast-food hamburger-flippers are today. And like the burger-flipper, the life of a shepherd was no doubt extremely monotonous and boring. When you and I have insomnia we try "counting sheep" in order to bore ourselves to sleep. The shepherd also counted sheep at night, yet not so he could go to sleep. He counted sheep in order to make sure they were all safe and accounted for. Because the occupation of shepherding was so excruciatingly dull, I can understand why Luke chooses the shepherds to be included in this extraordinary event. They deserve to have something interesting happen to them. They have paid their dues.

When Gabriel appears before a group of shepherds on the night of Jesus' birth they are terrified out of their minds, as any of us would be. This is especially true for men whose idea of fun is trying to entice sheep to jump over a stick. (This is not true where I grew up. In Texas the men are men and the sheep are scared, or so I have heard.) Sensing the fright of these poor, simple men, Gabriel implores them not to be afraid and then proceeds to tell them about the birth of the future Messiah, someone all the good Jewish folk had been looking and hoping for. The shepherds are so excited they seemingly drop everything and go to Bethlehem to see the new baby. I wonder who took care of the sheep while they were gone. It had to be Gabriel, right? (Assuming he was an hourly wage-earner rather than salaried.)

Why do shepherds figure so prominently in this story? Most people probably assume that their presence in the story is only incidental. That is, Gabriel could have appeared to, let's say, a bunch of fishermen or an office of tax collectors. Unfortunately, plumbers were not an option in that day. I believe there are very important reasons why those poor, illiterate, dirty, sleepy, hungry, boring, bored, and depressed shepherds are the ones who get a prime role in the birth narrative.

Perhaps the most popular reason the shepherds figure so prominently in the story is to link Jesus with the greatest king in the history of Israel, David, who grew up as a shepherd boy. Scholars have known for a long time that the Gospels go out of their way to make connections between Jesus and various characters from the Hebrew Scriptures, including David and Moses.

Other than the fact that David was a shepherd, and Luke is trying to connect Jesus to David, there is another important reason the shepherds figure so prominently in the birth narrative of Jesus. We are given a hint of this reason from the ancient Roman poet, Virgil, who said that an ideal ruler would be a shepherd of the people, born among simple shepherds. Luke, then, is trying to tell us what kind of Messiah Jesus will be (or was, because Luke is written decades after Jesus' death), and what kind of people he would include in his kingdom. The word "kingdom," by the way, is no longer politically correct in progressive Christian circles. However, it is appropriate in terms of linking Jesus to David . . . who was a king . . . and a darn good one at that. Jesus' kingdom will be so inclusive, Luke is telling us, that it will even include shepherds.

We often note how Jesus included all kinds of outcasts in his ministry. There were the poor, sick, blind, lame, sinners (of all sorts), prostitutes, tax collectors, and so on. One group of people we often fail to include in this list of lowly people is the shepherds. The revelation of the birth of the Messiah to shepherds living in the fields would have been shocking to the typical Jewish reader (much as the revelation of the resurrection to Mary Magdalene would have shocked the patriarchal misogynistic readers of the first century). Shepherds were not regarded as being particularly pious. The more elitist members of that culture despised them.

As a native West Texan, I can't help but draw a parallel between the shepherds in the Gospel narrative and oil field workers who are called "roughnecks." By reputation they are not particularly pious either, and many people despise their occupation. I grew up near the Permian Basin of West Texas, which features two nearby small cities, Midland and Odessa. Midland is more or less the home of the oil executives, the professional elites of the oil industry. It boasts of several small downtown "skyscrapers." Midland's city motto is, "The sky is the limit." By reputation, Odessa is the home of the oil field workers, the roughnecks, and there are no skyscrapers in downtown Odessa. To me, having the first proclamation of Jesus' birth come to first-century shepherds would be much like it coming to twenty-first century roughnecks who were out working on the rig at night.

Although shepherds may have been cultural outcasts in first-century Judaism, their reputations fared better in the surrounding east Asian and Greek cultures. In those cultures, the occupation of shepherding was well pleasing to God (or the gods). The shepherds reminded people of the time when gods still had dealings with human beings because they lived a contemplative existence and were still able to hear divine voices. The story of Moses comes to mind, who, as a shepherd, heard the voice of God telling him to go back to Egypt to deliver the Israelites from slavery. Cynically, I could argue that anyone who spends their entire days and nights surrounded by sheep will probably go a little insane and start hearing all kinds of voices.

There is much more to the birth story of Jesus than meets the eye, such as the fact that it compares closely with the birth stories of other famous men of antiquity, including Alexander the Great, Caesar Augustus, and Plato, all of whom, according to legend, were born as a result of a union between a divine father and human mother. As far as I know, however, their births were not announced to lowly shepherds by an angelic messenger from God. Nor did they spend their first days in a germ infested smelly animal trough. There is something about this that smacks of "good news," perhaps because Jesus' ultra-humble beginnings provide some perspective and counterbalance to the future messianic figure.

THE GOOD NEWS BEARS

Because Gabriel appeared to those poor shepherds and scared the bejesus out of them, he had to say, "Dudes! Don't be afraid! I've got some good news." Like everyone else, I love it when someone has good news for me. When people tell me that they have received a good medical report, when someone volunteers to do something in the church that no one else wants to do, when someone tells me they want to join my congregation . . . all good news. As a pastor I often feel like an angel has visited me in person when I receive really good news that relates to the life of my congregation.

Of course the only reason there is good news in the world is because it contrasts so radically with the bad news. There's nothing worse than bad news (a statement confirmed by Captain Obvious). I cringe when people preface their remarks to me by saying, "I've got some bad news." When someone in my family says that to me my heart starts pounding and I prepare myself for what usually turns out to be fairly insignificant. I'm pretty sure my family does this on purpose just to ruffle my feathers. One day an unnamed family member said, "I've got some bad news," and before I could faint, this person said, "We've run out of iced tea." See what I mean? That's just cruel. On the other hand, there are times when the statement, "I've got some bad news" is followed by genuinely bad news. I have learned to associate a phone call that comes before 8 am and after 10 pm as potential bad news. One morning in February 2003, my telephone rang at 5:30 am. I answered the phone half-asleep and heard my dad's voice say, "Jimmy, everyone is okay, but I've got some bad news." I'm glad he prefaced his remark with "everyone is okay" or else I would have had a stroke. And yet the news *was* bad: my folk's mom and pop grocery store had burned to the ground. Thirty-three years of running a grocery business had come to a halt.

The other thing that drives me crazy is when someone says: "I have some good news *and* some bad news." This creates the age-old conundrum: Which should we hear first, the good news or the bad news? Personally, I like to end on a high note, so I always request the bad news first. Fortunately, Gabriel didn't say to the shepherds, "I have some good news *and* some bad news." He (and I'm assuming Gabriel was a male angel, although I don't know what gender means for angels) just said, "I have some good news." I assume Gabriel was a male angel because a brother of one of my high school classmates was named Gabriel. Still, I'm pretty sure angelology is a gender-neutral discipline.

For most people in my large circle of friends, except for my vocal atheist Facebook friends that I truly love to discourse with, the story of Jesus of Nazareth is good news. The news has been so good in fact that we keep coming back for more details each and every Sunday. Much like a drug addict keeps meeting up with his or her connection once a week, those of us in the Christian tradition just can't get enough of the spiritual high of going to church, talking about a myriad of topics that relate to the Jesus story, singing familiar hymns, and hearing a sermon. Whatever the addictive element is—and it's different for different folks—we keep coming back for more. At the very least we perceive the Jesus story as good news.

On the other hand, we have to acknowledge that the gospel and the religion we call Christianity has not always been good news for everyone. One reason this is so is because Christians have not always acted in the name of

Jesus in a way that befits his—for lack of a better word—goodness. Jesus has been used on more than one occasion for harm rather than good. Obvious examples in the history of Christianity come to mind. The Crusaders had a knack for using the sword as an evangelism technique. Throughout much of Christian history heretics have been tortured, beheaded, hung, or burned at the stake. Suspected witches have been murdered. Wars have been fought on numerous occasions in the name of Jesus. None of this could be construed as good news for the victims or even for the perpetrators.

John Cobb, the process theologian, wrote an essay entitled, "Can Christ Become Good News Again?"[2] In this essay he gives several examples of when the gospel has been bad news rather than good news. Let me share some of these examples with you. First, he says that Christ has often been bad news for the Jews. The Holocaust serves as an obvious example. Recently, the church has admitted its complicity and passivity in response to the Nazi persecution of Jews and other people. The first Christians, of course, were Jews, but ever since then there has been a great deal of hostility between Christians and Jews. Not too many years ago the president of the Southern Baptist Convention claimed that God does not hear the prayers of the Jews. Many Christian groups have stated publicly that it is their duty to convert all the Jews to Christianity. My feeling is that if Christians continue to make statements like that, then Christ will continue to be bad news for the Jewish faith. The same could be said for people from all the other great religions in the world. Christians have often abused the name of Jesus and have made him offensive to people from other faiths. While the name "Jesus" is music to our ears, it has become irritating if not frightening noise to people from other faiths.

Another example concerns the targets of much of our missionary work in the last few centuries, especially in Africa. It has been said that the Christian missionaries were good at giving religion to the African natives and, at the same time, taking their land away from them. Bibles were traded for land. While the influence of Western Christianity has helped in the development of some parts of Africa, it has also led to loss of culture and loss of political sovereignty. One would have to stretch the realities of history to claim that overall Jesus has been good news for Africa.

A third example involves the environment and non-human animals, which have also been a victim of the Christian religion. This is a complicated issue. The Western world, which is primarily Christian, has been blamed for much of the environmental problems in the world today. This is an old argument. Back in the 1970s a professor named Lynn White wrote an essay

---

2. Cobb, *Can Christ Become Good News Again?*, 89–104.

famously making this point. A lot of the debate hinges on the word "dominion." The writer of Genesis suggests that God has given us dominion over all of creation, including the environment and other creatures. Unfortunately, conservative Christians tend to interpret the word "dominion" to mean that we can do whatever the hell we want to with the non-human world. In reality, the word translated as "dominion" in Genesis 1:28 is a word more closely related to the notion of stewardship, which means God wants us to be caretakers of the world.

Further examples in Cobb's essay include historically oppressed people. Women have been oppressed by the patriarchal, male-dominated emphasis in traditional Christianity, people of color have been oppressed due to the self-interests of people who benefit from slavery and a segregated society, and homosexuals have suffered from Christians hanging on to an uncritical reading of about six "clobber" passages in the Bible.[3] Other groups of people who might want to argue that Christ is no longer (or never has been) good news for them includes children that have been molested by clergymen, divorcees (at least in some churches), and the poor, whose continuing poverty has been historically justified by a misuse of Jesus' statement that the poor will always be with us.

Obviously, if people perceive a religion or worldview as bad news for them they will turn to other religions or worldviews that have more potential to be good news for them. In America people turn to everything from consumerism to Buddhism. I do not wish to criticize where people find good news because all of us have a right to life, liberty, and the pursuit of happiness. The question is not whether people should ignore all the shortcomings of historical Christianity and find a way to be addicted to regular worship. The question is whether or not the Jesus story can become better news than it has been.

Cobb makes the argument that the Christ who is bad news for various groups of people is not Christ at all. The Christ that is bad news is a result of the beliefs and practices of people who claim the Christian label and who, simultaneously, work against the wellbeing of others. Cobb's elegant answer is that Christ can become good news if the gospel is not so much a particular set of beliefs and practices, but a way of being in the world that is open to what others have to say and ready to change as it learns from them.[4] If this happens then Christ can be good news to those who now feel alienated from the church.

---

3. Cobb, *Can Christ Become Good News Again?* 89–93.
4. Cobb, *Can Christ Become Good News Again?*, 99–100.

WAITING FOR THE OTHER SHOE TO DROP

Or not. When we hear good news we automatically wait for the other shoe to drop. We wonder, "What's the catch?" If the story of angels, shepherds, and the babe in a manger had any hint of reality to it, I wonder if that's how the shepherds felt that night when Gabriel told them he had good news of great joy for all the people. I wonder if they thought to themselves that this is too good to be true. Nevertheless, just as we have all received that terrible phone call early in the morning or late at night bearing bad news, most of us have received some good news on occasion as well. It may not have been good enough news to make us perform prenatal calisthenics, but good news nonetheless. Someone accepted our marriage proposal... our favorite team won the championship... a child is born.

No matter what the good news is, we can't help but wonder sometimes if it's too good to be true. Good news has to prove itself, does it not? It has to weather the storm. We have been tricked or burned or let down so many times when good news didn't turn out to be so good that most of us are automatically skeptical of good news. I remember when I first received an email from a Nigerian scam artist. I was promised $800,000, and I will admit that when I first read it I naïvely hoped there might be something to it. After my natural skepticism took over the part of my personality that mimics a puppy dog with a chew toy, I called my dad to tell him about it. An uncle who was listening to the conversation informed me that he had read about the scam in the newspaper that very morning. It *was* too good to be true.

Like most people, I have become so jaded from hearing good news become not so good news that now I automatically wait for the other shoe to drop. The phrase, "waiting for the other shoe to drop" may have originated among apartment dwellers. A person in an upstairs apartment is preparing for bed. He sits on the bed, takes off the first shoe and lets it drop on the uncarpeted floor. Then he takes off the second shoe and lets it drop. If there is a long pause after the first shoe drops, the downstairs people are stuck waiting for the other shoe to drop.

Reading between the lines in Luke's story, it seems like the shepherds responded to Gabriel's good news by deciding to go and seek visual proof. So they left their poor sheep behind to go check it out. If even first-century uneducated superstitious shepherds were skeptical about the good news of the birth of a child who would change the world, then it's a safe bet to assume that twenty-first century educated rational cosmopolitan sophisticated Americans are going to be skeptical that the birth of Jesus represents anything other than a warm and fuzzy story about the ostensible founder of our religion. Have we simply created a nice story, a nice mythology, to help us through the winter doldrums, or is the birth of Jesus truly good news for the human race? I hear the dude upstairs taking off his shoes . . .

THE CHARMIN SIDE OF GOD

Admittedly, the Christmas story is kind of weird. Well, so is Christmas. What other time of the year do we sit around a dead tree and eat candy out of a stocking? On the other hand, as a briefs-wearing young boy, Christmas was a time to relish because my paternal grandmother's tradition was to buy all of her grandchildren new underwear for Christmas. How can you beat that? This was the essence of "good news" for me as a youngster. I love the feel of new underwear. And so do you. Just admit it.

Christmas is also weird because it upsets almost all of our normal routines. We spend several weeks building up to it, and we spend about another week in this weird holiday mood and then things get back to normal once again. One reason the holiday season is such a routine-buster is because many people do a lot of traveling. I always feel like I should be packing my bags, changing my oil, and hitting the highway like I did one year when my son and I took off from Kentucky for Texas after the eleven o'clock Christmas Eve service in order to beat an approaching ice storm. Whether we are traveling or not, the holidays do a good job of breaking us out of our normal routines. This is what happened on the first Christmas when Gabriel suddenly appeared to that group of shepherds. The most monotonous job in the world suddenly became interesting. The nightly shekel ante poker game came to an end. Trump, I mean, Luke says a "*yuge* angelic choir" appeared with Gabriel singing a praise song. I would have loved to have seen Elvis play the role of Gabriel in a movie, leading a choir of beautiful angels. But alas, it wasn't meant to be. Unless he's not dead yet.

Another reason the Christmas story is weird is because it introduced a relatively strange understanding of God to the world. For millions of future people, the face, reputation, and mission of the God of Western society would forever change. People often talk about how the baby Jesus changed history, but I say that the baby Jesus changed *God*, or at least our understanding of God. I'm not the only one who thinks this. Nadia Bolz-Weber is a heavily pierced and tattooed middle-aged pastor from the House for All Sinners and Saints Lutheran church in Denver, Colorado. Nadia is about as different as they come in terms of clergypersons. The late writer, Phyllis Tickle, said, "Nadia Bolz-Weber has probably done more than any other pastor in recent times to poke therapeutic fun at the misdemeanors and flaws of overly-churched Christianity and Christians."[5] Immediately I knew that I liked her when I read this. Nadia is one of the most interesting and provocative communicators of theology since Joan Osbourne's 1991 song, "What if God was one of us," where Osbourne asks whether God is "just a slob like one of us."

Let me share from a sermon Nadia Bolz-Weber preached Easter Sunday (in 2011) to a crowd of, well, sinners, saints, and everyone in between.[6] I've subtly changed the wording of this sermon to reflect my Christology:

> Once upon a time, the God of the Universe was basically fed up with being on the receiving end of all our human projections, tired of being nothing more to us than what we thought God should be: angry, show-offy, defensive, insecure, in short, the vengeance-seeking tyrant we would be if we were God. So, at that time, over 2,000 years ago, God's loving desire to really be known overflowed the heavens and was made manifest in the rapidly dividing cells within the womb of an insignificant peasant girl named Mary. And when the time came for her to give birth . . . there was no room in our expectations—no room in any impressive or spiffy or safe place. So this (child) was born in straw and dirt. He grew up, this Jesus of Nazareth, left his home, and found some, let's be honest, rather unimpressive characters to follow him. Fishermen, tax collectors, prostitutes, homeless women with no teeth, Ann Coulter and Charlie Sheen. If you think I'm kidding . . . read it for yourselves. These people were questionable. So, with his little band of misfits Jesus went about the countryside turning water to wine, eating with all the wrong people, angering the religious establishment and insisting that in him the kingdom of God had come near, that through him the world according to God was coming right to us. He touched the unclean and used spit and dirt to heal the blind and said crazy destabilizing things like the first shall be last and the last shall be first, and sell all you have and give it to the poor. And the thing that really cooked people's noodles wasn't the question 'is Jesus like God' it was 'what if God is like Jesus'. What if God is not who we thought? What if the most reliable way to know God is not through religion, not through a sin and punishment program, but through a person? What if the most reliable way to know God is to look at how God chose to reveal God's self in Jesus?

---

5. "Nadia Bolz-Weber." https://www.pts.edu/Being_Church_Bolz-Weber

6. See full sermon at: https://sojo.net/articles/reflection-easter-beyond-chocolate-and-new-bedding-true-gospel.

Exactly. What *if* God is like Jesus, and not the other way around? To be more specific and thought-provoking, what if God is like the baby Jesus? The next opportunity you have to hold a baby, tell yourself that this is how both humanity and divinity (whatever that is) is best revealed to the world. Now, that's weird, and it's also good news. This forces us to re-think how we understand God. Even if we don't realize what is happening to us, the Christmas story is like electroconvulsive or electroshock therapy to our souls. It induces a seizure of our theology. It forces us to see God in a different light.

For example, rather than see God through the eyes of Abraham, who almost sacrificed his firstborn son to a tyrannical god, or through the eyes of Noah, who built a giant ark in order to escape a species-ending flood, or through the eyes of an Old Testament prophet like Jonah, who was spewed out of a giant fish in order to preach to people who needed to "turn or burn," we are persuaded to see God through the eyes of poor, tired, dirty shepherds who gazed into the eyes of a newborn infant and somehow saw the depths of God's love.

If we think about this without our preconceived culturally formed understanding of God, we have to admit that getting a glimpse of divinity in a newborn baby is one of the strangest stories in the history of religion itself. Babies are too vulnerable, too helpless and powerless, too sweet to portray divinity. Babies change our view of reality in all kinds of ways. I remember when my first child was born, the attending nurse said to me as we walked down the hall to the birthing room, "The birth of a baby will make you believe in God." I smiled and took for granted what she said, yet since then I have come to understand that seeing the birth of my first-born child didn't just persuade me to believe in God; it compelled me to believe in God *differently*. This was the softer side of God, the "Charmin" side of God.

So what if God is like Jesus rather than the other way around? I'd like to offer an answer to that question. Without Jesus, specifically the baby Jesus, God's power is coercive. Think about all the stories in the Old Testament where God exercises power over people. Going back to the three stories I mentioned above, Abraham almost sacrifices his son because he felt coerced to do so. Noah is compelled to build an ark. Jonah is forced to preach to the Ninevites. God is a coercive God, sans Jesus. With Jesus, however, God's power is exercised in a different way. The Christmas story introduces us to the notion that God's power is persuasive rather than coercive. God persuades the world through the gentleness and warm fuzzies of a little baby. Again, the softer side—the "Charmin" side—of God. By the way, if I'm offending anyone by comparing God to toilet paper, I apologize. I would suggest, however, that the human waste system is a decent argument for the theory of Intelligent Design, except for the minor inconvenience of the odor. Other than that, Intelligent Design theory is just stupid.

In the Christmas story God comes to us in the soft skin of a baby, diaper rash and all, a weakened, vulnerable, crying, dependent infant. What if God is like the baby Jesus rather than the "Big Jesus" of much of the New Testament and Christian tradition? How would that change the way we treat one another, the way we treat our enemies, the way we treat the weak and the vulnerable? Wouldn't we lose our power, lose control, lose our competitive edge over other religions, other philosophies, other worldviews? Here's my answer: If the good news of a particular religion is predicated upon power, control, and a competitive edge, then that particular religion needs to be flushed down the toilet.

Luke 2:25–27

Now there was a man in Jerusalem whose name was Simeon; this man was righteous and devout, looking forward to the consolation of Israel, and the Holy Spirit rested on him. It had been revealed to him by the Holy Spirit that he would not see death before he had seen the Lord's Messiah.

THAT'S SO PREDICTABLE

ALLOW ME TO TRY my Jeanne Dixon impersonation and make a prediction or two about the future. In the spirit of the *Farmer's Almanac,* I predict that in the near future there will be sunshine and snow, hurricanes and tornadoes, and floods and droughts. I predict that one or more famous celebrity couples will get a divorce, that a celebrity will have a child (out of wedlock) and name it after a piece of fruit or some other object in nature. I predict that Americans will continue to argue about the size of government, welfare, taxes, immigration, same-sex marriage, abortion, war, capital punishment, and evolution/creationism. How am I doing so far?

If I sound a little pessimistic about the future there is good reason. People who try to predict the future tend to be pessimistic. Just read the so-called futurists as they describe our certain demise in the not-too-distant future due to an environmental, economic, or nuclear holocaust. They may eventually be right, and yet sometimes our pessimism about the future can make us sound rather stupid, especially with the benefit of hindsight.

In 1825, *The Quarterly Review* contained this statement: "What can be more palpably absurd than the prospect held out of locomotives traveling twice as fast as stagecoaches?"[1] Later, in 1901 in *Popular Science,* William

---

1. See: https://www.quotes.net/authors/The+Quarterly+Review+%28England%29

Baxter Jr. noted, "As a means of rapid transit, aerial navigation could not begin to compete with the railroad."[2] Similarly, in 1889, an article in *The Literary Digest* claimed: "The ordinary 'horseless carriage' is at present a luxury for the wealthy; and although its price will probably fall in the near future, it will never, of course, come into as common use as the bicycle."[3] In 1926, Lee Deforest, a scientist and inventor claimed, "While theoretically and technically television may be feasible, commercially and financially, I consider it an impossibility, a development of which we need not waste time dreaming."[4] In 1977, Ken Olson, President of Digital Equipment Corporation, stated, "There is no reason for any individual to have a computer in their home."[5] My favorite pessimistic prognostication of all time comes from the lips of Trip Speaker, the manager of the Cleveland Indians, commenting on Babe Ruth in the spring of 1921: "Ruth made a great mistake when he gave up pitching. Working once a week, he might have lasted a long time and become a great star."[6]

Although most predictions of the future tend to be rather pessimistic, there are a few eternal optimists out there. I suspect most of them are stoned. The Optimist Clubs around the country are smaller than my treehouse club when I was in elementary school. My treehouse club consisted of me and one other tomboy girlfriend. We called it the "Mary-haters Club," although the object of our scorn was not anyone named Mary. We used the name "Mary" so we wouldn't upset the true object of our scorn, whose name will continue to remain anonymous because, well, she's a mean person.

To explain either the optimist or the pessimist, it's best to use illustrations rather than definitions. For example, an optimist is the kind of person who believes a housefly is looking for a way out (or who believes all they need to do to get rid of the flies is to smack a couple of them). A pessimist is someone who, when told to "have a nice day," responds by saying, "No thanks, I have other plans." Pessimists suck.

How we think people will turn out in life has a lot to do with whether we are optimists or pessimists. Have you ever noticed that it seems that no matter how you turned out as an adult, someone always knew you would turn out the way you did? When I tell people back home that I am a minister,

---

%2C+March+1825.

2. See The Proud Americans: https://proudamericans.org/it-will-never-happen-2/.

3. See Liberty Tree: http://libertytree.ca/quotes/The.Literary.Digest.Quote.2BC7.

4. Quoted by Jim Whiddon in "The Wisdom Chronicle." https://crossexamined.org/the-wisdom-chronicle-27/.

5. See Quote Investigator: https://quoteinvestigator.com/2017/09/14/home-computer/.

6. Quoted in "The Experts Speak." http://www.falstad.com/experts.html.

inevitably someone from my childhood (an optimist) says to me, "I knew you had it in you," although most people respond with an overused acronym: WTF? If, on the other hand, I had grown up to be a habitual criminal there would be someone today (a pessimist) saying, "I knew he had it in him." (Perhaps the same characteristics and qualities exist in both future ministers and budding criminals.) Of course, hindsight is twenty-twenty, so looking back and remembering the things about a person that would help them evolve to become what they are today is much easier than predicting the future . . . especially if the one we are predicting about is still an infant. After all, what has an infant done that would give us any hint of his or her future?

This is the situation in Luke 2 where an elderly man named Simeon makes a prediction about Jesus while the latter is still an infant. Is Simeon's prediction an exercise in optimism or pessimism? Before I answer that, let me say a word about Simeon. Some people identify him as a first-century rabbi who was the son of Rabbi Hillel and the father of Rabbi Gamaliel, although I call BS on that. Both of these rabbis are historically significant. Gamaliel is especially important because he belonged to the Sanhedrin, the Jewish ruling council during Jesus' lifetime. Tradition says he was the teacher of the Apostle Paul. He is known to have advocated a generous interpretation of the Law (like Jesus) and, more famously, to have advised the Sanhedrin not to crack down on the emerging Jesus movement, instead allowing the future to determine whether or not it was blessed by God.

Whether or not this family history is true, the Simeon of Luke 2 was no dummy. However, did he have the ability to foresee the future? Did Simeon make a prediction about Jesus' effect on history, or is the event recorded in Luke 2 a matter of hindsight? That is, did the Gospel writer look back several decades after the life and death of Jesus and put words in Simeon's mouth, predictions about Jesus that turned out to be "true"? There is no way to know for certain, although if Luke is *not* looking back with twenty-twenty hindsight and has literally recorded the words of Simeon, then Simeon was a pretty remarkable fellow and perhaps should be celebrated in ways that have yet to be imagined in the Christian tradition. From a critical perspective we can assume that Luke has taken the literary license to create a character and a narrative that benefits the overall Jesus narrative.

Let's be idiots and assume for the moment, however, that Simeon *did* accurately predict Jesus' future. Does this make Simeon an optimist or a pessimist? Does he predict everything will turn out good for the baby Jesus, or will things go sour? If you've read the story then your answer is "yes." Simeon exhibits a mixture of both optimism and pessimism. First, he optimistically predicts that Jesus will bring promise to humanity. Luke writes that when Jesus' parents brought Jesus to the temple to be circumcised, the elderly rabbi took him in his arms and praised God by saying: "Master, now you are dismissing your servant in peace, according to your word; for my eyes have seen your salvation, which you have prepared in the presence of all peoples, a light for revelation to the Gentiles and for glory to your people Israel." I'm almost certain no one said anything like this about me when I was born, although there is the possibility that one of my maternal aunts was in a drunken celebratory mood and said, "That boy is going to make us all proud!"

As Christians we tend to focus almost exclusively on the "good news" of Jesus Christ, do we not? I've never heard anyone call it the "bad news" of Jesus Christ, although, as I noted above, Jesus *is* bad news for some people because of the way he has been used by some of his followers. Most of us, however, myself included, suggest that the birth of the Christ child has brought good things to the world. When we gather to worship in the tradition that bears his name we do so in a celebratory mood. For us, every Sunday is a holiday (i.e. "holy day"). Our religion is a religion of promise, even as many of our congregations continue to dwindle.

If Simeon would have ended his prediction of the effects of Jesus' life at verse 32, we would have reason to call him a sunny optimist. And yet Simeon was a man of complexity and brilliance. To give balance to what he has just said he adds a pessimistic note to his prediction. He predicts that Jesus will bring not just promise, but peril as well. A baby who will grow up to be what I call "Big Jesus" has to encompass elements of both promise and peril. Simeon looks at Jesus' mother and says, "This child is destined for the falling and the rising of many in Israel, and to be a sign that will be opposed so that the inner thoughts of many will be revealed—and a sword will pierce your own soul too." Because of this little baby, Simeon suggests, human beings will be in conflict with one another, and yet even Simeon could not have predicted the conflicts between the early Christians and the Jews, the Christians and the Roman Empire, the Crusades or wars between Christians and Muslims, the current conflicts in the Middle East which have all the trappings of a conflict between Christian and Muslim civilizations, and hundreds of other conflicts, persecutions, and pogroms in between. All because of the birth of Jesus.

Promise and peril. Salvation and sorrow. Redemption and remorse. Simeon's prediction of the effect of Jesus' life on humanity is characterized by both optimism and pessimism. Therefore, Simeon is neither an optimist nor a pessimist, but a *realist*. Was Simeon the inspiration for the twentieth-century theologian, Reinhold Niebuhr, the popularizer of "Christian Realism"? Someone needs to write a paper on that. Like Niebuhr, Simeon understood that with light comes darkness, with good comes evil, with the rising of some comes the falling of others, with the mountaintops comes the valleys.

One of my favorite times of the year happens to be the end of the year, primarily because my birthday falls on New Year's Eve. Along with the arrival of a new year I am tempted to think that everything will finally be copacetic. The beginning of a new year has a way of wiping the slate clean. Old Man Time is replaced with a baby . . . and his diaper is clean. The reason we make resolutions at the beginning of the year is because we are hyped with optimism. We can't very well make resolutions at any other time of the year because we don't have the same sense of starting over and getting things right. Psychologically, we need an injection of optimism that we get at the beginning of a new year. We need an occasion to focus on the positive, the promise, the hope that comes with a new beginning. But the wise old man Simeon knew instinctively that we need to prepare for other things as well.

A healthy spirituality, one that is well-balanced, is one that is rooted in reality. It cultivates a faith that is able to find its way in the darkness as easily as it does in the light. It nurtures a faith that can maintain its goodness even as it withstands the onslaught of evil. A healthy well-balanced spirituality produces a faith that continues to rise in quality even as one's circumstances decline. It grows a faith that is able to walk through the dark valleys of life with the same passion as camping out on the mountaintops.

Simeon's prediction for the baby Jesus is applicable for every generation. Like a psychic who practices cold readings, his words apply to us as much as it did for his own people. Those of us who follow the Christ child are asked to endure it all—the promise and the peril—in any given year. We don't need crystal balls or psychic abilities to know this, although reading a *Farmer's Almanac* couldn't hurt.

Luke 2:41–51

Now every year his parents went to Jerusalem for the festival of the Passover. And when he was twelve years old, they went up as usual for the festival. When the festival was ended and they started to return, the boy Jesus stayed behind in Jerusalem, but his parents did not know it. Assuming that he was in the group of travelers, they went a day's journey. Then they started to look for him among their relatives and friends. When they did not find him, they returned to Jerusalem to search for him. After three days they found him in the temple, sitting among the teachers, listening to them and asking them questions. And all who heard him were amazed at his understanding and his answers. When his parents saw him they were astonished; and his mother said to him, "Child, why have you treated us like this? Look, your father and I have been searching for you in great anxiety." He said to them, "Why were you searching for me? Did you not know that I must be in my Father's house?" But they did not understand what he said to them. Then he went down with them and came to Nazareth, and was obedient to them. His mother treasured all these things in her heart.

THE WANDER YEARS

When Jesus was a child what do you think people thought he would grow up to be, or be like? Have you ever wondered what Jesus was like as a youngster, during that period of time we call "the lost years"? I don't think he was such a bad kid that his parents ever considered throwing him off a cliff, and yet he did manage to cause his parents a little grief. The only story in the four Gospels that give any hint at all about his youthful years is found in the above passage. In this story, Jesus and his family have made the annual trip from Nazareth to Jerusalem for Passover, a major Jewish holiday. Jesus is twelve years old, which is the age at which a young Jewish male officially becomes an adult. Perhaps as a way of reveling in his new status as an adult, Jesus remains in the Temple to discuss theological matters with the local rabbis, even as his parents begin their trip back to Nazareth.

One reason Joseph and Mary may not have immediately noticed Jesus' absence is the possibility the married couples are not traveling together. The women and children usually got a head start on a long trip. Joseph and Mary may have thought that Jesus was with the other one. Joseph may have assumed that Jesus was still young enough to travel with the women and children and Mary may have assumed that since Jesus is now officially an adult he would make the trek back home with the men. His absence is discovered only when the men catch up with the women and children.

Why did Luke include this story in his Gospel? According to Marcus Borg and John Crossan, in their book, *The First Christmas: What the Gospels Really Teach About Jesus' Birth,* the purpose of this story is to make two points about Jesus' transition from late childhood to early adulthood. The first point is that he displayed extraordinary wisdom even at a young age. That is why the following comment is included as he is speaking in the temple to a group of rabbis: "And all who heard him were amazed at his understanding and his answers." The second reason Luke tells the story is expressed in the conversation between Jesus and his parents after they find him in the temple. He asks them, "Why were you searching for me? Did you not know that I must be in my Father's house?" This implies that Luke's Jesus is fully conscious of his divine status (whatever that means).[1]

Luke was not the only writer in the first century or beyond to try to imagine what Jesus was like during those lost years, the years before his ministry began in earnest when he was approximately thirty years old. With anyone who grows up to be famous, we want to know what they were like before they became famous. This is one reason biographies and autobiographies are so popular. What occurred during their formative years? What events helped to shape their life to make them the person they came to be? However, where would a person get this information? In the ancient world people couldn't just go to a library and read about a person. They didn't have access to film footage or the Internet. In that time and place, most of the information about a famous person's life story was passed on by word

---

1. Borg and Crossan, *First Christmas,* 19.

of mouth. Not the most reliable method of research there is, but it's all they had.

One person who attempted to write about the lost years of Jesus is the author of a document called *The Infancy Gospel of Thomas*, not to be confused with the better-known *Gospel of Thomas*. This is one of the many documents written in the first couple of centuries after Jesus' death that did not make it into the New Testament. About this document, the religious historian Bart Ehrman, writes, "Early Christians were naturally curious to learn the details of Jesus' life. As stories circulated about the inspired teachings and miraculous deeds of Jesus' public ministry, some Christians began to speculate on what he said and did before it began." Stories about Jesus' youth began to circulate throughout the church, although the story in Luke 2 is the only story that made it into the New Testament. Ehrman says, "Behind many of these legends lay a fundamental question: If Jesus was a miracle-working Son of God as an adult, what was he like as a child?"[2] *The Infancy Gospel of Thomas* is one of the earliest accounts of these legends of Jesus' childhood. Let me share a couple of these stories with you. If you have never heard these stories before, you will be shocked and awed. (Whatever you do, don't take them literally.):

> When this child Jesus was five years old, he was playing by the ford of a stream; and he gathered the flowing waters into pools and made them immediately pure. These things he ordered simply by speaking a word. He then made some soft mud and fashioned twelve sparrows from it. It was the Sabbath when he did this. A number of other children were also playing with him. But when a certain Jew saw what Jesus had done while playing on the Sabbath, he left right away and reported to his father, Joseph, 'Look, your child at the stream has taken mud and formed twelve sparrows. He has profaned the Sabbath!' When Joseph came to the place and saw what had happened, he cried out to him, 'Why are you doing what is forbidden on the Sabbath?' But Jesus clapped his hands and cried to the sparrows, 'Be gone!' And the sparrows took flight and went off, chirping. When the Jews saw this they were amazed; and they went away and reported to their leaders what they had seen Jesus do.[3]

Obviously, this story connects to stories of the adult Jesus' mastery of nature, references to sparrows, working miracles on the Sabbath, and the significance of the number "twelve" in ancient Israel. If you think Jesus seems a

---

2. Ehrman, *Jesus*, 66.
3. Inf. Gos. Thom. II 1–5.

little rebellious in that story, the next story in *The Infancy Gospel of Thomas* casts a more negative light on the youthful Jesus:

> Now the son of Annas the scribe was standing there with Joseph; and he took a willow branch and scattered the water that Jesus had gathered. Jesus was irritated when he saw what had happened, and he said to him: 'You unrighteous, irreverent idiot! What did the pools of water do to harm you? See, now you also will be withered like a tree, and you will never bear leaves or root or fruit.' Immediately that child was completely withered. Jesus left and returned to Joseph's house. But the parents of the withered child carried him away, mourning his lost youth. They brought him to Joseph and began to accuse him, 'What kind of child do you have who does such things?'[4]

(I overheard my school principal utter these words to my parents on more than one occasion.)

I think we can understand why these stories and others like them didn't make it into the New Testament. I can also understand why they were written. What Christian in the early centuries before the New Testament was put together wouldn't be curious about Jesus' childhood? So, what was he really like as a kid?

If there is any truth to the story in Luke 2, we can say that at the very least Jesus was extremely intelligent. When people talk about Jesus' characteristics in general (even as an adult) his intelligence is not often highlighted. I find this curious because that's the first thing I notice when I read the Gospels. To me, the parables and many of his other teachings are proof that what we have here is a first-rate mind. We could even say that Jesus was a savant. Don't misunderstand what I'm saying. This word "savant" is often associated with people who have neurological disorders like autism and yet are profoundly intelligent in a particular area.[5] When I say Jesus was savant I don't mean it in that way. I don't think Jesus had profound intellectual skills along with neurological disorders. Rather, a savant, by definition, is sim-

---

4. Inf. Gos. Thom. III 1–3.

5. An obvious example is Dustin Hoffman's character in the movie *Rain Man* (directed by Barry Levenson. MGM, 1988). *Rain Man* is based on the life of one of the most famous savants in the world, Kim Peek, who died on December 19, 2009. Kim was born with severe brain damage. Before he died, his elderly father bathed and dressed him and took him to the public library each day where Kim read books, fast, one page with one eye, and the other page with the other eye and remembered ninety-eight percent of what he read. He knew every city in the United States, postal codes, area codes, zip codes, radio stations, all the presidents and their wives. It was hard to stump him on a history question. Give him any date in the last two-thousand years and he would immediately tell you what day of the week it was on.

ply a person of profound or extensive learning, a scholar, a learned person. Does this best describe the young Jesus? Was he already an accomplished scholar at the age of twelve? Some Jesus historians say no. They argue that although Jesus was very intelligent and wise, he was illiterate, which was the fate of most people in that time and place. As far as we know he never wrote anything and may not have been formally educated, and yet we have ample evidence of his brilliance.

Scholars today point out that Jesus' teachings have more of a sage quality than a scholarly quality to them. His Sermon on the Mount, his parables, and his short sayings or aphorisms would not have required an extensive education, only a keen mind, a "beautiful mind," to use the phrase popularized by a movie about a schizophrenic genius played by Russell Crowe.[6] (And no, I don't think Jesus was schizophrenic either.) I believe Jesus was a profoundly wise sage, if not a learned savant. And I believe he was already showing signs of his wisdom at age twelve. The young Jesus seems to have been very precocious. This means that he matured earlier than normal. The fact that he stayed behind to converse with the scholarly rabbis in the temple suggests that he was precocious enough to think he didn't need his parent's permission.

So, what was Jesus like as a kid during these so-called lost years? Who knows? One thing seems certain. The adult Jesus and the Jesus that Christian tradition would build up to "Big Jesus" status had his roots in a mysterious childhood that continues to titillate our curiosity.[7]

---

6. *A Beautiful Mind*, Universal Pictures, 2001.

7. For an explanation of what I mean by "Big Jesus," you're going to have to put this book down and pick up a copy of my earlier work, *Big Jesus: A Pastor's Struggle with Christology*.

Luke 3:2b–6

. . . the word of God came to John son of Zechariah in the wilderness. He went into all the region around the Jordan, proclaiming a baptism of repentance for the forgiveness of sins, as it is written in the book of the words of the prophet Isaiah, "The voice of one crying out in the wilderness: 'Prepare the way of the Lord, make his paths straight. Every valley shall be filled, and every mountain and hill shall be made low, and the crooked shall be made straight, and the rough ways made smooth; and all flesh shall see the salvation of God.'"

ROAD WORK AHEAD

Much of what we do in life is preparation. We prepare ourselves hygienically in the morning. We prepare breakfast or coffee. Students prepare for school. Workers prepare for the day and for their future retirement. Personally, I spend a great deal of time preparing sermons, prayers, reports, etc. More often than not, however, other activities effectively crowd out crucial prep time for that which I love to do most: preach. Some weeks I have funerals or weddings, or I need to serve communion to shut-ins, visit the sick, attend social engagements, speak at other venues, or attend countless meetings at church or in the community. The possibilities for distractions from sermon preparation are countless. The golf course has its own special allure.

The season of Advent, when the above passage is typically read in a liturgical congregation, brings its own unique set of preparation headaches: preparing Christmas cards to mail to friends and relatives, preparing to travel or preparing to have holiday visitors, preparing gifts with wrapping paper and bows, and preparing holiday snacks and meals. We are so busy preparing at this time of the year that someone needs to invent a new drug called "Preparation H" ("H" for "holidays").

All of that is rather mundane. Spiritually speaking, our task for the season of Advent is to prepare for something much more mysterious, and yet much more rewarding. The biggest cliché uttered during Advent is "prepare the way of the Lord." And yet, what does that even mean? Some of the more pious among us (meaning they probably have something to hide) might assume that it means preparing for the birth of the Christ child, which, in case you haven't heard, has already occurred. Others might claim that it simply means preparing for Christmas, readying our hearts and minds for the more spiritual aspects of the holidays. And still others on the loonier fringes of Christianity might argue that the phrase "prepare the way of the Lord" has something to do with the "Second Coming" of Christ. The problem with all those answers is that none correspond to the reason the phrase was originally uttered.

The phrase was first penned in the fortieth chapter of the book of Isaiah, at the beginning of a section known as "Deutero" or "Second Isaiah."[1] Second Isaiah is thought to have been written around the time the Persians were conquering the Babylonians in the late sixth century BCE. Decades earlier, the Babylonians had taken many of the Jews from their homeland and exiled them in Babylon. Now, thankfully, the Jews are looking forward to the return home. In anticipation of this event, Second Isaiah writes these words:

> Comfort, O comfort my people, says your God. Speak tenderly to Jerusalem, and cry to her that she has served her term, that her penalty is paid, that she has received from the Lord's hand double for all her sins. A voice cries out: "In the wilderness prepare the way of the Lord, make straight in the desert a highway for our God. Every valley shall be lifted up, and every mountain and hill be made low; the uneven ground shall become level, and the rough places a plain." (Isaiah 40:1–4)

In this original context, the meaning of the phrase "prepare the way of the Lord" is quite simple. The exiled Jews needed to return home from Babylon (modern-day Iraq) to Palestine through the desert, and they needed a sixth century BCE version of a highway, one that was as "straight" as possible. None of that forty-year wilderness wandering stuff for them. Of course, it would take an enormous amount of roadwork to build a straight highway

---

1. Isaiah 40–55. The before and after sections of Second Isaiah are traditionally called First (Proto) Isaiah (1–39) and Third (Trito) Isaiah (56–66). Not the same guy.

through the valleys and mountains of this desert terrain. Literally speaking, it couldn't be done, yet Isaiah's words reflect the hope they had for a safe and speedy journey home, accompanied by the Lord.

Now let us fast-forward to the first century CE when the Gospels are written. All four of the Gospels quote Isaiah's "prepare the way of the Lord" refrain, and yet only Luke quotes it in its entirety. Obviously, the historical context has changed. The Gospel writers apply Isaiah's words to the story of John the Baptist. This makes sense because John was a wilderness preacher. He lived out in the desert. And so when the people came to see him they would have had to endure the harsh climate and terrain of the Judean desert. In many ways it would have resembled the journey home of the exiled Jews hundreds of years earlier.

So now the phrase "prepare the way of the Lord" has taken on new meaning. John is preparing the "way" for Jesus. The Gospel writers characterize John as a precursor or preparer of Jesus' ministry. Jesus preached a similar message of baptism and repentance of sins, although he seems to have fine-tuned John's message and added a larger dose of compassion. Jesus built upon John's ministry, perhaps even borrowing many of his followers after John was executed. Therefore in the Gospels the phrase "prepare the way of the Lord" has become less about the hope for a safe and speedy journey across the desert and more about John and his followers preparing for a new spiritual path. To get to that way, however, requires some roadwork, metaphorically speaking. It requires a straight highway or path (that is, no wandering around). And a straight highway in the ancient world would entail valleys that have been lifted up, lower mountains and hills, crooked roads made straight and rough ways made smooth.

This straight highway or path is a wonderful metaphor for the spiritual journey and informs much of Jesus' teachings. We are all on the "way," and yet our journey is beset with many obstacles. We spend much of our time wandering around like the children of Israel in the desert after escaping Egypt, lost and aimless with no clear direction. We spend much of our time dwelling in valleys of depression and despondency, while on occasion dwelling on mountaintops of joy. Many of us are spiritually bipolar. We go up and down like yo-yos, depending upon our circumstances. Our spirituality is ungrounded, so we are tossed to and fro by the chance happenings of everyday living. We are truly in the wilderness, so we need "roadwork." We need the crooked paths made straight and rough roads smoothed over. And that takes a heck of a lot of preparation.

Spirituality resembles road work. All religions have produced what we call spiritual "disciplines" to help people stay focused on that aspect of their lives. Spirituality resembles roadwork because it's all about making a nice, smooth, straight path, a way for us to journey through life, with all its bumps, pot holes, road blocks, dangerous curves, and detours. Spirituality resembles road work because it's all about making it down that highway of life without getting lost, run over, or broken down on the side of the road. This imagery is captured well in *The Message*, Eugene H. Peterson's contemporary language paraphrase of the New Testament:

> Thunder in the desert!
> "Prepare God's arrival!
> Make the road smooth and straight!
> Every ditch will be filled in,
> Every bump smoothed out,
> The detours straightened out,
> All the ruts paved over.
> Everyone will be there to see
> The parade of God's salvation." (3:4–6)

I love the end result of all that spiritual roadwork: a parade. Even as the roads are made straight and smooth, the new sidewalks are built, all the ditches are filled in, the bumps are smoothed out, the detours are eliminated, and the ruts are eradicated, we get a parade. I say "even as" because, as we well know, the roadwork never ends. Drive through Indiana some day and you'll discover what I mean.[2]

---

2. Speaking of another state where the roads are suspect, I recently learned that there are only two seasons in the state of Montana: winter and road work.

Luke 3:21–22

Now when all the people were baptized, and when Jesus also had been baptized and was praying, the heaven was opened, and the Holy Spirit descended upon him in bodily form like a dove. And a voice came from heaven, "You are my Son, the Beloved; with you I am well pleased."

GOING ROGUE

THERE'S ALWAYS SOMEONE IN a crowd who wants to be different, unique, non-conformist, or independent. Or, to put it another way, there's always someone who wants to go rogue. "Rogue" became in vogue (sorry, couldn't resist) after Sarah Palin published her book titled *Going Rogue: An American Life* (HarperCollins, 2009). She didn't just pluck that title out of thin air. About ten days before the election in 2008, tensions were high between Governor Palin and aides to Senator John McCain. CNN reported that McCain's people became frustrated with what one aide described as Palin "going rogue."

What exactly does that word mean anyway? The dictionary defines a "rogue" as a scoundrel, a dishonest person, or a mischievous person. None of those definitions seemed to me to describe exactly what the McCain people meant when they used that word in reference to Sarah Palin. But then I found another definition. To describe someone as a rogue can mean that they are merely a "problem." A "rogue nation," for example, is a nation that has become a problem to the rest of the world mainly because they don't want to play by everyone else's rules. One of my dictionaries actually has as an entry "rogue elephant" to describe a vicious elephant that has been exiled from the herd. I would not describe Sarah Palin as "vicious" either, and yet I do find it ironic that the symbol for the Republican Party is the elephant.

Whether you agree with Sarah Palin's politics or not, you had to admire her ability to be a pain in the backside, a non-conformist, and a person with an independent streak. Interestingly, the word "maverick" (McCain's label), in this context, is someone who takes an independent stand in politics. The point is that Palin turned someone's derogatory remark about her "going rogue" into the title of a best-selling book, although I did notice shortly after the Palin phenomenon faded away that her book was easily found in abundance on discount racks in chain bookstores. I have no idea why. .

To one degree or another, most people have a roguish streak in them. Human beings enjoy their uniqueness. Sometimes we just want to be part of the crowd; other times we want to stand out in a crowd. Sometimes we just want to be like everyone else; other times we want to be our own person. Sometimes we want to do things like everybody else does things; other times, like Frank Sinatra, we want to do it "my way." And sometimes when we do it our own way we become a bit of a problem to others. As Antonio Porchia said, "They will say that you are on the wrong road, if it is your own."[1] This is primarily what it means to go rogue.

It seems that in terms of religion there are more people going rogue in America than ever before. Mark Penn was Hillary Clinton's chief campaign strategist during the 2008 presidential campaign. Penn writes a column for *Wall Street Journal* called "Microtrends." He also published a book several years ago with the same title. Penn does statistical analysis of various trends in America and around the world. In a column called "Religious Independents: God Without the Religion," he makes the argument based on statistical analysis that Americans are more religiously and politically independent than ever before.[2] According to a recent *American Religious Identification Survey*, only 76 percent of Americans identify as Christians, down from 86 percent in 1990. But these non-Christians are not choosing another religion such as Islam or Judaism. Nor are they choosing atheism. Instead they are choosing what Penn calls a "secular Third Way" in religion. According to a 2008 Gallup poll, 15 percent of Americans—up from 8 percent in 1999— say they don't believe in a traditional view of God as expressed by the major world religions, and yet they do believe in a "Higher Power" or "Universal Spirit." They also reject the authority of the New Testament, the Torah, and the Koran. Penn claims that this growing group of Religious Independents

---

1. In *Voces*, 1943, translated from Spanish by W.S. Merwin.

2. Penn, Mark. "Religious Independents: God Without the Religion." *Wall Street Journal* (2009). https://www.wsj.com/articles/SB126101681731094729.

is much like political independents, a group that has also reached record highs, people that vote but refuse to affiliate with a political party.

So, what we have now are a couple of paradoxes in American life. First, overall participation in the political process is growing, but identification with a political party is diminishing. Second, overall belief in a Spiritual Being is rising, but participation in organized religion is declining. This poses a problem for those of us in organized religion. How do we reach out to the independents? How do we reach out to those who have gone rogue?

Going rogue, religiously speaking, is not a new phenomenon. Every important religious leader who has ever lived began as a rogue in the sense of going his or her own way, usually to the point of becoming a problem for the dominant religion of the day. Jesus of Nazareth, of course, is a good example. His independent streak resulted in his execution by the Roman government, supported by the religious leaders. Before we ever get to Jesus, however, we are introduced to a man known as John the Baptist. If there ever was a person who could write an autobiography titled *Going Rogue*, it was John the Baptist. Here is a man who wore a camel's hair garment and ate locusts and wild honey. Here is a man who, when seeing the elite religious leaders of his day coming to him for baptism, called them a "brood of vipers." Here is a man who was operating outside of the Jewish temple in Jerusalem, the center of religious and political authority in first-century Palestine. He did it *his* way. He asserted his independence. He went and became a nuisance, a problem.

John really became a problem when he condemned Herod Antipas, son of the late Herod the Great, for marrying his brother's wife, Herodias. Antipas had John arrested and eventually beheaded at the request of Antipas' wife and dancing daughter. The problem was no more, except for the fact that a young man named Jesus picks up where John left off and eventually becomes an even bigger problem for the religious and political authorities, mainly because of his ability to gather large crowds of peasants together (which worried the Romans), and his tendency to preach against some of the major tenets of first-century Judaism (which worried the religious leaders).

Other than John the Fetus jumping for joy in the presence of Jesus the Fetus, we first see an encounter between John the Baptist and Jesus the Christ at the latter's baptism. This compels me to make a rather roguish statement: Baptism is one of the most extreme acts of independence a person can do (if an adult makes that decision on behalf of him/herself). Christian baptism has its origin in the ministry of John the Baptist. Because we do not live in that place and time we may miss the original meaning and purpose of John's practice of baptism. So let me try to set the scene.

John was an eschatologist, that is, he believed that God was coming soon to avenge and purify a world of impurities and injustices. He believed that Roman oppression was a punishment for the sins of Israel. John Dominic Crossan writes, "What was needed, therefore, was a great sacrament of repentance, a popular repetition of ancient Israel's coming out of the desert, crossing the Jordan, and entering the Promised Land."[3] John's ministry was a criticism of the oppression of the Roman Empire and the injustices of Rome's puppet king, Herod Antipas. Like Jesus, John's ministry was also nonviolent, although John believed God would do some kind of "Divine Cleanup" at some point in the near future. God doesn't just have a "Charmin" side; according to John the Baptist, God has a "Bounty" side as well.

Nevertheless, when you are convincing people to come way out into the desert to undergo a moral cleansing, symbolized by the physical washing of baptism, you are feeding people's hostility toward the authorities, both secular and religious, because you are implying that they have failed in their duties. You are encouraging people to go rogue, much like the American people in recent years who attended those weird Tea Party rallies. Crossan writes, "No matter how nonviolent (John the Baptist's) proclamation was in theory, (he) was planting ticking time bombs of eschatological expectation all over the Jewish homeland."[4] John's ministry of baptism was an act of sedition, stirring up a rebellion against the Roman and Jewish authorities. For John, and then perhaps for Jesus, repentance and baptism were overtly political acts of anti-imperial subversion. Somewhere I read that baptism was a symbolic act that would have been comparable to burning draft cards.

I would never suggest that when we are baptized we are taking part in an act of sedition, subversion, or roguish behavior, mainly because our practice of baptism has become little more than a symbolic gesture of benign faithfulness. And yet we must recognize that the historical roots of our sacrament of baptism were risky, courageous, non-conformist acts of religious and political independence. I can imagine that this is exactly what was going through Jesus' mind as he was baptized and he allowed his own imagination to see that "heaven was opened, and the Holy Spirit descended upon him in bodily form like a dove" and he listened as "a voice came from heaven," saying, "You are my Son, the Beloved; with you I am well pleased." It was at that moment that Jesus knew he was going rogue.

---

3. Crossan, *God & Empire*, 111–12.
4. Crossan, *God & Empire*, 112.

Luke 4:1–13

Jesus, full of the Holy Spirit, returned from the Jordan and was led by the Spirit in the wilderness, where for forty days he was tempted by the devil. He ate nothing at all during those days, and when they were over, he was famished. The devil said to him, "If you are the Son of God, command this stone to become a loaf of bread." Jesus answered him, "It is written, 'One does not live by bread alone.'" Then the devil led him up and showed him in an instant all the kingdoms of the world. And the devil said to him, "To you I will give their glory and all this authority; for it has been given over to me, and I give it to anyone I please. If you, then, will worship me, it will all be yours." Jesus answered him, "It is written, 'Worship the Lord your God, and serve only him.'" Then the devil took him to Jerusalem, and placed him on the pinnacle of the temple, saying to him, "If you are the Son of God, throw yourself down from here, for it is written, 'He will command his angels concerning you, to protect you,' and 'On their hands they will bear you up, so that you will not dash your foot against a stone.'" Jesus answered him, "It is said, 'Do not put the Lord your God to the test.'" When the devil had finished every test, he departed from him until an opportune time.

WAY TOO MUCH TIME ON HIS HANDS

TEMPTATIONS. WE ALL HAVE them. I've been having them ever since I figured out a way to grab "girlie" magazines from my parents' grocery store and take them out back for a peek. Even Jesus had temptations, although he never had to withstand the wiles of *Hustler*. One of the best known stories in the Gospels is the "temptation of Christ" story. We find it in Matthew, Mark, and Luke. We probably don't find it in John's Gospel because John's Jesus is a little too divine for something as human as being tempted. This story, by the way, is not to be confused with the movie and novel by Nikos Kazantzakis, *The Last Temptation of Christ* (Bruno Cassirer, 1955), which was a fictional account about Jesus' temptation to climb down from the cross during his crucifixion. The movie (Universal Pictures, 1988), starring Willem Defoe, is awesome. I once managed to cross a picket line of sober Baptists in order to see it with a couple of other determined recovering-Baptist buddies.

The account in the above passage is about Jesus' first temptation, or rather, temptations. According to the story, after Jesus is baptized he is led by the Spirit into the wilderness, presumably the Judean desert, for a period of fasting. In the biblical tradition, fasting usually implies that a person is engaged in a great spiritual struggle. This story may help us understand the thoughts that were swirling around in Jesus' head after his baptism. The writer tells us that Jesus fasted for forty days and nights. Elijah and Moses in the Hebrew Scriptures fasted for forty days and nights as well. There's nothing magical about the number "forty." To the ancients it simply meant "a large amount." "Forty days and nights" means "a long time." Also, fasting does not necessarily mean a complete abstinence from food. One couldn't survive that long without food. Instead, it means that people only have access to sparse amounts of food while they are in a place like a desert.

So why did Jesus do this? It was at his baptism that he seems to have received his calling as the Christ or Messiah, the anointed One of God. He needed time to reflect on this so he seeks some alone time. While in the desert we are told that he is tempted by the "devil." If you are not inclined to believe that a man with fiery red skin, horns on his head, a lashing tail, and a pitchfork in hand actually carried on a conversation with Jesus, then think of this as a man struggling with his own thoughts. If you've ever been alone for a long period of time you can probably understand the dynamic at work here. The phrase "alone in one's thoughts" implies that a person has a lot of uninterrupted time to think.

We can imagine that Jesus had many more thoughts during his time in the wilderness that are not recorded by the storyteller and would not be classified as temptations. Many of them may have been thoughts about his life as a child, thoughts about his loved ones, fearful thoughts, happy thoughts, and yes, even some idle or wasteful thoughts such as we all have during the course of a day. Nevertheless, the storyteller wants us to know that a big portion of Jesus' internal thoughts were temptations that most people rarely if ever have.

Jesus struggled with three specific things. First, whether or not to make bread out of stones to relieve his hunger. Second, whether or not to worship the devil in order to have political authority in all the kingdoms of the world. Third, whether or not to throw himself down from the top of a pinnacle, most likely the temple in Jerusalem, and rely on the angels to break his fall. Kind of weird, huh? This story has often been used to argue that Jesus had temptations like every other human being. I don't buy that. Maybe I have never been this hungry, yet I have never thought for one moment that I could make bread out of stones, I have never had a desire to rule all the nations on the earth (or worship the devil), and I have never been tempted to jump from a high place.[1]

Truth be told (because I am under oath), I am somewhat afraid of heights. I might even have a phobia. When I was a youngster my relatives on my dad's side spent many weekends at a park fishing, swimming, and playing poker. One of the favorite activities of the clan was to dive headfirst from the top of a bridge into the river below. I couldn't even muster up the courage to stand on the guardrail in order to jump. All I could do was climb over the guardrail and hang on to the bottom of it and let go feet first into the water below. Even that scared the-you-know-what out of me (ironically, it scared the devil out of me). So, no, I can't relate to any of the temptations Jesus faced in the desert. The only temptation I would have had would be to get out of the desert as fast as I can and find the nearest Dairy Queen.

Nevertheless, I can relate to temptations in general, as we all can. In fact, as a minister I probably face more than my fair share. I found a list of ten temptations that often torture me and my fellow clergypersons. The list was offered at the 2007 National Pastors Convention in San Diego by John Ortberg. Ortberg argued that clergypersons are tempted to be inauthentic, live for recognition, live in fear, compare myself to others, exaggerate and plagiarize, live with a chronic sense of inadequacy, be proud, manipulate people, envy, and be angry. Of that list, I think the biggest temptation for me is to be inauthentic, that is, to be someone I am not.

I spoke about this one night at an Ash Wednesday service, using the word "hypocrisy." Hypocrisy is being someone you are not. I argued that this is not always a bad thing because sometimes we have to act better than we are to become better than we are. We have to practice being someone we might not actually be in order to (hopefully) become the person we want to be. Still, there has to be at least a modicum of authenticity in a person's life. Even while we are struggling to be better than we are there has to be some

---

1. I will admit, however, that in my younger days I ate a lot of bread while I was "stoned."

frank acknowledgement of who we are, what we do, and what we think or believe. To be inauthentic is a big temptation for many ministers.

One doesn't have to be a minister to experience temptations. Everyone can produce a long list of personal temptations. Despite the Tiger Woods phenomenon, not all temptations have to do with sex (or fame, fortune, and food). Temptations are insidious because they are often more mundane than any of those things. The worst temptations are not the ones that are so obvious; they are the ones that are more ambiguous, such as the temptation to envy. When a temptation is mundane, common, ambiguous, or unobvious we are less likely to try to overcome it because we don't recognize it as a temptation. Those are the truly insidious ones.

Sometimes we are confused about whether something is a temptation or not. There's the humorous account of the person who walked into an open church for a few minutes of contemplation and found a purse in the pew in front of him. Since no one else was in the church, a question promptly rose in his mind: Was this a temptation, or an answer to a prayer? There is a lot of ambiguity about this temptation business.

One other thing I have observed about temptations is that they are more obvious among people who have power, and therefore more easily spotted. Again, Tiger Woods, one of the most recognized persons in the world because of his fame and fortune, is a case study in this. Bill Clinton also comes to mind. I don't mean to compare Tiger and Bill with Jesus, yet there is a connection in terms of their personal power. In Luke's story, Jesus has just been called by God to be the Christ, the anointed One. Don't you think the temptations of that "office" would be considerable?

Notice that Jesus' temptations were all about power: economic power to produce bread out of rocks, political power to control the world's governments, and physical power to jump from a tall building and land safely on the ground. People with power have more obvious temptations. This applies to people high up the ladder in governments, corporations, and other institutions that have power. Their temptations are great. Because of this should we cut them some slack? Nah.

Luke 4:16–30

When he came to Nazareth, where he had been brought up, he went to the synagogue on the Sabbath day, as was his custom. He stood up to read, and the scroll of the prophet Isaiah was given to him. He unrolled the scroll and found the place where it was written: "The Spirit of the Lord is upon me, because he has anointed me to bring good news to the poor. He has sent me to proclaim release to the captives and recover of sight to the blind, to let the oppressed go free, to proclaim the year of the Lord's favor." And he rolled up the scroll, gave it back to the attendant, and sat down. The eyes of all in the synagogue were fixed on him. Then he began to say to them, "Today this scripture has been fulfilled in your hearing." All spoke well of him and were amazed at the gracious words that came from his mouth. They said, "Is not this Joseph's son?" He said to them, "Doubtless you will quote to me this proverb, 'Doctor, cure yourself!' And you will say, 'Do here also in your hometown the things that we have heard you did at Capernaum.'" And he said, "Truly I tell you, no prophet is accepted in the prophet's hometown. But the truth is, there were many widows in Israel in the time of Elijah, when the heaven was shut up three years and six months, and there was a severe famine over all the land; yet Elijah was sent to none of them except to a widow at Zarephath in Sidon. There were also many lepers in Israel in the time of the prophet Elisha, and none of them was cleansed except Naaman the Syrian." When they head this, all in the synagogue were filled with rage. They got up, drove him out of the town, and led him to the brow of the hill on which their town was built, so that they might hurl him off the cliff. But he passed through the midst of them and went on his way.

THE SUFFERER'S CLUB

Regardless of race, ethnicity, sexual orientation, age, ability, or religion there are certain things that all people have in common. Perhaps the most common experience among people of every persuasion is *fear*. If you have never feared, you have never lived. I'm talking about everything from first day of school jitters to the intense fear we feel when a loved one's life is in danger. There have been very few times in my life that I have experienced that level of fear. As a teenager I was in a bad accident, but didn't realize my life had been in serious danger until later.

In early 2010, however, I was as fearful for the life of a loved one as I have ever been. My son was in a terrible fire and was fortunate to survive. He is doing very well now, thank you very much. Some of you have lived through similar experiences. As one lady wrote to me at the time, letting me know that she had gone through something very similar, "I have lived through every parent's worst nightmare: getting a phone call from someone telling you something bad has happened to one of your children." My son's accident was life-altering for me in many respects, yet the one thing I learned above all else is that I'm not alone in this by any stretch of the imagination. Almost every parent will have to face the fear of losing a child at one time or another, as my parents had to back in 1974 when I almost died in a motorcycle accident.

Although parenthood is usually accompanied with many great rewards, it is also fraught with potential heartache, sadness, and even tragedy. And yet you don't have to be a parent to experience these things. You merely have to love another human being. Loving other human beings makes one vulnerable to suffering, and the fear of that potential loss is always just under the surface of one's conscious awareness, ready to awake from its light sleep whenever the phone rings in the middle of the night. I tremble when I think of how many people receive heart-wrenching phone calls, emails, or text messages about loved ones after the natural disasters or acts of terror and war that seem to plague our planet.

The possibility of loss, heartache, and suffering binds all of us together in our common humanity. We all belong to the same club, so to speak. I remember after my dad had open heart surgery he proudly exclaimed that he was now a member of the "zipper club." After fearing for the life and future well-being of my son I now feel as if I have joined a not very exclusive club. And suddenly, perhaps for the sake of self-survival, I have become very interested in the common human experience. What are those things that bind us together?

Religion, of course, is one place where this binding together occurs. The word "religion" itself stems from a word that literally means "to bind fast," or "a bond between humans and gods." At its core, religion—all religion—exists to bind us all together in common human experiences, the most common of which is suffering. As the Apostle Paul succinctly said, "If one member (of the body of Christ) suffers, all suffer together with it" (1 Cor 12:26). One of the key themes of most religions is that we are all in this together, from Haitians to Afghans to Americans, from Hindus to Muslims to Christians. We all bleed red and we all worry about our children.

My denomination, the United Church of Christ, is an ecumenical denomination. The word "ecumenical" comes from a Latin word for "general" or "universal." At its root it means that we are all in the same "house." Ecumenism reminds us that regardless of race, color, or creed, we are bound together in our common house or humanity. And again, the one thing that all people have in common is the potential for suffering.

The story above gives us a glimpse of our common human experience of suffering. Luke sets up this narrative as Jesus' inaugural sermon. Like a newly ordained minister he appears in his hometown synagogue and reads from the book of Isaiah, chapter 61:

> The Spirit of the Lord is upon me, because he has anointed me to bring good news to the poor. He has sent me to proclaim release to the captives and recovery of sight to the blind, to let the oppressed go free, to proclaim the year of the Lord's favor.

Afterwards he takes ownership of these words by claiming that "today this Scripture has been fulfilled in your hearing." That is, Jesus claims he will continue the prophetic tradition of bringing God's love and grace to suffering humanity. It's a very simple straightforward agenda, not clouded with cumbersome doctrines and theological systems.

The sufferers mentioned here are the poor, the captives, the blind, and the oppressed. A brief look at almost any ancient culture reveals that most people were impoverished, many people were unjustly imprisoned, a great many people suffered from loss of eyesight and other physical ailments, and most people were politically oppressed. So overall this is a good description of the general plight of people in the ancient world. We have to ask, therefore, what all four of these groups have in common. What binds them together with all other human beings, including you and me? Not to sound redundant, but the answer is: the potential for suffering.

If you have never suffered—severely or even trivially—someday you will. It is our common lot as human beings, if not all God's sentient creatures. It's what binds us together. Eventually, if we live long enough each and every one of us will be disabled in some way or another. Because of this, I have come to believe that religions exist primarily to give meaning to suffering. Certainly Jesus understood his mission in this way. For much of the Gospel record Jesus was known and celebrated for his healings and exorcisms. In a day with virtually no medical technology—yet teeming with superstitious explanations for suffering—a healer and an exorcist was the most sought-after member of society, which explains the large crowds that followed Jesus' every move. Christianity, then, was born in the common human desire to alleviate suffering.

Buddhism, a religion from the East, is also rooted in this desire to eliminate suffering, or *dukkha*. The Four Noble Truths of Buddhism are: All existence is suffering; suffering is due to grasping for existence and craving for the pleasures of sense and mind; the cessation of suffering comes with giving up all craving and grasping; and the practice that leads to the cessation of suffering is the Noble Eightfold Path.[1] The point is that in the prominent religion of Buddhism, the cessation of suffering is its ultimate goal. Buddhism is just one attempt to answer the question, "Why is there suffering?"

One of the great questions in the philosophy of religion is, "If God is all-loving, all-knowing, and all-powerful why do the righteous suffer?" This is called the *theodicy* problem which is an attempt to justify God's behavior. There is no answer to the theodicy question that satisfies all religious thinkers. Pat Robertson tried to blame the earthquake in Haiti a few years ago on a pact with the devil that the Haitians made while under French colonial rule.[2] Most people with any common sense reject such idiotic justifications for massive human suffering.

Regardless of why suffering occurs, the message we need to absorb is that the primary purpose, goal, or mission of Jesus, and therefore, Christianity (and almost all other religions) is to alleviate or eliminate suffering. This sounds like an impossible task, but it is our mandate. In terms of how this applies to our lives, let me offer three very simple lessons. We can reflect on how each one will be fleshed out in our own lives. First, do no harm; this is popularly recognized as the "Hippocratic oath." It's a great place to begin. Second, seek opportunities to help those who suffer without any thoughts of being rewarded; this is called "altruism," an unselfish concern for the welfare of others. Finally, never forget that we are all in this together.

A good way to conclude this essay is to quote Hellen Keller, a person who knew much about human suffering: "Although the world is full of suffering," she said, "it is full also of the overcoming of it."

---

1. This consists of right view, right resolve, right speech, right conduct, right livelihood, right effort, right mindfulness, and right union. As far as I know it has nothing to do with the alt-right.

2. James, Frank. "Pat Robertson Blames Haitian Devil Pact For Earthquake." https://www.npr.org/sections/thetwo-way/2010/01/pat_robertson_blames_haitian_d.html.

LUKE 4:16-30

DOWN (AND UP) WITH THE SYSTEM!

Every four years people come out of the woodwork to offer themselves as candidates for president of the United States. They have to attend numerous fundraisers and give countless speeches for almost two years leading up to the election. If you follow a candidate's path to their party's nomination you can watch them develop as a public speaker. Jesus was not a politician, but he did do some public speaking. The first time he gave a public speech is recorded in Luke 4. Luke tells us that after Jesus was baptized and spent a time of temptation in the wilderness, he makes his first public appearance in his hometown of Nazareth. As was his custom, he goes to the local synagogue on the Sabbath day. Somehow he is given the opportunity to speak. We don't know if he simply walked up to the front unannounced or if he had been invited to speak. Perhaps the people demanded to hear from this local boy who had been away for a while and had grown into manhood. Perhaps he had recently earned the status of "rabbi" and the people wanted to give him an opportunity to teach. Perhaps he just muscled his way up there.

Regardless, he opens the scroll and reads the aforementioned passage from Isaiah 61. Afterwards, "he rolled up the scroll, gave it back to the attendant, and sat down." Rabbis in that day taught while sitting down, so Jesus is now seated in front of the entire congregation for the purpose of commenting on the Scripture he had just read. All eyes were fixed on him. And then, like a shooting star, he catches the people totally by surprise, saying, "Today this Scripture has been fulfilled in your hearing."

This is a radical claim. Not only does Jesus link himself with the prophet Isaiah, one of the most revered of all Israel's prophets, he makes a not-so-subtle claim to Messiah-ship by claiming that the Spirit of the Lord had anointed *him*. The word "messiah" literally means "the anointed one," so according to Luke's Gospel Jesus made a claim of special identity in this, his first public appearance. We could say this is Jesus' public outing. And yet many people had made this claim over the years. There were more messiah wannabes running around in that day than there are people on psychiatric medication in our day. (Well, not really, but ironically some of those on medication today have what we call "a messianic complex." There were probably many people in Jesus' day that could have benefited from psychiatric medication. For the record, I don't think Jesus was one of them.)

It wasn't necessarily his claim to be anointed that caused a lot of eyebrows to be raised. It was his claim about what he was going to do. He said he was going to set people free from bondage to poverty, prison, blindness,

53

political oppression, and (one I failed to mention earlier) debt.[3] Jesus chose to read from Isaiah 61 for a purpose. He was sending a message about what he was going to do. Did he succeed? To be honest, he succeeded only on a very limited basis. Aside from telling the poor that they were loved by God, aside from (presumably) healing a few blind people, and curing a few souls, Jesus died before he could accomplish his bold, aggressive agenda. Even if Jesus had lived to a ripe old age, his determination to rid the world of the evils of bondage would have been incomplete. Bondage is a universal human condition. It has always been with us, and always will be, yet Jesus rightly understood that he was anointed or called to do something about it. In fact, the "kingdom of God," as Jesus understood it, was an image of the world without the evils of bondage.

One reason bondage is so universal is because it is usually systemic. Human bondage is often part of a larger system over which we as individuals have very little control. Political and economic systems are out of our control. Legal systems are out of the control of individuals. And because all these types of bondage are largely systemic we don't know how to confront it. One way we often deal with bondage is to blame the victim. We determine that evil in general, and bondage in particular, is usually caused directly by individuals who simply make poor choices. Let me illustrate this way of thinking with the contemporary issue of poverty, one of the examples Jesus used.

Poverty, of course, is still with us today and is a definite form of bondage. We often deal with the problem of poverty by claiming that it is a result of poor choices by morally bankrupt people (pardon the pun). People say, "The American dream is available to anyone who is disciplined, moral, and enterprising. The poor are by definition lazy and immoral—simply not willing to lift themselves by their bootstraps." Poverty is a form of *self*-bondage, people claim. We put ourselves in bondage with poor choices. Do you see how easy this approach to poverty is? It's a nice cop-out because it doesn't require much from the non-poor, other than a few charitable acts accompanied with derogatory statements. If Jesus had had this view of bondage he would have said something like this:

> The Spirit of the Lord is upon me, because he has anointed me to tell the poor to get off their lazy asses and get to work. He has sent me to build more prisons for the captives and to tell the blind they can only have eye surgery if they have health insurance (which, if they don't have it, it's because they're lazy), to

---

3. The "year of the Lord's favor" is likely the "Year of Jubilee," which was, theoretically, a massive debt-forgiveness program.

tell the oppressed to stay in their own country and don't even try crossing our borders, to proclaim that people who get into debt should be smart enough to pay off their credit cards each month.

That doesn't quite sound like Jesus, does it? No, because Jesus understood that bondage in all its manifestations is not as simple as immoral people making bad choices. The evil of bondage is largely systemic. That doesn't mean that individuals are always powerless to help themselves, yet it is a recognition that the problem is more systemic than not.

A systemic thinker (like Jesus) will have a different approach to the problem of poverty. A systemic thinker will look at a more complex set of factors such as educational disadvantages, cultural biases, the hangover effect of slavery and racism, entrenched institutions, as well as, yes, some government policies that have created an environment of dependence. Systemic thinkers see the growing gap between rich and poor as something more than just a natural consequence of a free market. Because Jesus understood that bondage is largely systemic he courageously declared to his hometown audience that his mission would be to fight the system as best he could. After he died the early Christians took up the fight against the evils of human bondage to varying degrees of success.

One of the more enlightened passages in the Bible from a systemic perspective is 1 Corinthians 12:12ff. Here, the Apostle Paul makes the argument that just as evil is systemic, so is good. He describes the church as a "body" of "members," each one contributing to the whole. The church is called to be "the body of Christ," working to continue Jesus' legacy of fighting the systems of bondage. Paul understood that we are all part of a larger system, the institution of the church, and if we all work together, like the members of a human body, then we can accomplish more than we ever could as individuals. Just as the causes of evil are often complex and systemic—including the evil of bondage—so are the causes of good.

Earlier I mentioned the ecumenical movement and the role of my denomination, the United Church of Christ, in that movement. The purpose of this movement is in fact to create a system of good to counter the systems of evil. The ecumenical movement recognizes that we can do more good works together than separately. Looking at the list of social ills Jesus quotes from the book of Isaiah, the ecumenical movement has worked tirelessly around the world in the last century to fight poverty, to free political prisoners, to offer health care, to end oppression of all kinds, and to help eradicate debt in Third World countries. The story of the ecumenical church is the continuation of the goals Jesus set for himself in Luke 4 when he stood in front of those who knew him from childhood and told them what he wanted to do. Yes, the systemic forces of evil eventually killed him for his efforts, and yet the systemic forces of good, bearing Jesus' name, continue to break the chains of bondage with God's help.

STUFF WE WON'T HEAR ANYWHERE ELSE

Why do people go to church? Don't laugh. I'm asking a serious question. What is it that compels some of us to crawl out of bed on a Sunday morning and drive to our favorite sanctuaries? Let me offer a few obvious reasons before I offer one that you may not have ever thought about before.

One answer is that we come to worship God. True, but can't we worship God in other places that are more quiet or serene? Furthermore, is God really so egocentric or insecure that s/he actually needs our worship?

Some people attend church because they want to learn more about God and/or religion. True, but can't we do this by reading books, attending a couple of seminars, or hiring a spiritual guru? The Internet has a lot of handy info as well.

Many people come to church because they want to experience community. This is a good reason too, yet can't we experience community at work, at the local pub, at the Country Club, with a civic group, or over morning coffee at the local Dairy Queen?

Others belong to a church because they want to learn how to be good. Okay, but didn't our parents teach us how to be good? Can't we learn how to be good by observing other role models?

I guess what I'm trying to ask is whether or not there is anything we can find in church that we can't find somewhere else. (In case your answer is "pews," then you haven't been in a courtroom lately.) In Barbara Brown Taylor's book *Leaving Church* (HarperOne, 2006), she actually offers one of the best arguments I have ever heard for *staying* in church. Talk about irony. Describing her experience on Sunday morning she writes, "We had nowhere else to go and nothing else to do but sit there together, saying sonorous words in unison, listening to language *we did not hear anywhere else in our lives.*" When I read this I nearly jumped out of my chair I was so excited. You would have thought I had discovered the fountain of youth or a cure for AIDS or a secret button on my television remote control that actually finds a good program. Taylor is exactly right. Where else are we going to hear words and phrases like "take heart," "go in peace" or "bear fruit," to give the examples she uses? In our liturgy on Sunday mornings we see and hear words that, I dare say, are rarely ever heard in everyday conversations, and if they are, they are often used in very different contexts. Many congregations often begin worship by "passing the peace." In what other setting in your day-to-day activities does someone offer you "the peace of Christ"?

One doesn't have to dig very deeply in the Bible or our liturgy to find words that bless and inspire us. The prophet Jeremiah, to give one example, claims that he believed the "word of the Lord" came to him, saying, "Before I formed you in the womb I knew you (Jeremiah 1:5)." Before these words came to be used in a contentious way in the modern abortion debate, they were words of grace for a man who struggled with his calling to be a prophet of Israel. These words offered him a sense of meaning, purpose, and self-worth, and they do for us as well.

In a typical Sunday morning worship service you and I will hear and say words like "trust," "delivers," "rescues," "refuge," "saves," "created," "accepts," "affirms," "love," "embrace," "mysteries," "faith," "worship," and "empowers." Our lives are enhanced with words like "consecrated," "discipleship," "service," "encounter," "grow," "insights," "hope," "expand," "hearts," "welcome," and "transform." We might hear one or two of these words per week outside of worship, and yet we hear words like these frequently in a worship environment. Where else would we be inspired to sing in words set to music, "O for a thousand tongues to sing," or "I love to tell the story," except in the confines of Christ's sanctuary? Where else would we find words like the following from 1 Corinthians 13: "Love is patient, love is kind"?

Taylor convinced me that the one thing that separates good religious institutions from other institutions, as worthy as they might be, is *words*, words that inspire, words that add meaning to our lives, words that compel us to love our neighbors as ourselves, words that Jesus spoke over and over again. In chapter 4 of the Gospel of Luke we are given an early account in Jesus' ministry in which he elicited a response from people because of his words. As I mentioned above, he had come to the synagogue in his hometown of Nazareth to speak, opening up the scroll to Isaiah 61, reading inspiring words such as "anointed," "good news," "release," "recovery," "free," "proclaim," and "favor." Although these words were first penned by the prophet Isaiah, there must have been something moving in the way Jesus spoke them. Luke says of his audience's response, "All spoke well of him and were amazed at the *gracious words* that came from his mouth."

The Gospels are full of the gracious words of Jesus, from his aphorisms to his parables, from his metaphors to his commands. Why else do we call his message and his story "the good news"? He would never have made the six o' clock news because gracious words are not newsworthy, at least not according to the wisdom of those who write the news. Sadly, they are probably right. I often wonder whether Jesus' story would have been remembered if his sensationalized death had not been such a compelling story. It makes me think that gracious words from gracious people are not enough. We need a good murder mystery to go along with it.

The task of the church, of course, is to carry forth Jesus' legacy of gracious words, words that we rarely hear outside of the church. Yet what happens when the church decides that the gracious words of Christ are only for them, that they are not meant to be spoken to others? Even before the church was born, this was already occurring. Luke tells us that after Jesus' hometown audience sat there "amazed at the gracious words that came from his mouth," they began to question in their minds the authenticity of his words. Perhaps they thought what he said was too good to be true. How could words like that come from one of their own?

In response to this criticism Jesus began to share stories from their own religious tradition—stories that confirmed that God's grace is available even for those outside of their religious tradition. He reminded them of the story of Elijah who was sent to a gentile widow for sustenance because God had blessed her with food and water. He reminded them of the story of Elisha, who healed a gentile leper. Here's why Jesus reminded them of those old stories: He could sense that his audience believed that his gracious words were only for them, so he reminds them that the grace of God exists even in the lives of those outside of their tradition. Luke tells us that "when they heard this, all in the synagogue were filled with rage." They literally ran him out of town—his hometown!

This may be the trickiest part of being disciples of Jesus. We can apply his gracious words to the world around us, including those who worship other gods or no gods at all. We can live the words "love is patient, love is kind" to all who cross our paths. Still, there is the possibility, if not probability, that our gracious words will create rage in the ones who believe those gracious words apply only to them.

IRRATIONAL BEHAVIOR

After Jesus offered his gracious words to his hometown synagogue the people from Nazareth got so mad at him that they tried to kill him. I can understand why some people get mad when they get on the bathroom scales, yet I find it very difficult to understand why Jesus' hometown friends treated him so badly. Why would anyone behave like that?

The answer is a two-word phrase I discovered not too long ago: "value attribution." Value attribution is "our tendency to imbue someone or something with certain qualities based on perceived value, rather than on objective data."[4] To put in layperson's terms, value attribution occurs when we judge someone prematurely based on what we think we know about them. We attribute a level of value to them according to our own preconceived notions about "people like that." And when we judge someone prematurely, we are likely to behave irrationally toward them.

I came across this phrase, "value attribution," in a book I read called, *Sway: The Irresistible Pull of Irrational Behavior*.[5] One day, while my family and I were visiting my son in the hospital we decided to find a bookstore in order to find some reading material for the long hours we were not allowed in his room. I also wanted to find something for him to read, once his burned hands healed enough to hold a book. I spotted the book *Sway* and thought he might want to read a book about irrational behavior, given his circumstances, and yet I soon discovered that it's a book I needed to read as well. The authors are two brothers, Ori and Rom Brafman. For the book they collected stories that illustrate how people are often swayed to engage in irrational behavior. Because they are Jewish they may have been unfamiliar with the story from Luke 4:16–30, yet if they had been familiar with it they might have included it in their book.

Again, the question is why the people from Nazareth, Jesus' hometown, reacted so irrationally to Jesus' sermon? Why did they get so mad? They responded to Jesus in a way that seems to be the opposite of rationality. Luke writes that the people were "filled with rage." Why such rage? The answer is that they committed the sin of value attribution—twice in fact—leading to the irrational behavior of trying to hurl Jesus off the cliff. The first time they committed the sin of value attribution it was toward Jesus himself. Jesus was a hometown boy. He was raised in Nazareth and had very humble roots. He was "Joseph's son." To them, Joseph apparently was a "nobody" and therefore Jesus was a "nobody." Thus, the people couldn't help but imbue Jesus with certain qualities based on their perception of his family's value without considering the objective data in front of them.

At first, however, they seemed open to the possibility that this lowly person with humble origins just might have made something out of himself. The people are surprised because he spoke such gracious words as he read and commented on their Scriptures, specifically from the book of Isaiah. Jesus' audience would have made one huge assumption as they listened to these words. They would have assumed that the poor, the captives, the blind, and the oppressed that were to curry God's favor, were all Israelites. The

---

4. "Sway: Value Attribution and Diagnosis Bias." https://mattyford.com/blog/2014/4/4/sway-value-attribution-and-diagnosis-bias.

5. Brafman, Ori, and Rom Brafman. New York: Crown, 2008.

"year of the Lord's favor" refers to the Israelite "Year of Jubilee," which was a celebrated year of restoration in ancient Israel. Debt was supposed to be eradicated and property returned to the original owner, although it is unlikely this ever happened on a large scale.

Jesus' listeners would have assumed up until this point that he was declaring God's love and concern for the descendants of Israel—and only for the descendants of Israel—who suffered from these various troubles and afflictions. They would have believed this wholeheartedly, and so they were happy and "amazed at the gracious words that came from (Jesus') mouth." As someone who has had an opportunity to preach in one's hometown, I can tell you that one is greatly tempted to say things that one knows will be graciously accepted by the audience. The only criticism I received from the audience back in 1985 when I preached my first sermon at First Baptist Church in Sterling City, Texas came from my sister, who claimed that I stuttered "ugh" 37 times. She obviously wasn't paying attention to my sermon.

At first Jesus received nothing but accolades from his audience. There would have been people in the audience who were holding high hopes that Jesus would indeed fulfill Isaiah's vision and help them overcome their poverty and afflictions. Poverty was rampant in the ancient world, and given the lack of medical knowledge and technology in that day a big percentage of any population at any given time would have been suffering a great deal from physical problems. This would have been just as true for Jesus' audience. Although this was his first sermon in his hometown synagogue, Jesus had already established a reputation as a miracle worker and a healer due to his initial ministry in Capernaum, a city located on the Sea of Galilee.

Jesus knew what they were thinking as he read from the book of Isaiah: "Here is this hometown boy who has this great reputation, yet we know he's a 'nobody' like his father, Joseph." This is value attribution at its worst. Suddenly, Jesus' sunny disposition turned gloomy. He sensed that he was getting very little respect. Isn't it ironic that we are willing to trust the authenticity of people we don't know more than people we have known our entire lives? Do we know them too well perhaps? That's exactly what was going on here, and Jesus is earnestly disturbed by it. His famous, oft-quoted line is, "Truly I tell you, no prophet is accepted in the prophet's hometown." This is true precisely because of the human tendency to judge people based on the information we already have about them—value attribution. Once we think we know someone we are not very inclined to find out more about them. So, that was the first incident of value attribution in this story—the crowds' premature judgment of Jesus.

The second example of value attribution in this story concerned their premature judgment of gentiles, or non-Jewish people. Sensing this, Jesus reminded his audience, people who were steeped in the Hebrew Scriptures, that the prophet Elijah was sent to a gentile widow for food during a famine, and that only Naaman the Syrian, a gentile, was healed of leprosy from the hand of the prophet Elisha. Jesus' point: God loves even the gentiles. This didn't sit well with Jesus' audience. They did not value gentiles very much, much like ethnic majorities tend to devalue ethnic minorities in every nation in which ethnic diversity exists. This is value attribution at its worst. This is the kind of value attribution we might label prejudice, racism, or xenophobia. Their response, says Luke, was that, "When they heard this [when they heard Jesus attributing worth and value to gentiles], all in the synagogue were filled with rage." Jesus made a tactical blunder at least in terms of maintaining a decent relationship with his hometown peeps.

I can relate to this. Twice in my ministry I have made the same kind of tactical blunder. The first time occurred during my trial sermon at the first United Church of Christ congregation I was called to serve. It was January 1990, Martin Luther King Jr. Sunday. I decided to mention Dr. King in my sermon and talk a little about racial justice. After all, this was a UCC church. What better place to talk about social justice! After the sermon I was voted in as their settled pastor. The next night I received a visitor at my front door, slightly inebriated, who asked me if I were a "nigger lover." Why? I had implied that God loves African-Americans as much as Euro-Americans. I had not joined in his faulty value attribution of African-Americans.

My second tactical blunder occurred in December 1997. This time I allowed an African-American to fill the pulpit for me in my East Texas UCC church . . . emphasis on "East" Texas. This man was a retired Air Force chaplain, an ordained minister, and a tireless worker with the youth at church camp. He also claimed to be a friend of Colin Powell. Nevertheless, because a few of the people there thought I had allowed the pulpit to be "desecrated" I felt the need to resign a few months later . . . before I was fired. The point being that at least twice in my ministry I have experienced the kind of rage Jesus felt from his audience that day when he implied that God loves even those to whom some people do not attribute much value.

Value attribution—our tendency to imbue someone or something with certain qualities based on perceived value rather than on objective data—leads to irrational behavior. How else do we explain Jesus' hometown folks wanting to kill him *over a sermon* in which he implied that God loves gentiles? How else do we explain my former congregation running me off because I had allowed an African-American to fill the pulpit? Believe me, if there had been a cliff nearby, some of those East Texas folks would have acted like they were from Nazareth and tried to throw me off of it.

Perhaps the greatest lesson we can learn from these incidents can be encapsulated in some time-honored clichés like, "Don't judge a book by its cover," or "Don't jump to conclusions." And yet the lesson goes deeper than that. It's not just that we should refrain from irrational behavior that stems from value attribution. The greater lesson is that we worship a God who values us more than we value ourselves, a God who values people we do not value. I hope that doesn't piss you off.

Luke 5:1–11

Once while Jesus was standing beside the lake of Gennesaret, and the crowd was pressing in on him to hear the word of God, he saw two boats there at the shore of the lake; the fishermen had gone out of them and were washing their nets. He got into one of the boats, the one belonging to Simon, and asked him to put out a little way from the shore. Then he sat down and taught the crowds from the boat. When he had finished speaking, he said to Simon, "Put out into the deep water and let down your nets for a catch." Simon answered, "Master, we have worked all night long but have caught nothing. Yet if you say so, I will let down the nets." When they had done this, they caught so many fish that their nets were beginning to break. So they signaled their partners in the other boat to come and help them. And they came and filled both boats, so that they began to sink. But when Simon Peter saw it, he fell down at Jesus' knees, saying, "Go away from me, Lord, for I am a sinful man!" For he and all who were with him were amazed at the catch of fish that they had taken; and so also were James and John, sons of Zebedee, who were partners with Simon. Then Jesus said to Simon, "Do not be afraid; from now on you will be catching people." When they had brought their boats to shore, they left everything and followed him.

THE BIG WHOPPER

HERE'S THE THING ABOUT "fish stories": *Because* they are fish stories we tend not to believe them. Fish stories have almost become synonymous with lying (of the harmless variety, but lying nonetheless). Why do we think that is? I have a theory about this. First of all, I don't think it's because fishermen are by nature liars any more than any other group of people. Most fishermen, in fact, are something else other than fishermen. Unless a person is a professional fisherman or is unemployed and has to fish for survival, the likelihood is that a person who fishes lives a big part of their lives away from the rivers and lakes and oceans. Not only that, but the professional fisherman and the person who fishes for survival are actually unlikely to fabricate stories about their fishing prowess because they have no motive for doing so. It is the recreational fisherman—the occasional fishing hobbyist—that is more likely to tell a whopper.

The reason I believe this is because recreational fishing is something we usually do when no one else is around. A fisherman will intentionally seek places that are not frequented by other human beings. And, of course, any time human beings do something in relative secrecy, there is a temptation to stretch the tale of one's accomplishments.

Nevertheless, sometimes fish stories of the whopper variety are told even when a lot of other people are around. In the above passage we are offered a fish story that outdoes any whopper you or I have ever told. One day Jesus went to the Lake of Gennesaret, better known as the Sea of Galilee. Perhaps he wanted to get in a little fishing himself. All of a sudden a large crowd of people converge on him, wanting to hear his wonderful, inspiring teaching. Thinking it would be advantageous to be out on the water so everyone can see and hear him better, and so he can make a quick getaway if necessary, he climbs into Simon Peter's boat. Simon, a new acquaintance of Jesus, and his fellow fishermen had been cleaning their nets, getting ready for the next day when Jesus decides to get out on the water. He taught for a good while, probably stressing out Simon who may have been anxious to get home to his wife after a long day of unfruitful fishing. After Jesus was through teaching he asked Simon and his fellow fishermen to go out again, this time farther away from the shore into the deep part of the lake and cast their nets once again. The weary Simon says something to the effect of, "Look, we've been fishing all day long and haven't caught a thing, but if you insist."

At this point Luke feels compelled to tell a whopper. He claims their nets became so full of fish that they almost ripped apart. They even had to get help from their partners, James and John, who were in another boat. In fact, both boats were so full of fish that they almost sunk before they made it back to the shore; this, after a day when the fish weren't "biting" (or rather, landing in the net). I'm not going to speculate one way or another about the veracity of this story. All I know is that if a fisherman came home after an afternoon of fishing and told his wife he literally filled up two boats with fish I'm pretty sure she would ask for a divorce on the basis of being a terrible liar.

I'm not skeptical of this story just because of its claim of how many fish they caught. The main reason I am skeptical is because Matthew and Mark do not include the large haul of fish in their accounts of this story. Here is Mark's version of this account (which is almost exactly like Matthew's):

> As Jesus passed along the Sea of Galilee, he saw Simon *and his brother Andrew* [a point omitted by Luke] casting a net into the sea—for they were fishermen. And Jesus said to them, "Follow me and I will make you fish for people." And immediately they left their nets and followed him. As he went a little farther, he saw James son of Zebedee and his brother John, who were in their boat mending the nets. Immediately he called them; and they left their father Zebedee in the boat with the hired men, and followed him.

Do you see the difference? In Matthew and Mark there is no "fish story." The storyline is much simpler: Two pairs of fishermen brothers, Simon and Andrew, then James and John, leave their nets and follow Jesus. (By the way, the Gospel of John's version of the calling of Simon Peter is so different they shouldn't be considered parallel accounts.)

The question for serious readers of the Bible is this: Why does Luke add the whopper fish story? Why didn't he just stick with Mark's earlier version, copied almost verbatim by Matthew? Why did he apparently augment his version of the story? Before we answer that, let's first examine what these stories all have in common. In all three of the Synoptic Gospels—Matthew, Mark, and Luke—the conclusion is the same: several men drop their fishing nets and follow Jesus for the purpose of "fishing for people." What we can assume from this is that these men left their occupations, their sources of livelihood, behind to become followers, or disciples, of Jesus. The only motivation we can discern from this is that they must have believed this was an opportunity of a lifetime. To be invited to leave behind a difficult back-breaking underpaid job to follow a man with so much promise and hope . . . it doesn't seem to have been a difficult decision for them.

And yet notice how Luke's addition of the whopper fish story would have made their decision much more difficult. In Luke's version, Simon and his partners didn't have a good day at all. They hadn't caught a thing. Jesus then takes them out into the deep part of the lake. Maybe they hadn't been that far out before. Regardless, they produce a massive haul. Simon, in his typical overly-exaggerated way, responds rather dramatically: "Go away from me, Lord, for I am a sinful man!" He must have bought into the typical theological perspective of the day that God blesses the obedient and curses the disobedient or sinful. In Simon's mind, Jesus was blessed and he (Simon) was cursed, and yet no one is cursed on this day. Furthermore, isn't it likely, after this huge catch, that their desire to fish would have been reinvigorated? Wouldn't this large haul of fish excite Simon and his partners about the possibility of coming back the next day (after they cleaned all those fish)?

Luke's version of this story is more powerful than Matthew or Mark's version. The Simon Peter of Luke's story would have to give up more than just a meager profession. He would have to give up the possibility of success, wealth, status, and everything else that a monumental catch of fish would change about his life. This was the catch that would put him in the Fisherman's Hall of Fame. For Luke's Simon, catching people (as Jesus invited him to do) is not just a nice opportunity to do something different. It is a once-in-a-lifetime sacrifice after a once-in-a-lifetime catch. The same is true for his partners, James and John, sons of Zebedee, and presumably, Andrew as well. Notice, by the way, that after they bring the fish to shore they leave them there. I bet old Zebedee had a nice meal that night.

For Simon Peter and his partners, the lure to follow Jesus (pun intended) was a matter of priorities. Priorities are much more difficult to assess when there is great value in all the choices. Simon and his partners had to choose between the best day of their professional careers and the best day of their spiritual lives (a choice you and I seldom, if ever, have to make). Follow money and success or follow Jesus. It's interesting that so many of the stories in the Gospels are, at base, stewardship stories. Not only that, they are *radical* stewardship stories. Of course, not everyone can literally give up their careers or jobs or sources of livelihood to be disciples of Jesus. And yet if we did, think of all the fishing we could do.

Luke 6:20–26

Then he looked up at his disciples and said: "Blessed are you who are poor, for yours is the kingdom of God. Blessed are you who are hungry now, for you will be filled. Blessed are you who weep now, for you will laugh. Blessed are you when people hate you, and when they exclude you, revile you, and defame you on account of the Son of Man. Rejoice in that day and leap for joy, for surely your reward is great in heaven; for that is what their ancestors did to the prophets. But woe to you who are rich, for you have received your consolation. Woe to you who are full now, for you will be hungry. Woe to you who are laughing now, for you will mourn and weep. Woe to you when all speak well of you, for that is what their ancestors did to the false prophets."

BLESSED ARE THE CURSED

JESUS HAD A STRANGE view of blessedness. If I were making up a list of what makes us blessed (or happy), it would include: "Blessed are those whose wheels on the shopping cart turn the same way." Actually, I agree with an ancient Chinese proverb that says, "If you wish to be happy for one hour, get intoxicated. If you wish to be happy for three days, get married. If you wish to be happy for eight days, kill your pig and eat it. If you wish to be happy forever, learn to fish." Seriously, why do you think Jesus said we are happy or blessed when we experience such things as poverty, hunger, sorrow, and being excluded, reviled, and defamed? You probably realize these points are also included (with some variation) in the Gospel of Matthew's "Sermon on the Mount." Here in Luke's Gospel, Jesus is preaching this sermon on level ground. Luke's version is often called the "Sermon on the Plain." All you need to know is that Matthew and Luke are drawing on the same material, even though there are subtle differences between the two versions.

One way Luke's version of this sermon differs from Matthew's version is that after Jesus offers a list of the "blessed" he follows with a list of "woes": to the rich, the full, the laughing, and those who are liked by everyone. Should we interpret this to mean that God loves poor, hungry, and depressed people of ill repute, yet God doesn't love rich, well-fed, happy people who have good reputations? If that were true, then many of us better start packing for a nice long vacation in the hot place. To understand what Jesus really means, we need to probe into the sacred writings of Jesus' people—the Hebrew Bible or Old Testament. We need to understand the religious tradition in which Jesus and the first-century Jews lived. So let's take a journey back in history, before Jesus, so we can understand why Jesus is making such strange statements.

The ancient Hebrews had a tendency, much as we do today, to divide people into two groups: blessed and cursed. This was their version of good vs. evil that is so ingrained in our culture. Go to almost any movie these days, especially action movies, and the theme will almost always be the same: good guys vs. bad guys. The old western movie version of this was white hats vs. black hats. People, or groups of people, are either good or evil, with very little nuance in between. For example, on a national level, we used to consider all communists as evil. Today many Americans tend to believe that all Muslims or people from the Middle East are evil, whereas we are good. We always have to have an enemy, do we not? This good vs. evil mentality shows up in our political discourse as well. Our country is becoming increasingly polarized, meaning we have divided ourselves into sharply opposed political factions, namely the red states and the blue states. Some people even refer to what is happening in America as a culture *war*. All of this echoes the blessed vs. cursed mindset of the ancient world. The blessed were blessed because they were good or faithful to God. The cursed were cursed because they were bad or unfaithful. Read Deuteronomy 30:15–19:

> See, I have set before you today life and prosperity, death and adversity. If you obey the commandments of the LORD your God that I am commanding you today, by loving the LORD your God, walking in his ways, and observing his commandments, decrees, and ordinances, then you shall live and become numerous, and the LORD your God will *bless* you in the land that you are entering to possess. But if your hearts turns away and you do not hear, but are led astray to bow down to other gods and serve them, I declare to you today that you shall perish; you shall not

live long in the land that you are crossing the Jordan to enter and possess. I call heaven and earth to witness against you today that I have set before you life and death, *blessings and curses.*

Do you see how the ancient Hebrew religion divided people? God either blessed people or cursed people. But now, who was blessed and who was cursed? Obviously, if you obey the commandments, you will be blessed; if you disobey, you will be cursed. For further evidence of this ancient division of people into two groups, look at Psalm 1:

Happy are those who do not follow the advice of the wicked, or take the path that sinners tread, or sit in the seat of scoffers; but their delight is in the law of the LORD, and on his law they meditate day and night. They are like trees planted by streams of water, which yield their fruit in its season, and their leaves do not wither. In all that they do, *they prosper.* The wicked are not so, but are like chaff that the wind drives away. Therefore the wicked will not stand in the judgment, nor sinners in the congregation of the righteous; for the LORD watches over the way of the righteous, but the way of the wicked *will perish* (that is, *not* prosper).

Psalm 1 is a very important Psalm because, obviously, it sets the tone for the entire collection of Psalms, which were used in worship in Jesus' day. And I don't think Psalm 1 can be any clearer: Happy (or blessed) are those who *prosper;* cursed are those who do not prosper. How do you know if someone has been obedient and faithful to God? They have been blessed financially (prosperous). And how do you know if someone has been disobedient and unfaithful to God? They are not prosperous.

If you like to watch television preachers you know that one of their favorite themes is "prosperity." Televangelists—many of them—love to talk about how God prospers us, financially, physically, and on occasion, spiritually. We even have a couple of names for this: "the prosperity gospel" and "the health and wealth gospel." The roots of this theology lie in the Old Testament, including the book of Deuteronomy and the first Psalm. We also find this type of theology in the prophets. Look at Jeremiah 17, beginning in verse 5. Here we find more evidence of the ancient view that God blesses, or prospers, the good and faithful people, and God curses those who are not good and faithful:

Thus says the LORD: *Cursed* are those who trust in mere mortals and make mere flesh their strength, whose hearts turn away from the LORD. They shall be like a shrub in the desert, and shall not see when relief comes. They shall live in the parched places of the wilderness, in an uninhabited salt land. (In other words, they will not prosper.) Blessed are those who trust in the LORD, whose trust is the LORD. They shall be like a tree planted by water, sending out its roots by the stream. It shall not fear when heat comes, and its leaves shall stay green; in the year of drought it is not anxious, and it does not cease to *bear fruit* (or prosper).

You can see that this is a very prominent stream of thought running throughout the Old Testament. Did the Jews of Jesus' day believe that God blessed the good and faithful and cursed the disobedient, unfaithful folks? Absolutely.

So let's connect the dots. If you were wealthy, had plenty to eat, had much to laugh about, and had a good reputation, then obviously God had blessed or prospered you because you were ostensibly obedient to God. On the other hand, if you were poor, had little to eat, had much sorrow in your life, and people hated you, then God had cursed or caused you not to prosper because you were disobedient to God. In other words, the ancient Hebrews believed there was a *moral* reason why people suffered. You suffer if you've been bad, disobedient, or unfaithful to God.

We Americans have inherited a little of this type of thinking. How many times have you heard (or said) that so-and-so is poor because he or she is lazy or has made poor choices, both of which are moral judgments? The poor, hungry, sorrowful, and those of ill repute are often thought to be in such a miserable state because of their lack of morals. They are "bad" people. As much as we try to hide our opinions about the down-and-outs of our society, the view that they are in some way cursed because they are bad is always in the back of the minds of the relatively well-to-do, well-fed, happy, good citizens of our world, which includes most people who are reading this book. But at least we try to hide our thoughts for the sake of political correctness.

In Jesus' world, the view that the down-and-outs were cursed by God was a view that was extremely popular and taken for granted. There was no question about it. If you were living out of trash heaps or begging for food, then you were not a good and faithful member of the kingdom of God. All of this makes Jesus' words in Luke 6:20–26 rather strange and controversial. He might as well have written a Facebook post in big, bold letters: BLESSED ARE THE CURSED! Imagine how this would have affected his audience, people who had been raised to believe that the only reason bad things like poverty, hunger, sorrow, and ill repute happen to them is because they have been unfaithful to God. Through Jesus, the cursed people heard that they were blessed. There is nothing he could have said that would have been more radical and earthshaking. He completely redefined the religious status of the general population.

So here we are, two thousand years later. We continue to hear Jesus speak words of blessedness, and yet we are still labeling people as cursed. Only we don't often use that word. It smacks of witchcraft. Usually we say someone is bad, evil, hypocritical, unrepentant, unfaithful, heretical, lost, unsaved, un-Christian, immoral, unethical, shameful, sinful, etc. I believe that the task of every generation of Christians is to do exactly what Jesus did: Tell the cursed that they are blessed. We must redefine people in a way that emphasizes their worth and value. It doesn't matter who they are. That's our job. We are to be like Jesus, not like the religious leaders of his day who had developed a religious system that constantly told the general population they were cursed.

This may be our toughest task as followers of Christ. If *we* don't redefine people in order to emphasize their blessedness, then who will? Without giving any examples of people that we devalue—which would be an obvious list—just think about any person or groups of people that usually inspire negative comments from us. Think real hard. To use the language of Jesus, these are the people whom we consider to be cursed, and these are the people we are prone to verbally curse. We need to stop looking at appearances, circumstances, and reputations, and stop making unjustified value attributions about people.

A PARALLEL UNIVERSE

Human beings are limited in their ability to grasp all the mysteries of the universe, although we do have the ability to grasp much smaller mysteries. Either through our vocational training, our natural talents, or our hobbies, all of us have some level of expertise about something. Some of us may have uncovered a few mysteries about gardening or golfing, fishing or philosophy, sewing or salesmanship, nursing or needlepoint. Few of us, however, have mastered the mysteries of *justice*. In fact, most of us can't even offer a definition that would do justice to the word "justice." There is confusion about what it actually means because there is more than one definition of justice.

One view is that justice involves avoiding or preventing harm to people. We treat people justly when we do no harm to them. Another view is that it involves treating people according to their "just deserts." We give them what they deserve, reward or punishment. The criminal justice system is based on this definition of justice. Another view is that people should be treated according to their needs (rather than what they might deserve). If people need food, for example, justice demands that we provide it for them. The welfare system is based on this kind of justice. Another way to understand justice is that people should be treated fairly and impartially. The image of "blind lady justice" comes into focus here.

The moral theorist, John Rawls, in his book, *Theory of Justice*, argues that the best way to practice justice is to put on blinders when making moral decisions that can affect people's lives.[1] We are to be blind to our own identity, blocking from our minds the knowledge of whether we are the oppressor or the oppressed. To practice justice that is fair and impartial we should tell ourselves that we do not know if we will benefit or not from our decision. So we should base our decision solely on how the most vulnerable people will be affected.

Take the issue of affirmative action. Have you ever noticed that those who would benefit from affirmative action are usually for it, and those who would not benefit from it are often against it? This is clear evidence that we usually make moral decisions with blinders *off*. We are too aware of how a decision will affect us or our own particular community. According to Rawls, however, a moral decision based on justice is made with blinders on, not knowing how the decision will affect us or our community.[2] Usually this translates into justice for the vulnerable and oppressed.

Of course, this kind of "blinders on" impartial justice may be impossible in our universe. And yet, who knows, it might exist in a *parallel universe*. Science fiction buffs know what I'm talking about. According to the parallel universes theory, all the possibilities for every action exist somewhere as an alternate universe. Whereas you woke up late this morning, in another universe you woke up early. Whereas you failed that exam last week, in another universe you may have aced it. Whereas you drove through an intersection yesterday and got hit by another car, in another universe you hesitated before going through and avoided the accident. And whereas this universe is full of injustices, in another universe, blind, impartial justice is practiced.

I'm not too sure what I think of the parallel universes theory, and yet it has me thinking of all the possible universes out there. It has me thinking that in some parallel universe there is no war, hunger, prejudice, or even illness. We can only dream of the possibilities of a more just universe out there. However, because we live in this universe we simply have to do our best to create a more just universe here. As Christians we have a mentor in

---

1. Rawls, "Theory of Justice," 622.
2. Rawls, "Theory of Justice," 622.

this regard, a man who taught and practiced justice on an entirely new level. I'm talking about Jesus, of course.

We get a glimpse of Jesus' understanding of justice in Luke 6:20–26, Luke's version of Matthew's Sermon on the Mount. Here, Jesus gives us a glimpse of a world built upon a foundation of justice, but not justice in the way we usually think of it. I get the feeling that if Jesus could construct his own parallel universe, justice would be much more than the fair, impartial, and unbiased version of justice that we usually strive for. In Jesus' universe, justice would be partial and biased. It would favor the poor and not the rich. It would be partial toward the hungry and not those who have plenty to eat. It would be biased toward those who weep and not toward those who laugh. It would tip the scales in favor of those who are hated and excluded and away from those whom others speak well of. The scales of justice in Jesus' parallel universe would not be fair, impartial, and unbiased. His thumb would weigh heavily in favor of the poor, the hungry, the sorrowful, and the despised. Our sense of morality tells us that we should always try to be fair and impartial, that we should never apply a heavy finger to the scales of justice. Jesus, however, had a big thumb, and he put it on the scales of justice to favor those who are needy, vulnerable, and oppressed. There was nothing "blind" about the way he understood justice.

If we apply Jesus' view of justice to the issue of race then we can claim that racial justice is the practice of favoring those who have been oppressed or discriminated against because of race. It's not a matter of impartiality; it is a matter of partiality in favor of racial minorities or other segments of the population who are oppressed. The question for us is whether we want to be a part of Jesus' parallel universe, what he called "the kingdom of God." The kingdom of God is the way the world would be if we acknowledged Jesus' God as the ruler of the universe. It would be a universe characterized by political power for the poor, full bellies for the hungry, uncontrollable laughter for those who weep, and total inclusion for those who are now excluded. This is clearly not the universe in which we currently reside. Perhaps Jesus' parallel universe is more "upside down" than parallel. It takes the values of our world and reverses them. Regardless, Jesus calls us to help turn this parallel universe into reality.

Luke 6:27–38

But I say to you that listen, Love your enemies, do good to those who hate you, bless those who curse you, pray for those who abuse you. If anyone strikes you on the cheek, offer the other also; and from anyone who takes away your coat do not withhold even your shirt. Give to everyone who begs from you; and if anyone takes away your goods, do not ask for them again. Do to others as you would have them do to you. If you love those who love you, what credit is that to you? For even sinners love those who love them. If you do good to those who do good to you, what credit is that to you? For even sinners do the same. If you lend to those from whom you hope to receive, what credit is that to you? Even sinners lend to sinners, to receive as much again. But love your enemies, do good, and lend, expecting nothing in return. Your reward will be great, and you will be children of the Most High; for he is kind to the ungrateful and the wicked. Be merciful, just as your Father is merciful. Do not judge, and you will not be judged; do not condemn, and you will not be condemned. Forgive, and you will be forgiven; give, and it will be given to you. A good measure, pressed down, shaken together, running over, will be put into your lap; for the measure you give will be the measure you get back.

THERE'S PLENTY MORE WHERE THAT CAME FROM

Every year in my congregation we have the annual "We are short of cash so please consider giving more" Sunday, otherwise known as Stewardship

Sunday. In terms of financial stewardship, there's only one response a minister ever wants to hear from a parishioner when asked/begged/emotionally manipulated for more money: "There's plenty more where that came from." I love that expression. I have heard it in various contexts, but the three that come to mind include a schoolyard scuffle (I remember someone taking a beating at the hands of a bully and the bully saying to this person, "There's plenty more where that came from."), from a customer in a bar who was trying to get good service from a waiter (He tipped the waiter and said, "If you keep the drinks coming, there's plenty more where that came from."), and from a host who had cooked a big meal for me and my family (She kept telling us, "Eat all you want, there's plenty more where that came from."). When people use that line (in a positive context) they are trying to claim that there is an unending reservoir of some particular commodity, such as more tip money or more food from the kitchen. It is designed to give people the impression of extravagant generosity.

Extravagant generosity is reflected in the words of Jesus from Luke 6:38, where he says, "Give, and it will be given to you. A good measure, pressed down, shaken together, running over, will be put into your lap." During the fall of the year, when we observe Stewardship Sunday, I can't help but think about bags of gathered leaves when I read that quote from Jesus. In the fall, many people have the back-breaking task of filling up large lawn bags with leaves from their yards. It is amazing how many leaves one can cram into one of those bags. Just when you think you've filled the bag, you give it a good pressing-down, shake it, and you have suddenly created more space for more leaves. And yet even as you fill up the generously receiving bag, the trees in your yard are saying to you, "You think this is a lot of leaves? There's plenty more where that came from." Even as your back muscles start to cramp up from raking up all the leaves, you can't help but appreciate how extravagantly generous the trees are for giving their leaves. Likewise, we are encouraged to be extravagantly generous, like a thirsty tipper in a bar, like a host serving a home-cooked meal, like a tree shedding its leaves in autumn, like a lawn bag creating more and more space for more and more crushed leaves. Those are all images of extravagant generosity.

I would be disingenuous to claim that the extravagant generosity of Christian stewardship is about more than just giving money. It *is* about more than just giving money, but giving money is a big part of it, if not the biggest, at least in our teaching emphasis on stewardship. Even if we try to hide it or sugarcoat it, we cannot escape the fact that the church needs financial resources to continue in its current manifestation. I suppose a congregation could exist in some form or fashion without financial resources, yet it would look very different than most congregations look now, and it would certainly not be in a building. You get what you pay for, as the old adage says. So let me be very clear about this: If parishioners want the services of professional staff, if they want the availability of a nice facility, if they want to do collaborative mission work in the world, then they have to "cough it up."

Tough economic times notwithstanding, an extravagant attitude of generosity will say to those who ask for money for a good cause: "There's plenty more where that came from." In fact, I would encourage congregations to make that their motto for at least one year. I realize mottos are largely feel-good phrases that usually have very little transformative power in our lives. Not too many years ago, Congress spent a useless amount of time and energy debating whether the national motto is "e pluribus unum" or "In God we trust," as if that makes any difference in our day-to-day existence. Nevertheless, imagine the transformation that would occur in our lives if we sincerely adopted as our motto the phrase, "There's plenty more where that came from," and used it anytime someone asked us for money for a good cause. We might end up broke, but we would be transformed.

To be good financial stewards, to be extravagantly generous, requires the opening up of one's pocketbook or wallet. However—and I don't wish this to sound like a cliché—good stewardship is about more than just giving money. Money is certainly the most tangible of all the acts of generosity we can practice, but generous financial giving does not exactly set us apart as Christians. A lot of people—Christian and non-Christian alike—practice generosity with their pocketbooks. There has to be more to it than that.

From a biblical standpoint we need to remember that Jesus' audience consisted mainly of very poor people. It is very doubtful that he meant to sound like a contemporary American televangelist who preaches the "prosperity gospel." The prosperity gospel claims that if you give to someone's ministry you will prosper beyond your wildest expectations. The prosperity gospel only "works" in societies that know what prosperity looks like. The preacher can point to his gold watch or her diamond necklace or his or her yacht and say, "If you give to my ministry, it will be given to you. A good measure, pressed down, shaken together, running over." Jesus' audience would have laughed until their emaciated stomachs split wide open if they had thought he was telling them that giving to the local synagogue would make them wealthy or prosperous. Besides, you never hear the televangelists finish Jesus' sentence, where he says, "for the measure you give will be the measure you get back." How can you get rich if you only get back what you have given? That's not even as good a return rate as a savings account.

So, again, let me be very clear as I state the obvious: You will not get rich or become prosperous by giving your money to a church. That's not even close to being a law of the universe or of God. However, by giving money to your church you will get to enjoy sermons from know-it-all clergy-types, sit on hard pews in buildings with bad lighting and leaky roofs, and listen to people next to you sing off-key. Now, that's a good return on your investment.

Seriously, what Jesus was talking about in Luke 6 had less to do with tangible things like money and more to do with the intangibles because, again, he was talking to poverty-stricken people. Jesus is speaking these words not to those who read *Wall Street Journal*, but to those who are sick, poor, hungry, sorrowful, hated, excluded, reviled, and defamed. From a biblical standpoint, Christian stewardship doesn't flow from an abundance of tangible things like wealth; it flows from an abundance of *intangibles*, things that may be even scarcer in our lives than money. Things like love for our enemies, acts of goodness for those who hate us, blessings for those who curse us, prayers for those who abuse us, forgiveness for those who have done us wrong. Can we, with a straight face, say that we are doing those things today, and add, "There's plenty more where that came from"? Are there plenty more episodes of cheek-turning in our future? Do we have an unlimited number of shirts to give those who have taken our coats? Are we able to tell the beggars in our life—those who stand on the street corners and those family members who keep showing up on our doorstep—that "there's plenty more where that came from"?

That's just enabling bad behavior, right? Well, Jesus wasn't a very good student of psychology. He doesn't seem to have a whole lot of what we call "common sense." In Luke 6, Jesus echoes the same logic, or illogic, that he proclaims all throughout his teachings. Let me put it this way: If we can say, "There's plenty more where that came from," *and there is*, then one is not being generous. Instead, Jesus is calling his followers to give *what they don't have*—and again, I'm not *just* talking about money.

A lot of things Jesus said sounds very idealistic, impractical, and naïve. Because they were. And ironic. It's almost as if they were meant for another universe, another world, another place, or another time. I believe, however, his words were meant for our universe. None of it makes much sense unless we open our eyes to the possibility that maybe God is just as idealistic, impractical, and naïve as Jesus was. Maybe God has a big lawn bag for each one of us and all of us as a whole, and is constantly cramming into that bag a good measure of love, justice, peace, goodness, blessings, forgiveness, mercy, and grace.

And just when we think no more can fit into our bags, God presses it down, shakes it all together, and adds more and more until it runs over in our laps. "My cup runneth over," said the writer of Psalm 23. He could have said, "My leaf bag runneth over." And if God does that for us, we are called to do the same for others. That's Christian stewardship. That's extravagant generosity. And there's plenty more where that came from.

Luke 7:36–50

One of the Pharisees asked Jesus to eat with him, and he went into the Pharisee's house and took his place at the table. And a woman in the city, who was a sinner, having learned that he was eating in the Pharisee's house, brought an alabaster jar of ointment. She stood behind him at his feet, weeping, and began to bathe his feet with her tears and to dry them with her hair. Then she continued kissing his feet and anointing them with the ointment. Now when the Pharisee who had invited him saw it, he said to himself, "If this man were a prophet, he would have known who and what kind of woman this is who is touching him—that she is a sinner." Jesus spoke up and said to him, "Simon, I have something to say to you." "Teacher," he replied, "Speak." "A certain creditor had two debtors; one owed five hundred denarii, and the other fifty. When they could not pay, he canceled the debts for both of them. Now which of them will love him more?" Simon answered, "I suppose the one for whom he canceled the greater debt." And Jesus said to him, "You have judged rightly." Then turning toward the woman, he said to Simon, "Do you see this woman? I entered your house; you gave me no water for my feet, but she has bathed my feet with her tears and dried them with her hair. You gave me no kiss, but from the time I came in she has not stopped kissing my feet. You did not anoint my head with oil, but she has anointed my feet with ointment. Therefore, I tell you, her sins, which were many, have been forgiven; hence she has shown great love. But the one to whom little is forgiven, loves little." Then he said to her, "Your sins are forgiven." But those who were at the table with him began to say among themselves, "Who is this who even forgives sins?" And he said to the woman, "Your faith has saved you; go in peace."

SEX IN THE CITY

I HAVE NOTHING AGAINST sex, whether we are talking about sex in the city, sex in the country, or sex in the suburbs. Unless you never watch television or movies, read popular magazines, or listen to contemporary music, you are surely aware that our society is becoming more and more open about its sexuality. We are moving from a sexually repressed society to a sexually permissive society—and we have been for several decades now. Perhaps the epitome of open, permissive sexuality was seen in what was originally an HBO series called, appropriately enough, *Sex in the City*.

Sex in the City is about four women who live in New York City. They are either single or separated from their husbands and they experience romances, heartbreaks, and yes, one night stands. The main character, played by Sarah Jessica Parker, is a columnist that writes about relationships. Her columns are inspired by her and her friend's experiences. I am very critical of this television series, but not because it contains nudity and profanity. My real problem with *Sex in the City* is that it supports the double standard about sexuality in our culture.

A double standard is defined as "a set of principles permitting greater opportunity or liberty to one than to another, especially the granting of greater sexual freedom to men than to women." The double standard guarantees that women will acquire a very different reputation than men for the very same activity. Sexually permissive women are called all kinds of names that I won't mention here, whereas sexually permissive men are said to be just "sowing their wild oats" or they are called "red-blooded" (as if women have a different color of blood). This is a double standard that has been around forever, mainly because men have been the primary authors of history and formulators of sexual mores. Therefore, women have always been known as "temptresses" and men as their unsuspecting victims who just can't help themselves and who are only doing what comes natural to them. In Hebrew mythology, although Adam and Eve both ate the forbidden fruit, it was Eve's fault. Although it takes two to tango, in the ancient world and in some cultures even today, only the female adulteress is stoned, not the man.

This double standard continues to be a reality in contemporary Western society. Isaac Asimov tells the story about a mother who bought into the double standard. He said, "A woman I know was once telling me of the many conquests of her son, a handsome fellow who had no trouble doing well with the girls. 'Of course,' she said, 'I can't say that I approve of the girls. They seem willing to get into bed with him on slight acquaintance. I can only conclude that they must be disgustingly promiscuous.' 'But,' I protested, 'it seems to me that your son has as slight an acquaintance with the girls as they have with him. Isn't he equally promiscuous?' At which she turned on me fiercely and said, 'He's entitled!'" Obviously, women will never obtain equal status with men as long as so many women continue to enforce the double standard in favor of men.

The nameless woman in Luke 7:37–50 is undoubtedly a victim of the double standard. Given a name, a pretty face, and upscale clothing, she could have been the fifth member of the cast of *Sex in the City*. In verse 37 Luke calls her "a woman in the city." This phrase was as loaded then as it is now. "A woman in the city" by definition was, and is, a sinner. We are never told what sin she had actually committed, and yet we can guess that it was sexual in nature because sin and sex are almost always synonymous with one another.

According to the story, this woman came to the home of Simon the Pharisee where Jesus was dining. She seemingly walked in without invitation, used her tears to wash Jesus' feet and her hair to dry them. Then she began kissing his feet and anointing them. All of this is very strange, almost erotic, behavior. Of course I say that because I am a man, one who has been brainwashed by the double standard. (Isn't self-awareness grand?) She does this because she has found love, acceptance, and forgiveness. She is simply showing her gratitude in the best way she knows how. We don't know what Jesus did to solicit this kind of gratitude. He could have simply been kind to her immediately before he went to the Pharisee's home. Talking to women, especially a woman with a stained reputation, was a social taboo, so his kindness would have been both startling and liberating for this woman. Or, she may have just heard him talk to the masses with general words of love and forgiveness, words that she may have taken to heart personally. Whatever Jesus did, this woman was eternally grateful.

She probably didn't have to do much of anything to get a reputation. After all, she is a woman—probably a single woman—from the city. She is a reincarnation of Eve, bringing forbidden fruit to anyone who will partake. Simon the Pharisee probably suspected she was there to tempt Jesus (because that's the way men think). Still, we need to be fair to Simon. He is simply reflecting conventional views. Most societies have viewed women as the more evil of the two genders. This anti-woman bias has had an enormous effect on the status of women in the church. Until recently, ordination to the ministry was closed to women—still is in many circles—for no other reason than the fact that men have controlled the church and the teachings of the church for two thousand years. Many churches continue to teach that women are second-class citizens, and wives are unequal to their husbands.

Perhaps the real irony of this story is that the Pharisee never asks Jesus for forgiveness. He doesn't think he needs it. After all, he's not a single woman who lives in the city. He's a man . . . and a religious man at that. The Pharisees were one of the groups that had the religious power in Jesus' day and therefore they got to determine who was righteous and who was unrighteous, even if they engaged in the same activities as the unrighteous. I suspect Jesus knew the Pharisee was applying a double standard to the woman. We shouldn't get too excited, however. Jesus probably never used the term "double standard."

A double standard is evident in other areas besides gender relationships. In any area of life where one person or group has power over another person or group, there is usually a double standard. We see this in religion, when one group is deemed more righteous simply because they belong to a particular religion; in race relations, when one group is deemed morally superior just for having a certain color of skin; and in international politics, when one group or nation is deemed to have more value and worth only because they are a certain nationality. One way to interpret the Gospel, or good news of Jesus Christ, is to see it as a bulldozer trying to knock down all of the unjust and ignorant double standards of humanity. This theme was articulated in the strongest terms by the Apostle Paul who wrote, "There is no longer Jew or Greek, there is no longer slave or free, there is no longer male and female; for all of you are one in Christ Jesus" (Gal 3:28). If Paul were writing today his list would be much longer. He could just as well have said, "There should no longer be a double standard applied to any of our human relationships. Period."

DOMINATRIX SYSTEMS

Recently, the Monday evening discussion group at the congregation I currently serve engaged in a study about Reinhold Niebuhr, perhaps the preeminent American theologian of the twentieth century. He was born and raised in Wright City and St. Charles, Missouri—just down the highway from my church in Ferguson, Missouri. Niebuhr and his family, including the formidable H. Richard Niebuhr, hail from the E-side of the E & R tradition of the United Church of Christ. The E & R tradition consists of two German immigrant denominations in America: the German Evangelical Synod of North America and the German Reformed Church. Don't worry, they all fly 'Merican flags in their sanctuaries.

Much of Niebuhr's writings are about "power." He said things like: "Goodness, armed with power, is corrupted; and pure love without power is destroyed."[1] Niebuhr could be a little difficult to understand at times.

---

1. https://www.brainyquote.com/quotes/reinhold_niebuhr_385301.

Speaking of power, as we were engaged in our study of Niebuhr, we were once again witnessing the jockeying for power—the pursuit of power—as another election season unfolded. You may remember this election as the one where a lady named Hillary Clinton destroyed her opponent Donald Trump. Wait, what?

At the end of Niebuhr's teaching career at Union Seminary in New York City, he had a colleague named Walter Wink. Wink, who died in 2012, is, in my mind, one of the greatest American biblical scholars and theologians of our era. For some reason he was denied tenure at Union Seminary and ended up teaching for many years at Auburn Theological Seminary, also in New York City. Wink was surely influenced by Reinhold Niebuhr, although they had their differences. Both, however, studied, understood, and wrote about *power*. Listen to the titles of Wink's most popular books: *Naming the Powers* (1984), *Unmasking the Powers* (1986), *Engaging the Powers* (1992), *When the Powers Fall* (1998), and *The Powers that Be* (1999). Did you notice a theme?

Wink described "the powers that be" in every era in history as "domination systems."[2] Like Niebuhr, he saw the ugly side of power exercised more in *systems* or institutions than in individuals. When we see a power-hungry individual, in other words, they are usually supported and propped up by some kind of system—a nation, an institution, an organization, a corporation, a church, a family etc. Individual people don't have much power outside of a system that supports them. According to Wink, our task as Christians is to name, unmask, engage, and help befall the oppressive powers of the world—the domination systems. Sounds like fun, right? We'll get right on that.

The story above is interesting because it implies four specific domination systems that were operating in that time and place in history. To help us understand them, I need to briefly retell the story: Jesus is invited to eat at the table of a Pharisee. While there, a woman of ill repute crashes the dinner party, bows at Jesus' feet, cries, wipes her tears off his feet with her hair, and anoints them with an expensive ointment. This irritated the host of the party, Simon the Pharisee. So Jesus responds with a nice little parable about forgiveness. His basic argument is that those who are most in need of forgiveness will be most grateful for that forgiveness. There are other people at the party, of course, and they are, let's say, startled, that Jesus had the audacity to forgive this woman of her sins. That's a job for someone else, namely, the priests in the temple in Jerusalem.

---

2. See Wink, *Powers That Be*, 37–62. I named this section "Dominatrix Systems" because, after all, we were talking about sex earlier.

That's the story in a nutshell. Therefore, what are the four domination systems at play in this story? The first one is the *Law of Moses*. The Law of Moses comes into play when Luke, the writer, refers to the woman in the story as a "sinner." She is a sinner because she is a "woman in the city," which means she is a common person. The Pharisees believed that common people, what they referred to as "people of the land," did not properly follow the Law of Moses. Therefore, whether this woman was a prostitute or not—which is a common assumption—she is by definition a "sinner." The interpreters of the Law of Moses said so. She is ritually unclean according to the Mosaic Law. There are in many cultures what we call "purity codes" or "holiness codes," which are designed to keep people ritually or religiously pure and holy. The purity codes of first-century Judaism were broken when this woman—a sinner—touched Jesus with her tears, her hair, and her hands. This made Jesus ritually unclean—although he doesn't seem to mind it one bit. Yes, Jesus was a red-blooded American male. Wait, what?

The second domination system in this story is Simon the Pharisee's *table*. Even more than today, who one ate with was socially significant. Simon's table is closed to the woman, again, because she is a woman of the city, a sinner. By the way, the word "Pharisee" means "separate ones." Historically, people are separated at tables. This is why that old classic movie about the young white woman bringing her black boyfriend to meet her parents is called, *Guess Who's Coming to Dinner* (Columbia Pictures, 1967). It was a surprise because it was taboo. Tables can either be places of separation or places of fellowship. Even today, in many churches around the world, the table is closed to people who don't "deserve" to be there.

The third domination system in this story is *patriarchy*. Patriarchy is defined as a social system in which males hold primary power, predominate in roles of political leadership, moral authority, social privilege, and control of property. In traditional patriarchal families, fathers or father-figures hold authority over women and children. The woman in this story is not just a common person, she is a *female* common person. The patriarchal domination system is working against her here.

Finally, the fourth domination system in this story is the *temple in Jerusalem*. The temple was the only institution in first-century Judaism that had the power to forgive. And yet here is Jesus forgiving this "sinner" woman. He should be ashamed of himself.

Now, why am I pointing out to you the four domination systems at play in this story? My purpose is one of awareness and action. It is to help the reader realize that much of the underlying storyline of the entire Bible is dedicated to doing exactly what Walter Wink talked about in his books: naming, unmasking, engaging, and befalling oppressive systems of power in the world. So where are the domination systems today, I ask? No need to answer. Just know that they are still in our world today, and our job, says Wink, is to name them, unmask them, engage them, and help to befall them (i.e., kick their asses). Sounds like fun, right? It also sounds daunting. Where do we begin? Maybe we should begin with Reinhold Niebuhr's famous Serenity Prayer: "O God, give us serenity to accept what cannot be changed, courage to change what should be changed, and wisdom to distinguish the one from the other."

Luke 8:26–29

Then they arrived at the country of the Gerasenes, which is opposite Galilee. As he stepped out on land, a man of the city who had demons met him. For a long time he had worn no clothes, and he did not live in a house but in the tombs. When he saw Jesus, he fell down before him and shouted at the top of his voice, "What have you to do with me, Jesus, Son of the Most High God? I beg you, do not torment me"—for Jesus had commanded the unclean spirit to come out of the man.

COMMON SENSE

CONVENTIONAL OR TRADITIONAL WISDOM, otherwise known as "common sense," tells us that bad apples can spoil the entire barrel. It says you don't hang around with the wrong crowd or you wind up being as bad as they are. We've all heard this kind of wisdom before. Common sense tells us that we must separate ourselves from anything that might contaminate us or make us dirty. People start with the premise that they are good, pure, clean, or holy and therefore there are certain things and people from which they should keep separate because these things and people are, in some sense, contagious. History is full of examples of our desire to maintain our holiness and goodness by being separate. It all begins in elementary school when little Johnny doesn't want to sit next to Sally because Sally has cooties. (Sorry, Sally. I don't mean you.) As we get older, our parents tell us not to hang around with the wrong crowd or else we might become as bad as they are. Of course, this advice becomes a problem when *we* are the wrong crowd. One of the biggest shocks of my life was the day I told my son not to hang out with the wrong crowd and he informed me that those words were more appropriate when uttered by the parents of his friends.

As we get even older, the separation mentality becomes more serious. Racial conflict is rooted in the human desire to stay separate so as not to be contaminated. Segregation, criticism of so-called mixed marriages, and white flight from the cities are examples of white people's desire for racial purity. Similarly, Catholics and Protestants used to want to keep themselves separate and holy by forbidding or discouraging religiously mixed marriages. Perhaps one of the most important symbols of maintaining racial, ethnic, or religious purity and holiness by separation is the cemetery fence. When I was an interim pastor in South Texas years ago, one of the biggest issues in the community at that time was whether or not to knock down a fence in a cemetery that separates whites from Hispanics. Much to the chagrin of some of the white purists, they knocked the fence down. The same thing occurred in Jasper, Texas in 1998 when three white supremacists dragged James Byrd Jr. to his death behind a pickup truck. After that, a cemetery fence separating blacks and whites was knocked down, symbolizing the desire of the majority of Jasper's citizens to no longer be seen as separatists.

Another example of separation so as not to be contaminated is how people relate to certain illnesses. When people became aware of the HIV-AIDS virus in the 1980s, many people became afraid to even touch AIDS patients for fear of literally being contaminated. As a result of this, AIDS patients were often treated like the lepers of old.

The desire not to be contaminated by others pops up in a lot of different places and scenarios. In 2008, the Southern Baptists held their annual convention in Indianapolis. Almost every issue they voted on was a separation issue. First, they voted to separate from the World Baptist Alliance because they perceived this larger group of Baptists to be too liberal. Southern Baptists apparently do not want to be contaminated even by other Baptists. On the other hand, to show they're not too exclusionary, they voted down a resolution that would have encouraged parents to pull their children out of the godless public schools. Many Southern Baptists believe their children will become contaminated with secularism if they remain in the public schools, and yet apparently the majority of Southern Baptist delegates thought that was going a little *too* far with the separation mentality.

The need for holiness understood as separation from that which is unclean is a dominant theme in the Hebrew Scriptures. Leviticus 20:26 states, "You shall be holy to me; for I the Lord am holy, and I have *separated* you from the other peoples to be mine." After the Babylonian exile was over and many of the Jews went back to their homeland, Ezra explained that the exile had been a consequence of mixed marriages and so marital purity was now in order. Ezra said, "The people of Israel, the priests, and the Levites have not *separated* themselves from the people of the lands." Ezra then forced the people to separate themselves from "the people of the lands and from the foreign wives" so that "the fierce wrath of our God on this account is averted from us." This fear of God's wrath in ancient Israel led to laws that distinguished things and behaviors into categories of "clean" and "unclean." Leviticus 10:10 says, "You are to distinguish between the holy and the common, and between the unclean and the clean." Certain animals were declared to be unclean, including pigs. Lepers were unclean and had to dwell outside the community. Corpses were unclean and therefore one would become unclean by hanging around burial places. These are just a few examples.

With all this in mind, it is easy to understand why the Gerasene demoniac is separated from his community. He is about as unclean and impure as any person could be. He is the poster-child of unholiness. He is living among the tombs, in Gentile territory in proximity to swine, and he is possessed by a legion of unclean spirits. As a tomb-dweller he may have taken on the role of a grave-digger, which means he was in constant contact with corpses. From an Old Testament perspective, this man doesn't have a chance. Common sense suggests that he at least be chained up to keep him from folks who don't want to be contaminated. Actually, they tried to do that but he broke free of the chains and made his way out to the tombs, a place he figured would be safe from anyone who is looking for him.

Fortunately for him, Jesus found him. Jesus had a different perspective about all this separation nonsense. For Jesus, holiness isn't something that needs to be protected from contamination. Instead, holiness is a dynamic power that conquers that which is unholy. Jesus didn't have a lot of *common* sense. That is, he didn't care much for conventional or traditional wisdom. He had a running dispute with the Pharisees. He did not believe, as they did, that we must keep ourselves separate from the world for fear of contamination. He believed, on the other hand, that holiness is contagious, not unholiness. Holiness is a transforming power, not something that needs to be protected and insulated from sources of defilement.

Jesus touched and placed himself in the vicinity of just about everyone the Law had claimed to be unclean. He touched lepers. A woman with a bloody discharge touched him. He even touched corpses. Again, this doesn't show a lot of common sense. Even *we* know not to touch these things. One day my son brought home a dead squirrel, hoping we could bring it back to life. Of course, we can't bring dead squirrels back to life, so we told him to get rid of it and wash his hands because dead animals are unclean. Actually, his hands were probably cleaner playing with a dead squirrel than they normally were. But that's conjecture on my part. I'm not a scientist.

We do have to have a little common sense about what we touch, where we go, what we do, who we hang around with, and so forth. And yet as Christians we must also be aware of the one who made something good out of every occasion in which he refused to be separate from the unholy, the unclean, the impure, and the sinful. Holiness is not something to be protected and insulated from defilement. Holiness is contagious. Love is contagious. Goodness is contagious. That may sound too idealistic and not like common sense, yet it should become more common.

Luke 9:28–36

Now about eight days after these sayings Jesus took with him Peter and John and James, and went up on the mountain to pray. And while he was praying, the appearance of his face changed, and his clothes became dazzling white. Suddenly they saw two men, Moses and Elijah, talking to him. They appeared in glory and were speaking of his departure, which he was about to accomplish at Jerusalem. Now Peter and his companions were weighed down with sleep; but since they had stayed awake,* they saw his glory and the two men who stood with him. Just as they were leaving him, Peter said to Jesus, 'Master, it is good for us to be here; let us make three dwellings,* one for you, one for Moses, and one for Elijah'—not knowing what he said. While he was saying this, a cloud came and overshadowed them; and they were terrified as they entered the cloud. Then from the cloud came a voice that said, 'This is my Son, my Chosen;* listen to him!' When the voice had spoken, Jesus was found alone. And they kept silent and in those days told no one any of the things they had seen.

GETTING OUR FIX

Have you ever had the experience of sitting down to watch television with someone, let's say your mother, and a commercial comes on about something embarrassing, usually some medication designed to help with a specific bodily function—I'll let your imagination run with that. If you were sitting by yourself the commercial wouldn't bother you, and yet watching it with someone else makes you very uncomfortable. So what do you do?

You have three choices. First, you can talk over the commercial. Always have a topic in mind that you can start talking about at a moment's notice—the weather, politics, sports, even religion. Second, you can suddenly announce that you need a bathroom or kitchen break. If so, jump up quickly and stay in the bathroom or kitchen until the embarrassing commercial is over. Third, you can play dumb and oblivious. This is the best option when you either can't think of a topic to talk about, or aren't able to jump off the couch quick enough to get out of the room. So just play dumb, like you don't even realize what the commercial is about.

About the only time of the year I watch commercials is on Super Bowl Sunday. These days, most of my television viewing is through Netflix and Hulu, so I go weeks and months at a time without watching a television commercial. On occasion I attend Super Bowl parties with people I may not know very well. In those situations, I am totally prepared to employ one of these three techniques if I'm sitting there watching the game with, let's say, someone who reminds me of my mother, and a commercial comes on that makes my face turn red. And yet I *do* watch Super Bowl commercials. Although I do enjoy a good football game, perhaps the primary reason I watch the Super Bowl is because the best, most creative, most colorful commercials are produced for this one particular night of the year. Since I don't watch many other commercials during the year, the Super Bowl is my way of getting my commercial fix.

Getting a fix has a bad reputation because it suggests one is addicted to something. A heroin addict needs to get his or her fix. We could, however, be addicted to things that are less dangerous, like for example, good books or Chinese food. Getting a fix could apply to just about anything that is habitual to one degree or another. My wife will tell you that if I don't get my unsweetened iced tea fix in the morning I am fit to be tied. I know some of you get the same way if you don't get to drink some of that hot black brew first thing in the morning.

As a Christian, I occasionally need a Jesus fix. Even though I am a clergy person, and I probably get about as big a dose of Jesus as a human being possibly can—heck, I even wrote a book about him—there are still plenty of other things that life throws in front of me to keep Jesus out of my reach. To use a football analogy, sometimes I get blocked, if not completely knocked down, before I can tackle Jesus. Sometimes it feels like Jesus runs away from me before I can get to him. The good thing about needing a Jesus fix is that we won't suffer from physical withdrawals if we have to go a few days without him. Unlike some of our other habits, like surfing the Internet or playing on our cell phones, we don't have to rely on fickle technology to keep in touch with him. So how do we get our Jesus fix? Some people get their Jesus fix by praying to him. Some, who are of a more mystical bent, get their fix abiding in his presence. After all, the dude abides. Some simply get their fix by reading about him, either in the pages of the Bible or in the pages of books written about him.[1]

Can you imagine being one of Jesus' first disciples, the men and women who actually followed him around and got to hang out with him? How about that for a Jesus fix? Furthermore, can you imagine being one of Jesus' *closest* friends? How exciting, interesting, and sometimes perplexing that must have been. According to the Gospel writers, three of Jesus' disciples seem to have fit that bill: Peter, James, and John. We often call them "the inner circle." The story above is a good example. Peter, James, and John have the privilege of accompanying Jesus on a hike up a mountain. They go there to pray to get their God fix.

Mountains are important in the worldview of the biblical writers because God was thought to be *up there*. Therefore, a mountain got you as close to God as humanly possible. In the modern world we have had to rethink our understanding of where God is because we know "up there" is a lot of empty space, planets, stars, and galaxies. Still, I don't think many modern people would argue that there is not something about mountains—and nature in general—that make us feel closer to something that is wholly and holy other. If you want a God fix, a climbable mountain or hill is a good place to go if for nothing more than the solitude it provides.

So Peter, James, and John accompany their friend and leader up the mountainside to pray. While they are praying, something extraordinary occurs (according to this fanciful story). Jesus' countenance changes and his clothes become dazzling white. Note that in the ancient world, *no one's* garment was ever "dazzling white." They didn't have laundry detergent, bleach, or washing machines, and, more importantly, they were always walking around in the dirt. In that place and time, nothing was very clean by today's standards. Frankly, I don't know why a Madison Avenue advertising agency has not yet picked up on the idea of using this story to advertise the superiority of their client's laundry detergent. Don Draper would be all over it. To me, that would be a commercial worthy of a Super Bowl spot. This story—what we call the "Transfiguration Story"—is like a big Super-Bowl-style television commercial with the sole purpose of trying to *sell Jesus*. Like all good commercials, it employs a little exaggeration while effectively communicating the central truth. And the central truth of the Transfiguration Story is that Jesus is One. Very. Important. Person.

---

1. I hear a really good book about him is titled, *Big Jesus: A Pastor's Struggle with Christology*.

Think about all the imagery in this story that elevates Jesus' status: In a time and place where everyone is dirty, Jesus becomes pristinely clean. Two of the most important historical figures in the Jewish faith pop up out of nowhere: Moses, who represents the Law, and Elijah, who represents the prophets. A cloud appears, reminding us of the pillar of clouds that led Moses and the Israelites through the wilderness. The voice of God speaks from the clouds, reminding us of Jesus' baptism. Not only does God repeat what was said at Jesus' baptism that he is God's "beloved" or "chosen" Son, the voice demands, "Listen to him!" Again: One. Very. Important. Person.

Moses and Elijah share something else in common with Jesus: their deaths are shrouded in mystery. There are no bodies to be found. The book of Deuteronomy tells us that Moses died and was buried in the land of Moab, with this added caveat: "but no one knows the place of his burial to this day." That's the storyteller's way of saying, "Moses was too awesome to die like the rest of us." Elijah, of course, didn't really die, according to the book of 2 Kings. As if he is hailing a cab, Elijah is picked up by a chariot and horses of fire and lifted up in a whirlwind. And then there's Jesus, who dies, is placed in a borrowed tomb, and is raised from the dead. All three—Moses, Elijah, and Jesus—are biblical jabs at the power and finality of death.

We get the point: the storyteller is trying to *sell* Jesus. To use the language of television commercials, Jesus is a "new and improved" version of the Law and the Prophets, the two pillars of Jewish religion. This is savvy, creative storytelling, enough to make any Madison Avenue advertising agency envious. In Super Bowl terms, the Transfiguration story is the Gospel's "halftime event." It's a great commercial break for the church. Think about it. It's read every year at the end of Epiphany and the Sunday before Ash Wednesday. It serves as a bridge between the Advent-Christmas-Epiphany stories of the beginning of Jesus' life and ministry and the concluding stories of Jesus' life and ministry that we celebrate during Lent, Holy Week, Easter, and Pentecost. It helps us make the transition between these two great clusters of seasons on the Christian calendar.

So, the next time you go to a Super Bowl party and a commercial about erectile dysfunction pops up (sorry, couldn't resist), and you're sitting by someone who reminds you of your mom, get up, go into another room, open up the pocket Bible that you managed to smuggle into the party, and read the Transfiguration story. Then, after you get your Jesus fix, go enjoy the game.

Luke 9:57–62

When the days drew near for him to be taken up, he set his face to go to Jerusalem. And he sent messengers ahead of him. On their way they entered a village of the Samaritans to make ready for him; but they did not receive him, because his face was set toward Jerusalem. When his disciples James and John saw it, they said, "Lord, do you want us to command fire to come down from heaven and consume them?" But he turned and rebuked them. Then they went on to another village. As they were going along the road, someone said to him, "I will follow you wherever you go." And Jesus said to him, "Foxes have holes, and birds of the air have nests; but the Son of Man has nowhere to lay his head." To another he said, "Follow me." But he said, "Lord, first let me go and bury my father." But Jesus said to him, "Let the dead bury their own dead; but as for you, go and proclaim the kingdom of God." Another said, "I will follow you, Lord; but let me first say farewell to those at my home." Jesus said to him, "No one who puts a hand to the plow and looks back is fit for the kingdom of God."

THE MOST MISUNDERSTOOD MAN IN THE WORLD

I ONCE POSTED ON Facebook as my doppelganger the Most Interesting Man in the World, the handsome gentleman featured in the Dos Equis beer commercials. I really don't look like him—in fact, I've been told I look like a younger version of Jeff Bridges or Kenny Rogers—but a guy has to do what a guy has to do. As a minister, however, I feel less like the Most Interesting Man in the World and more like the Most *Misunderstood* Man in the World. This is due to my accent and faulty grammar more than anything else.

If I have occasionally been misunderstood, then I stand in good company because Jesus himself was, and is, often misunderstood. However, he has been misunderstood not because his speech was unclear, not because like a modern-day celebrity he has been misquoted in the media (allegedly), not because his words have been taken out of context, and not because he talked over people's heads. Jesus was, and is, misunderstood because he kept saying and doing things that butted heads with conventional wisdom. Marcus Borg, the late great Jesus scholar, refers to Jesus' teachings as "subversive" wisdom.[1] While not everything he said was new, taken as a whole he brought to humanity a brand of wisdom that was, and is, radically new and different and subversive of the status quo. He was, and is, misunderstood because understanding him is often too much of a shock to one's system.

The above passage serves as a great example because it reveals some of our most obvious misunderstandings and misapplications of Jesus' teachings. Jesus taught the kingdom of God as a way of peace . . . and yet many folks believe that in the kingdom of God violence is often justified. Jesus was all too familiar with violence. In verse 53 we are told that he "set his face to go to Jerusalem." He knew the possibility of a violent fate in Jerusalem, the city that "kills the prophets." He knew that his fellow humans have a tendency to solve their political, social, and even religious problems with violence. Nevertheless, he was so determined to get to Jerusalem that he decided to take a shortcut through Samaria. Samaria was located between Galilee in the north, from which Jesus came, and Judea in the south, where Jerusalem is located. Samaria, of course, was occupied largely by the hated Samaritans, folks that were scorned by both the Galileans and Judeans.

Like many of us who are fearful to travel through an inner city ghetto, most Jews in Jesus' day would travel *around* Samaria because they were either fearful of Samaritans or they just didn't like them. Apparently Jesus thought it would be safe to travel through the slums of Samaria, so he sends messengers ahead of him to warn a Samaritan village he and his entourage would be passing through. Unfortunately, the Samaritans did not desire to show them any hospitality, perhaps because they were just passing through. Maybe they felt slighted or ignored. Maybe *they* felt misunderstood or under-appreciated. Regardless, two of Jesus' disciples, James and John (the hot-headed sons of Zebedee), felt the best course of action would be to command fire to come down from heaven and consume the inhospitable Samaritans. Other than the fact that they were delusional for thinking they actually had the power to do that, Jesus rebuked them for even considering taking such vengeful and violent measures. His solution was to simply head on to another village.

---

1. Borg, *Meeting Jesus Again for the First Time*, 70.

Today we live in a nation that would rather command fire to come down from heaven and consume our enemies rather than peacefully head on to another village or nation. We understand that Jesus taught the way of peace, yet we misunderstand its application. For us, peace is a method to be used only when others are peaceful toward us, whereas violence is the preferred method against violence. We will likely continue down this path; still, we ought to at least confess that doing so is to completely misunderstand what Jesus was talking about.

Jesus also taught the kingdom of God as a way of self-sacrifice . . . even as many of us understand the kingdom of God to be all about comfort and prosperity. Everyone wants to be happy. The Fourth of July is partly a celebration of the pursuit of happiness, the American Dream, which is most often thought of in terms of material comfort and prosperity. We will purchase any book, read any pamphlet, or watch any financial guru that shows us how to attain this kind of happiness. I would imagine that this desire was especially strong in Jesus' time because much of the population was poor or destitute. They had very little in terms of material possessions. They were not very comfortable and they certainly were not prosperous. They would naturally follow someone who might help them in this regard.

Jesus knew that as his popularity increased among the peasants, there was bound to be this misunderstanding that following him would bring physical and material comfort and prosperity. As he and his disciples were traveling to the next village in Samaria, someone said to him, "I will follow you wherever you go." Perhaps this person was free to travel because there wasn't much to keep him at home. He may have assumed that life would be better on the road with Jesus. He must have thought that traveling for "Jesus, Inc." would be better than staying home in a meaningless job (or no job at all). However, Jesus quickly lets him down by saying to him, "Foxes have holes, and birds of the air have nests; but the Son of Man has nowhere to lay his head." Unfortunately, there were no Holiday Inns on Jesus' itinerary, and no limos, lunch buffets, or executive suites. There was some serious roughing it going on.

I don't think Jesus is saying in absolute terms that his followers must "do without." If he did, and we took him literally, there would be virtually no Christians in the world today. So I think we misunderstand him if we forsake everything and become a roaming, homeless ascetic. But I also think we misunderstand him if we believe that following him means that our mission in life is to have as much comfort and prosperity as possible, or that this is the reward for being a faithful Christian. What Jesus taught, over and over again, is that faithfulness often requires self-sacrifice—even self-denial—so that we become attuned to those who truly have nowhere to lay their heads.

Finally, Jesus taught the kingdom of God is our primary obligation ... even as we often understand the kingdom of God to be secondary. Luke tells us about two prospective followers of Jesus who can't seem to prioritize their commitment to him. They want to follow Jesus but they have other obligations. The first is a man who responds to Jesus' call to follow him by saying, "Lord, first let me go and bury my father." Jesus says to him, rather sarcastically it seems, "Let the dead bury their own dead; but as for you, go and proclaim the kingdom of God." I doubt seriously that the man's father had just died. There is no way Jesus would have objected to a man wanting to give his father a funeral. It is more likely that this man was merely looking after an aging father and was telling Jesus, "I'll become your follower once my family obligations are finished."

Then there is the prospective follower who first needed to "say farewell" to those at his home. More family obligations it seems. And yet Jesus says to him, rather harshly, "No one who puts a hand to the plow and looks back is fit for the kingdom of God." Again, I doubt that Jesus would literally have a problem with someone going to his home and saying goodbye to his loved ones before taking off on a potentially long and dangerous journey. What is more likely is that Jesus sensed this person, like the one before him, would always have other obligations. Jesus is fighting against a slippery slope argument here. That is, once we assign the status of primary obligation to anything other than the kingdom of God, the kingdom of God becomes no obligation at all.

For many reasons, Jesus was, and is, the most misunderstood man in the history of the human race. (Please don't misunderstand me here. I love hyperbole.) He initiated a spiritual movement that pushes human wisdom to the brink of nonsensicalness. Most people find all this rather absurd: that peace is the proper response to another's hostility, that self-sacrifice and denial is the only reward for following Jesus (rather than comfort and prosperity), and that the way of peace and self-sacrifice is our primary obligation. This is subversive wisdom at its best, and because of its perceived lunacy we are prone to apply this wisdom only when it suits us best. We are prone to practice peace only when we think it will work better than violence, we are prone to deny ourselves comfort and prosperity only if we have no viable means of attaining such things, and we are prone to put God's kingdom first in our lives only if we have no other obligations. I don't know if Jesus has a doppelganger today. If he does, that person is likely to be grossly misunderstood.

A POST-LIBERAL CHURCH

Many people like to wax nostalgic about the church of the 1950s and 1960s. For example, do you miss the day when the pews were filled to overflowing? Do you miss the day when the church was the center of the community? Do you miss the day when an American was assumed to be a Christian? Do you miss the day when people from other religions lived in other countries, when no one used words such as "multiculturalism"? Do you miss the day when no one criticized the exclusive language we use in our hymnals and Bibles, when no one was pushing us to use politically correct inclusive language? Do you miss the day when the ordination of women and/or homosexuals was not an issue? Do you miss the day when prayers were uttered in the public schools? Do you miss the day when no one questioned the offering of prayers at football games? ("Dear God, make sure I don't get a concussion today." "Okay," God says, "then you get to sit on the bench.") Do you miss the day when no one tried to remove the phrase "under God" from the Pledge of Allegiance? Do you miss the day when we had blue laws and everyone, it seems, observed a Sabbath day of rest? Do you miss the day when children did not play soccer on Sunday mornings and the schools didn't assign homework on Wednesday nights so the children could go to Wednesday night services?

In the 1950s and early 1960s, the church was the center of the cultural life in America. The church gave its blessing to almost everything that was happening in our society. Scholars refer to this former state of the church in a couple of different ways. First, "Christendom"—literally, the kingdom of Christianity—implies that Christianity was the most powerful institution in Western society. Second, "civil" or "civic" religion is the notion that being a citizen of a country and being a member of the church is considered to be one and the same thing. If you practice a civil religion then you are likely to confuse the notion of being a citizen of the United States with being a Christian.

Christendom and civil religion are good ways to describe the church of that era. The Christian church was the most influential institution in America and being an American and a Christian were virtually synonymous. Back then, the air we breathed was Christian. Having just won World War II, we assumed that soon the whole world would be Christian. Nothing would stop us. In 1954 the phrase "under God" was added to the Pledge of Allegiance because it seemed obvious to us that we were a nation that lived under the blessings of Almighty God. And yet, even then, when the church was reaching its peak in America, we noticed the political and cultural power of the church slowly begin to fade away.

In that same year, 1954, the power of the church in the South was weakened by a Supreme Court decision, *Brown vs. the Board of Education*. This decision declared segregation in the public schools unconstitutional. White Southern Christians had been the strongest supporters of segregation, so they must have felt like they were losing some of their power and influence in the larger culture. In 1963 the Supreme Court declared that mandated prayers in the public schools were no longer constitutional. This decision still sends shock waves through our society. It signified that the culture was becoming less and less specifically Christian and more and more secular. Christendom was disappearing. Then, when *Roe v. Wade* became the law of the land in 1973, many Christians became convinced that the power of the church was forever losing its grip on America's values. That was the straw that broke the camel's back . . . until gay marriage became the law of the land and the camel's back was snapped in two.

Christians in America reacted to this string of events in two very different ways. The more conservative Christians made desperate attempts to reestablish the power and muscle of the church. Before this time in history, conservative Christians saw very little need to be politically active because the laws of the land generally supported their views and values. With the rise of secularism, however, politically active conservative Christian groups arose like Jerry Falwell's "Moral Majority" in the 1980s and Pat Robertson's "Christian Coalition" in the 1990s.

Meanwhile, progressive/liberal Christians started thinking, "This secular business isn't so bad. Secular values are very much like our own. We believe in equal rights for women and minorities, civil liberties, abortion rights, and the separation of church and state." And yet at the same time they began to ask themselves, "If there is no difference between being a liberal Christian and being a non-Christian secularist, if our values are pretty much the same, then why am I wasting time in the church?" This began a mass exodus of people out of the liberal denominations. The irony is this: Even though secular values are more in line with liberal Christianity, liberal Christianity has become largely irrelevant in terms of social power.

Today, as the membership of the politically active conservative churches continues to hold their own and continues to work hard to reestablish Christendom (which will never happen), the membership of mainline liberal denominations continues to diminish. The "mainline" church has become the "sideline" church. Conservative Christianity has become the public face of Christianity. When the secular public hears the word "Christian" they almost always have the more conservative Christians in mind like the ones they see on television. I can't name one popular television preacher that is from a liberal, mainline denomination. No one knows who we are. On the rare occasion the general public is introduced to a liberal Christian they tend to dismiss him or her as just a secularist who dresses up on Sunday morning.

The main reason for this dilemma is that liberal Christians and secularists talk the same language. Let me illustrate what I'm talking about. Before Paul Sherry became president of the United Church of Christ, he was executive director of the Chicago Renewal Society, a social service agency that has Christian roots. On one occasion he was invited to speak at the dedication of a new youth center. Another of the speakers was Harold Washington, then mayor of Chicago. After the ceremony Mayor Washington invited Paul Sherry to a local diner for a cup of coffee. When they sat down, the mayor quickly got to the reason for his invitation: "You know, Paul, I appreciate all of your efforts in getting this center opened, and I also appreciated your remarks today. But you are a Christian minister and I didn't hear you say anything today that couldn't have been said by somebody else. We need to hear something else from you. We need to hear something from the gospel!" When Paul Sherry was president of the United Church of Christ I'm sure he tried his best to help us become the United Church of *Christ* rather than just the United Church of *Culture*. Still, the sad fact remains that the general public has a difficult time distinguishing between liberal Christianity and secularism because we practically speak the same language. Therefore, we have become largely irrelevant.

What are we going to do about this? I believe, as many others do, that the solution to our dilemma is for our denomination and other mainline churches to evolve from being a liberal church to a "post-liberal" church. This is a very complicated subject. I will simplify matters by saying that post-liberal Christians are Christians with liberal values who speak *as Christians* and not just as secularists who like to dress up on Sunday mornings. To say it another way, post-liberal Christians are people who have moved beyond their secularism to an authentic Christian faith. Their values are rooted in the gospel and not in secular, rational thought. They have accepted the fact that everyone in our society will not be Christian by default, and therefore the church needs to actively engage in Christian formation. We have to learn to disciple people once again.

What I like about our current situation is that we have the opportunity once again to be the church, rather than just American citizens who like to dress up on Sunday mornings. Our situation today is actually very similar to that in the early church when most people were not Christian. In fact, our situation is very similar to the very beginning of the Jesus movement when Jesus himself was trying to recruit people to follow him. In the text above from Luke 9, Jesus and his small group of disciples are traveling through

Samaritan villages on their way to Jerusalem. As I stated above, this is a shortcut from Galilee in the north to Judea in the south. His movement is building momentum but he needs more disciples. And he certainly can't assume that everyone he meets will accept him and his message. As you can imagine, once Jesus explains to people that "Foxes have holes, and birds of the air have nests; but the Son of Man has nowhere to lay his head" a lot of wannabe followers decide that kind of life just isn't for them. A few follow him; most do not.

This scenario is eerily similar to our situation today in the liberal mainline church. We say we are willing to follow Jesus, we get up on Sunday mornings and come to church, yet we feel more comfortable living, breathing, and talking in a secular way. This has worked for us very well for a long, long time. Why change now? Again, that day is gone. As Jesus says, "No one who puts a hand to the plow and looks back is fit for the kingdom of God." In other words, the past is over. The days of Christendom have expired. The civil, or secular, faith that has worked so well for us in the past is no longer a viable option. We need to look forward, not backward. We need to become authentically Christian, to speak a language of faith, to be the church. We can no longer assume that the larger culture is in partnership with the Christian faith. We can no longer assume that people born in this country will automatically be Christian. We now must get busy with the task of forming people in the Christian faith.

For those of us in the liberal/progressive denominations, like the United Church of Christ, our dilemma is this: Are we Christians or are we secularists who like to dress up on Sunday morning? Should we continue to be liberal Christians or should we become post-liberal Christians, that is, Christians in liberal denominations who are able to say, "Lord, I will follow you wherever you go?" A lot has changed since the 1950s, yet one thing has not changed: Jesus is asking us to follow him . . . whether we look like him or not.

Luke 10:1–4

After this the Lord appointed seventy others and sent them on ahead of him in pairs to every town and place where he himself intended to go. He said to them, "The harvest is plentiful, but the laborers are few; therefore ask the Lord of the harvest to send out laborers into his harvest. Go on your way. See, I am sending you out like lambs into the midst of wolves. Carry no purse, no bag, no sandals; and greet no one on the road.

PLAYING IT SAFE

According to this passage, Jesus played it safe by sending out his disciples in pairs. There is safety in numbers, right? Jesus was realistic enough to understand the potential danger of their mission, "like lambs into the midst of wolves," he said. This is probably why he told them not to take a purse, bag, or sandals and not to greet anyone on the road. If the journey truly was that dangerous, then someone might steal their purse or bag because that's where people kept their money. Or they might forcibly take their sandals away from them because sandals were a precious commodity in a place and time where people walked everywhere. Good sandals were a first-century version of Nike's Air Jordans. People would kill for them. Furthermore, telling them not to greet anyone on the road was for the purpose of not drawing attention to oneself. Jesus could play it safe as much as anyone. He wasn't stupid; he was just being realistic.

In reality, however, Jesus was not playing it safe at all, or he would have told his followers to go back to fishing. I don't mean to mix metaphors, but the harvest is out *there*, says Jesus, not in *here*, although it feels to me like most of our congregations are more comfortable seeing the harvest as something that occurs only in their sanctuaries on Sunday mornings. This is our version of playing it safe. Unless folks begin seeing the harvest as something that takes place outside of the four walls, however, no one is ever going to have a harvest.

Playing it safe is not always the wrong the thing to do, of course. Congregations do need to be cautious, prudent, and realistic. They need to stay as grounded as possible. And yet, on occasion, they need to risk being ungrounded and climb the proverbial water tower. When I was a teenager, I marveled at the bravado of my older cousin, Buddy, who seemed to have no fear climbing the ladder on the water tower in my little West Texas hometown. I always thought he would make a great street evangelist. I don't agree with street evangelism theology, however, I always thought this sort of thing would require oversized *cojones*, which he apparently had, and which come in pairs, by the way.

If Jesus is our model, congregations need to mobilize their constituents to offer an inside-the-walls extravagant invitation while, at the same time, taking it to the streets like a Doobie Brothers song. Just make sure you keep your money in your fanny packs.

Luke 10:9b

"The kingdom of God has come near to you."

DID THE KINGDOM OF GOD COME TO AMERICA?

Every Fourth of July we celebrate the day our American forefathers and mothers walked through the relatively unknown door of freedom. As the years went by, their genius produced such liberating documents as the Declaration of Independence, which contains the following words in the Preamble: "We hold these truths to be self-evident: That all men are created equal; that they are endowed by their Creator with certain unalienable rights; that among these are life, liberty, and the pursuit of happiness." A few years later they produced the Constitution of the United States of America. Its Preamble states, "We the People of the United States, in order to form a more perfect union, establish justice, insure domestic tranquility, provide for the common defense, promote the general welfare, and secure the blessings of liberty to ourselves and our posterity, do ordain and establish this Constitution for the United States of America."

The primary goal of both of these documents was political freedom from Great Britain. As time went by we have amended the Constitution in order to add other freedoms. These freedoms include the freedom of speech and the press, the right of assembly and petition, the right to keep and bear arms, property rights, the rights of persons accused of crimes including the right of trial by jury, and finally, the abolition of slavery and the right to suffrage for minorities and women. We need to understand how unique these freedoms are in the annals of human history.

Perhaps the most significant freedom sought by our foreparents was religious freedom. What a gift we brought to the world. Today we almost certainly take religious freedom for granted, yet in the Western world of the eighteenth century there was very little religious freedom and tolerance. The states, or governments, controlled the church. There were no independent churches at that time. The monarch presided over both church and state. At first, our American ancestors had a difficult time envisioning and practicing religion freedom. Although many of them came to our shores to escape religious intolerance and discrimination in Europe, there was still a fair amount of discrimination against Catholics, Jews, and atheists in colonial America. South Carolina even proclaimed that "the Christian Protestant religion shall be established as the religion of this state,"[1] and it limited office-holding to Protestants and voting to religious believers.

However, for the most part during the Revolutionary era in America, religion became disestablished, or separated from the states. This was a phenomenon without precedent in history. The disestablishment of religion, freedom of religion, or separation of church and state was not to be found in the Old World until well into the nineteenth century. But in the New World of the United States something new and different was happening. Because the first real glimpse of religious freedom and independence occurred in the United States, many people began to assume that God was doing something very special in America.

There was even a widespread notion that the history of the world had come to a climax with the American Revolution. Abiel Holmes, the father of the poet Oliver Wendell Holmes and grandfather of Justice Oliver Wendell Holmes wrote a history of the United States. His book begins with the expulsion of Adam and Eve from the Garden of Eden and ends with American independence, the climax of all history. Clearly, people thought something very special was happening. Americans have often seen themselves as the new "chosen people," the New Israel. In fact, some have argued that what we see in America is none other than the kingdom of God on earth. We may scoff at this assertion, but it does force us to ask the question, "Did the kingdom of God come to America?" Is the history of America a history of God's unique blessing on a chosen people? If not, when and where has the kingdom of God occurred?

The timing of the kingdom's arrival has provoked heated scholarly debates. Let me offer four brief answers to the question of the timing of the arrival of the kingdom of God, and then I will try to answer the question, "Did the kingdom of God come to America?"

The first possible answer is that Jesus thought the kingdom was present in his own ministry. In Luke 10:9 Jesus said, "The kingdom of God has come near to you," and in Luke 11:20 he suggests, "The kingdom of God has come

---

1. Commager, "Religion and Politics in American History," 46.

upon you." Both of these sayings, along with others in the Gospels, imply that the kingdom of God was present during the life and ministry of Jesus.

A second possible answer is that Jesus expected the kingdom of God to come very soon, in fact at the end of his life or soon after his death. In Matthew 10:23 Jesus tells those he is sending out, "Truly, I say to you, you will not have gone through all the towns of Israel, before the Son of man comes." In Luke 9:27, Jesus says, "But I tell you truly, there are some standing here who will not taste death before they see the kingdom of God." These and other passages suggest that Jesus himself expected the kingdom to come in the lifetime of his followers.

A third possibility is that the kingdom of God will arrive in the future when Christ will literally reign on earth. This is the "dispensational" view, popular among fundamentalist Christians. According to this view, the kingdom isn't here yet. This is also the "Jesus is coming soon and he's really pissed" view.

Finally, a fourth possibility is that the kingdom arrived in the past, is here in the present, and will come in the future. "The kingdom of God is already, but not yet" is a popular way of saying it. I believe this fourth option is the most theologically sound answer. It simplifies matters without putting the kingdom of God behind a specific door marked "the kingdom of God," a door to which only certain privileged people have access. Can you imagine the deals Monte Hall could have made with people looking for that door?

If we were to argue that the kingdom of God came in the past, let's say when Jesus was walking around on earth, or when he resurrected from the dead, or when America won her independence—if we argue for any past event as being the moment of the kingdom's arrival, then we have effectively placed the kingdom of God behind a very specific door to be opened only by the "right" people. Likewise, if we say that the kingdom will arrive only at some point in the future, then nothing we do today has any value, and only those privileged few who know when and how the door will be opened will benefit from the kingdom's arrival.

I believe, on the other hand, that the kingdom of God can be found behind many doors in the past, the present, and the future. It would be arrogant for us to think we can point to any event in the past or future and say, "There is the kingdom of God." The kingdom of God is something that transcends our human understanding of time and place. It has come in the past, it bears fruit in the present, and we wait for it with expectation in the future. Looking for it behind a particular door is too limiting.

So, did the kingdom of God come to America? Yes it has, and it will. Furthermore, is the American experiment of democracy and freedom and justice for all the climax of the kingdom of God in human history? I hope not, because we haven't exactly been perfect in our implementation of what we might call "kingdom values." Let me quote from an essay entitled, "Religion and Politics in American History," by Henry Steele Commager. He writes, "On the larger stage we persist in believing that whatever we choose to do is righteous in the eyes of God and of history because our purposes are noble and our hearts are pure." He said we often have a "tolerance of deep and widespread social injustice and inequities in our treatment of the poor, blacks, women, and the 'dangerous and perishing classes' of society." Going beyond our borders, Commager claims that we have also had an "indifference to the claims of justice owed the hundreds of millions of men and women in less fortunate nations" and to "the rights of posterity to the natural resources of the earth."[2]

All of this is a fancy way of saying, "No, we haven't been perfect." It would be difficult to make an argument that the kingdom of God was inaugurated on July 4, 1776. And yet, there is something inside of us that stirs our souls when a small child waves an American flag in one hand while holding an ice-cream cone in the other. There is something that humbles us when fireworks are ignited and people gather around the barbecue pit and utter the word "liberty." There is a chord that strikes in our hearts when we sing "let freedom ring," "America, God shed His grace on thee," and "Mine eyes have seen the coming of the glory of the Lord." The door through which our foreparents walked—the door of freedom—may not be the only door or even the best door behind which we find the kingdom of God on earth. Nevertheless, as long as equality, human rights, life, liberty, the pursuit of happiness, justice, and tranquility remain the standard by which all nations are judged, we can say with some amount of certainty, "Yes, the kingdom of God came to America." Let's hope there's more to come.

---

2. Commager, "Religion and Politics in American History," 53.

Luke 10:25–37

Just then a lawyer stood up to test Jesus. "Teacher," he said, "what must I do to inherit eternal life?" He said to him, "What is written in the law? What do you read there?" He answered, "You shall love the Lord your God with all your heart, and with all your soul, and with all your strength, and with all your mind; and your neighbor as yourself." And he said to him, "You have given the right answer; do this, and you will live." But wanting to justify himself, he asked Jesus, "And who is my neighbor?" Jesus replied, "A man was going down from Jerusalem to Jericho, and fell into the hands of robbers, who stripped him, beat him, and went away, leaving him half dead. Now by chance a priest was going down that road; and when he saw him, he passed by on the other side. So likewise a Levite, when he came to the place and saw him, passed by on the other side. But a Samaritan while traveling came near him; and when he saw him, he was moved with pity. He went to him and bandaged his wounds, having poured oil and wine on them. Then he put him on his own animal, brought him to an inn, and took care of him. The next day he took out two denarii, gave them to the innkeeper, and said, 'Take care of him; and when I come back, I will repay you whatever more you spend.' Which of these three, do you think, was a neighbor to the man who fell into the hands of the robbers?" He said, "The one who showed him mercy." Jesus said to him, "Go and do likewise."

WHY DID THE SAMARITAN CROSS THE ROAD?

ONE DAY IN THE not-too-distant past, I took the liberty of goofing off for a few hours. While driving in my pickup I heard a variation on the "Why did the chicken cross the road?" joke on the radio and decided, you know what, I can do better than that. So I set about the task of coming up with new comedy material, inventing several new variations on the "Why did the chicken cross the road?" joke. Much to the chagrin of my Facebook audience, I shared all of them. The following is a sample of my comedic inventions as I sat outside in my square gazebo (I call it a "gazebo" because that sounds much classier than "a detached screened-in porch"):

Why did the playground equipment salesperson cross the road? To get to the other slide.

Why did the duck cross the road? Because she wasn't chicken.

Why did the Protestant cross the road? Because he didn't know how to cross himself.

Why did Donald Trump cross the road? To part his hair on the other side.

Why did Hillary Clinton cross the road? She didn't. She used email.

Why did the chicken cross the road? Because she had yet to be introduced to the poetry of Robert Frost. (I don't mean to sound condescending. I'm referring to Frost's poem, "The Road Not Taken." If you don't know what I'm talking about, then I'm also referring to "The Freshman Literature Class Not Taken.")

Obviously, my creative juices ran dry. On that same evening I was sitting in my screened-in detached porch to look at the Gospel reading for the upcoming Sunday: "The Parable of the Good Samaritan." Unless you have been run over trying to cross the street, you know that this parable is about someone who is willing to cross the road to care for someone who had been robbed and beaten half to death. It didn't take two seconds for me to realize that my sermon title for that Sunday would be, "Why did the *Samaritan* cross the road?"

Before I answer the "Why" question, let me first talk about the Samaritan in Jesus' parable. Notice that Jesus never calls him the "Good" Samaritan. He didn't need to. The Samaritan's goodness is implied in the story. The second reason Jesus doesn't call him the Good Samaritan is because this would have been an oxymoron, a contradiction in terms. No Samaritans were good from the perspective of Jesus' listeners. To refer to the Samaritan as good would have created a reaction at best of rolled eyes and a dismissive smile and at worst the lawyer would have spat on the ground, cursed, and walked away. A good storyteller, as Jesus was, would not want to sabotage his story by turning off the listener at such a critical point in the story.

According to first-century standards, Samaritans were ethnically and religiously below par. ("below par" in this sense means "not good." In golfing terms, however, "below par" means "really good." Such is the shortcomings, contradictions, and outright confusion of golfers contributing to the English language.) They had Jewish ancestry yet may have comingled with some gentiles during the time of the Babylonian exile over five hundred years earlier when the best and brightest Jews were forced into exile. The irony is that the word "Samaritan" means "Guardian of the Law" (or Torah). The Samaritans saw themselves as religious purists in that they believed they kept the original religion of Judaism intact. And yet to their neighbors to the north in Galilee and to the south in Judea, the Samaritans were ethnically and religiously impure and therefore looked at with contempt.

Because of that, their morality was suspect as well. When I first thought about this I wanted to compare them to a specific ethnic and cultural group today called the Romani, or Gypsies. For a long time people thought Gypsies were from Egypt, thus the connection in the name. The consensus now is that they originally descended from India about a thousand years ago and now live all over the world in different cultures, speaking different languages. They are pejoratively called "Gypsies," which has a connotation of being illegal and irregular. In fact, this label is where we get our word "gyp," which means to cheat or swindle. We've all heard the stories. I suspect that while Jesus is telling the lawyer a story about a Samaritan who is willing to cross the road to help a man that not even a priest or a Levite is willing to help, it would have sounded to him much like it would sound to us if someone told a story about a Gypsy crossing a dangerous road to help someone rather than rob someone who is lying there half dead. Listeners today might roll their eyes as well.

After what has occurred in my community, in Ferguson, Missouri, and in many other places in this country in recent years, I think we can safely say that the Samaritan is symbolic of the "other" in our midst. The "other" is defined by who we are. If we are white, the other is a person of color, and vice versa. If we are straight, the other is gay, and vice versa. If we are African-American, the other might be a police officer, and vice versa. If we are Christian, the other might be a Muslim, and vice versa. Just like if we were Jewish in the first century, the other was a Samaritan, and vice versa. Reading this parable of the Good Samaritan is just as relevant as it was then because the other doesn't seem to want to go away. And the one thing that can rock anyone's world is the notion that the other can be morally superior to us, no matter who "us" is. Crossing the road, therefore, is a metaphor for engaging the other when the others are bleeding to death, both literally and figuratively. Crossing the road is also a metaphor for recognizing the good in the other. Our task is to cross the road, no matter how dangerous we might think it is. By the way, I came up with a new phrase for Christians who are willing to cross the road: "Jaywalking for Jesus." You have my permission to use that.

So why is the road dangerous? The parable mentions the road from Jerusalem to Jericho. This road follows a wadi, specifically the Wadi Qelt, which is a deep ravine. Crossing a wadi to get to the other side of the road is dangerous because either wild animals or bandits could have attacked them as well, which is one reason the priest and the Levite in the parable were afraid to cross the road. It wasn't like crossing a path or a modern paved street. It really wasn't like jaywalking at all. It was climbing down into the ravine and climbing up the other side. Anything could happen. The Samaritan does so, courageously, and accomplishes four things. He stops the man's bleeding, takes him to a safe place, spends the night with him, and then leaves money for his care. This is why there are hospitals and many other charitable organizations around the world that have utilized the name "Good Samaritan" in their official titles.

So, why did the Samaritan cross the road? My first thought was, "To avoid the priest and the Levite." No, this is really a question about motivation. The Samaritan was motivated by compassion. The priest and the Levite were motivated by self-preservation, not compassion. They understandably didn't want to risk getting robbed and beaten themselves. Also, according to their laws they were not even allowed to touch a corpse or blood, both of which would make them ritually unclean. The last thing a priest or Levite wants to do is become ritually unclean. They would have to miss work for a few days. A Levite, by the way, was a priest that worked primarily in the temple in Jerusalem.

One might think the Samaritan didn't need to worry about either one of those problems—getting robbed or becoming ritually unclean. First, a Samaritan outside of his region would be in even more danger of physical harm. Here are a couple of modern parallel examples: a white person who is afraid to drive through a predominantly African-American neighborhood, and a black person who sees the lights of a police car in their rearview window. That's what it was like for the Samaritan to be traveling between Jerusalem and Jericho. Second, remember that the Samaritans saw themselves as religious purists—they are the Guardians of the Law. They would be even more concerned about touching blood or dead bodies. And yet, according to this oxymoronic story, the Samaritan, with so much at stake, is the one who crosses the road or ravine to get to the half-dead man. The question is, then, why would such a purist of the law be the one that sidesteps the law in order to practice compassion?

Perhaps because he was a purist, he knew the essence of the Law better than the Jewish priest or the Levite. Why did the Samaritan cross the road? Because he knew that obeying the Law should never get in the way of showing compassion. That's pretty much the essence of Jesus' religion. We can go for a walk now.

LIKE A GOOD NEIGHBOR

Again, Jesus never uses the word "good" in references to the Samaritan in this parable. He simply allows the story to make what would have been a radical assertion, that a Samaritan could indeed be good. Notice that his parable is a response to a lawyer's question about eternal life. (At this point the reader may insert a lawyer joke, especially one that implies lawyers have very little chance of inheriting eternal life.) In this context, lawyers studied religious laws, so it is curious that he would be asking Jesus such a simple theological question, one that he probably could have answered in a brief. (It is also curious that a lawyer can write a thirty-page document and call it a "brief.") Jesus knew the lawyer had all the answers he could possibly ever want in one of his big fat law books on his barrister bookshelf, so he asks him, "What is written in the law?" The lawyer, perhaps realizing that Jesus has wisely wiggled out of answering a very tricky question, decides to venture a guess.

He does so by referring to "legal precedent" (something our current Supreme Court might want to consider). He combines Israel's Shema on the love of God from Deuteronomy 6 with the love of neighbor of Leviticus 19. (Leave it to a lawyer to bring together two separate answers to form one answer.) From Deuteronomy 6 he says, "You shall love the Lord your God with all your heart, and with all your soul, and with all your strength, and with all your mind." Then, for good measure he quotes from Leviticus 19 which implores us to "love your neighbor as yourself." Please ignore the narcissism in that verse. Jesus, in his cut-to-the-chase way of speaking, says, "You have given the right answer; do this, and you will live."

Here's the thing about lawyers. They don't appreciate simple answers. They hate succinctness. They despise brief briefs. In fact, they probably call their writings "briefs" to make us think they could write another thirty pages if they wanted to. Lawyers love to parse, to break down each and every word in a sentence until they capture just the right essence of what was said or spoken. So, in typical lawyer fashion, he asks Jesus, "And who *is* my neighbor?" After all, one's neighbor could be limited to the lady next door who waters her flowers and turns out her lights by 9:00 pm or the young man who loans me his lawn mower at a time of desperation. Anyone could love those people.

By this time, Jesus knew that he would get nowhere with a person who would pick apart every single word he heard until the question, "What must I do to inherit eternal life?" would lose all practicality and relevance. So, he does the one thing that will stop this inquisitor in his tracks and leave him scratching his head. He tells a story. The parable of the Good Samaritan undoubtedly befuddled and provoked the lawyer and the crowd of listeners. Yes, there was a crowd because Jesus would not have shared such an important parable with only one person. He would not have given so much hay to just one or two cows. And yet we get no signal of a reaction. We can assume there was only dead silence. While waiting for this pregnant pause to transpire, Jesus looks the lawyer squarely in the eyes and asks him, "What do you think? Which of the three—the priest, the Levite, or the Samaritan—became a neighbor to the man attacked by robbers?" As embarrassing as it must have been for this Jewish scholar of the law, a man with many friends who were priests and Levites, he answers (begrudgingly), "The one who treated him kindly." Notice he didn't answer, "The Samaritan," much less "The *Good* Samaritan." There's no way those words were going to come out of his mouth.

After the lawyer holds his nose, crosses his fingers, and is barely able to say (if not grunt) that the Samaritan was the neighbor in Jesus' parable, Jesus rubs proverbial salt in the wound by saying, "Go and do the same." That is, go and be a neighbor like the Samaritan was a neighbor. My guess is that the lawyer's entire world collapsed around him. His worldview, that God has clearly marked those who are good, righteous, holy, and pure—in contrast to those who are not—evaporated, or at least was badly wounded, in a matter of a few seconds. His professional philosophy, that only those who love God in the proper way, with the proper theology, and who love their neighbors, which, as any first-century Jewish scholar knew, was limited to those who loved God in the proper way with the proper theology, was blown out of the water. Imagine spending your entire life preparing for and practicing a particular profession, one that you believe is enormously important and crucial for the well-being of your society. Then imagine one day, in a matter of seconds, all of this tumbling down like a house of cards. Imagine the foundation of your beliefs, the core of your values, the essence of your identity melting like salt on a bald head in the middle of July in Texas.[1]

---

1. I have seen this happen. Performing a weird wedding outside at 5:00 pm on a

The parable of the Samaritan is important for us today in ways that escape the notice of most Christians. We live in a nation and world that is becoming more and more religiously diverse or pluralistic. Diana Eck's book, *A New Religious America*, was published shortly after 9/11. In the introduction she writes, "For ten years I have gone out looking for the religious neighbors of a new America . . . I have celebrated the Sikh New Year's festival of Baisakhi with a community in Fairfax County, Virginia. I have feasted at the Vietnamese Buddhist 'Mother's Day' in a temple in Olympia, Washington, and I have delivered an impromptu speech on the occasion of Lord Ram's Birthday at a new Hindu temple in Troy, Michigan." She goes on to say, "It's one thing to be unconcerned about or ignorant of Muslim or Buddhist neighbors on the other side of the world, but when Buddhists are our next-door neighbors, when our children are best friends with Muslim classmates, when a Hindu is running for a seat on the school committee, all of us have a new vested interest in our neighbors, both as citizens and as people of faith."[2]

The world has always had religious diversity, and yet for most of human history, religions were largely geographically confined to particular locations. That's no longer as true as it once was. Today, because of improved transportation and mass migration, people of various religious persuasions are living next door to one another, and because of improved communications technology, we are all more aware of the presence of other religious persuasions around the world. We should therefore be less surprised than that first-century lawyer when a member of another religion acts more justly and compassionately than members of our own religion. The parable of the Samaritan, then, is a story that is even more relevant today than it was in first-century Palestine. It teaches us that neighborliness, compassion, mercy, and goodness are not the prerogative of one religion. It teaches us that we don't have to qualify a member of another religion with the word "good," such as "Good Samaritan," "Good Muslim," or "Good Buddhist," because their goodness is *not* an exception to the rule. Goodness lies in the hearts of most people regardless of ethnicity or religion.

The most radical point this parable is making, however, is one involving eternal life. Our awareness of the presence of so many religious persuasions in the world has created much consternation among evangelical Christians, Christians who believe that only Christians can inherit eternal life. And yet if this parable can be taken as "truth" on any level, then Jesus'

---

hot summer day in Texas, I sprinkled some salt on the groom's bald head as part of the ritual. It literally (I mean physically) melted on his head.

2. Eck, *New Religious America*, 2–6.

criteria for eternal life are far different than the typical American evangelical criteria. Whereas evangelical Christianity wants to exclude all who do not believe a certain way, Jesus wants to include all those who behave like a good neighbor, even those dirty Samaritans who have bad theology.

Luke 10:38–42

Now as they went on their way, he entered a certain village, where a woman named Martha welcomed him into her home. She had a sister named Mary, who sat at the Lord's feet and listened to what he was saying. But Martha was distracted by her many tasks; so she came to him and asked, "Lord, do you not care that my sister has left me to do all the work by myself? Tell her then to help me." But the Lord answered her, "Martha, Martha, you are worried and distracted by many things; there is need of only one thing. Mary has chosen the better part, which will not be taken away from her."

TO BE (IN THE KITCHEN) OR NOT TO BE (IN THE KITCHEN)

PERSONALLY, I THINK WORK is overrated, and yet if I were a betting man I would wager that most Christians identify with Martha rather than Mary. My impression of every congregation I have ever served is that they are full of Marthas (or Marks, to be more gender-inclusive). I am always impressed with how many good workers there are in my congregations. There is never a lack of workers, and yet there is often a lack of organization. One of my tasks as pastor, then, has always been to try to improve the coordination of the work that goes on in my congregations without interfering with the energy and creativity.

However, as valuable as church work is to the life of a congregation, we need to lift up the Marys, because that's what Jesus did. Of course, Jesus did not have a problem with people whose faith is practiced primarily through service to others. In fact, even though he refers to Mary's act of sitting at his feet and hanging on his every word as "the better part," I think he meant that it was the better part *at that moment,* because at that moment everyone in that house had an opportunity to listen to a pretty darn good teacher.

It's difficult to draw a parallel with anything today, and yet imagine that you are a Catholic and the pope has come to your home for a visit, or you are a Buddhist and the Dalai Lama has stopped by for lunch. If the leader of your religion began to talk about spiritual matters in your home, what do you think would be the better part, washing dishes or listening to that person speak? Again, I perceive that many of my parishioners have almost perfected the art of working in the church. They are "Martha-ites," the hands and feet of the faith. Martha-ites serve on committees, cook and clean for church functions, make arts and crafts, count the money, do handiwork, serve communion, run soup kitchens, etc. Without the Martha-ites, the church would simply cease to exist.

Nevertheless, sometimes the other side of life in the church needs more attention, the side represented by Mary. Jesus is lifting up what may be the most neglected side of the Christian journey: the listening, learning, contemplating, meditating, and introspective part of the faith. These "Mary-ites" are the heads and hearts of the faith. They include theologians, mystics, teachers, and pray-ers. Ministers tend to be one or the other. Martha-ite ministers tend to make better pastors, because they primarily see themselves in service to others. Mary-ite ministers tend to make better preachers, because they spend more time learning and reflecting on the Christian faith.

Those of you who are Martha-ites, I implore you to keep doing what you're doing. If you quit, give up, or get burned out, the Mary-ites will have nowhere to play. However, if you've been considering laying down your spatula, calculator, or hammer for a quiet moment at Jesus' feet so that you can "hang on his every word," then let Mary be your inspiration.

By the way, there are more Marys in the New Testament than in a large Catholic parish, so you might be a little confused about which Mary this is. First, she is probably not the mother of Jesus because if she were she would have had no desire to listen to him and would have gladly made her way to the kitchen. She would have thought to herself, "All this love and peace stuff—I've heard it all before." Second, some scholars speculate that this is the famous Mary Magdalene, the lady who keeps getting all the hype these days. The Magdalene is the preferred choice for having been Jesus' wife. I would personally never rule out the possibility that Jesus was married, and yet it's more probable that the Mary in question here is another Mary, Mary of Bethany, the sister of Martha and Lazarus. (You remember Lazarus, the brother who, as the King James Version said upon the occasion of his rising from the dead, "he stinketh.")

Now that I have *not* cleared up who this Mary is, let me offer a couple of reasons why I believe most of us prefer to operate as Martha-ites rather than Mary-ites. First, there is just something about Martha that makes her more, well, normal. We tend to measure normality numerically, that is, if most people are this way, or do things that way, then that is normal. Right-handed people are normal. People who eat all the various food items on their plate at the same time, rather than separately one at a time are normal. However, as children we learn that the normal way is not always the best way. Do you remember what your mom told you? "Even if everyone else jumps off the bridge, that doesn't mean you should!" So be cautious about what you consider to be normal. Normality doesn't always equal rightness. C. Wright Mills, the great sociologist, once said that if the majority of the people believe something, it is probably wrong. Normal people, in other words, should scare us.

Still, there is every indication that Mary was normally like Martha. Martha complains that her sister had "abandoned the kitchen," implying that this was her usual location when the two of them were hosting guests. Of course, as a woman the kitchen would have been the socially approved location for Mary in that day. That culture was even more patriarchal than our own. At least today women have a choice about whether to do the dishes or watch the football game (for the most part). In that day, unfortunately, there was no choice.

What Mary did was not normal. The same is true today. As a pastor I can attest that for most parishioners, service for the sake of Jesus is preferable to soul-searching, pulling our weight around here is preferable to prayer, and laboring for the Lord is preferable to learning. It is simply too difficult for most of us, the heirs of the Protestant work ethic, to lay down our metaphorical dishrags and listen to Jesus. This is why most Christians identify more closely with Martha. We feel we are not being faithful servants of Christ unless we are *doing* something. For us, scrubbing the toilets is more spiritual than studying the Torah.

This leads to the second reason most of us prefer to be Martha-ites rather than Mary-ites. Mary-ites are thought to be a little, well, lazy (at least in the eyes of many Martha-ites). Rather than girding up their loins and getting to work for a better world, they seem to be merely longing for a better world. We live in a culture that despises laziness. Years ago I lived in an area that used to be covered with potato farms. I heard an old story of a farmer who was extremely lazy. When asked what he was doing one day, he replied, "Waiting for an earthquake to shake the potatoes out of the ground." Sometimes the Mary-ites among us seem as if they are waiting for a spiritual earthquake to come along and help them to bear spiritual fruit. (I realize potatoes are not fruit.)

There's no doubt that some Christians are lazy. They may not be lazy at their respective jobs, in their own homes, or even around the church, but some Christians are spiritually lazy. Let's admit it. We don't always put forth a Herculean effort in terms of our faith. Mary, however, was not spiritually lazy. Not only do the spiritually lazy not make hospital visits or serve on the evangelism team, neither do they sit at Jesus' feet and hang on his every word. Time, of course, is a necessary commodity for both Martha and Mary activity, yet most of us have no excuses in this department. We actually have more opportunities today to be like Mary than at any time in the history of humanity because we have more leisure time. Still, leisureliness is something we value outside of the church rather than inside of the church.

In the 1960s, most people believed that the twenty-first century would be summed up in one word: leisure. A very lazy, albeit smart, person writes, "Many perfectly sober thinkers believed that the rising tide of automation, computerization, robotics, efficiency, modem management techniques, atomic power, instant communications and all that would so improve productivity, cut the need for labor, and create so much real wealth that people would not need to work so much."[1] Okay, so they blew that prediction. Arthur C. Clark, the science fiction writer, went so far as to say that technology would eliminate ninety-nine percent of all human labor, from the ditch-digger to the CEO. Most people, he said, wouldn't need to work much, if at all, and those who did would be restricted by law to only a few days a week and be expected to retire by age forty-seven.[2]

Some futurists, however, saw this leisurely future as a real social problem. They imagined a world where most of the population would have little to do except watch five hundred channels of television and listen to the robot lawn mower cutting the grass. With little to do we would quickly tire of our leisurely activities and sink into apathy and decadence. For proof of this, they ask us to look at celebrities who are unemployed most of the time even if they are successful. Do not many of them start acting bizarre or self-destructive? Charlie Sheen? Perhaps this is why only the elderly should retire because only the elderly are wise enough to keep out of trouble (and they don't have the energy to get into trouble in the first place).

Maybe this is why Martha wanted Mary to get up off her duff and do something productive. Maybe she was afraid that Mary wouldn't use her leisure time in a good way. Maybe this is why many Christians avoid sitting at

---

1. "Leisure." http://www.davidszondy.com/futurepast/leisure.html.
2. Quoted in "Leisure." http://www.davidszondy.com/futurepast/leisure.html.

the feet of Jesus and hanging on his every word. Maybe we are afraid that all of the prayer, meditation, study, reflection, and listening will be considered lazy. The truth is: Mary and Martha are both needed in the church. They are both needed within each one of us, if we want to be well-rounded people.

FOOTBALL VERSUS DISHES

Paradoxically, despite our increased opportunities for leisure time, life in our society is simply too busy. We are running around like a chicken with its head cut off . . . with less direction. We have got to slow down. We have created a fast-paced society. Many people are NASCAR revved up . . . even those who aren't ADHD. Only a mechanical problem like a bad knee or weak heart can slow us down. Our society is full of what psychologists call "Type A" personalities. Type A personality traits include a pattern of pressuring self and others to accomplish more because there is never enough time, a spirit of intense competition in all activities, an intense compulsion to win at all costs regardless of the activity or co-competitor, an inclination to dominate all social or business situations, being too direct and overbearing, a propensity to become irritated by the actions of others who do not conform to one's sense of propriety or correctness, a state of perpetual impatience with any waiting, delays, or interruptions, difficulty in sitting and quietly relaxing or reflecting, psychomotor facial signs of intensity and pressure such as muscle tension, scowling, glaring, or tics, and psychomotor voice signs such as irritatingly forceful speech or laughter, rapid and intense speech, and frequent use of obscenities.

Does this sound like you or someone you know? Does Martha sound like a Type A personality? Her behavior fits several of these characteristics. In the only other story in the Bible in which Martha has a significant role, John 11, she reveals her impatience with Jesus who had delayed his arrival to heal Lazarus, Mary and Martha's brother, before he died. Of course, the real Martha may have been different than what is revealed in the few references to her in Scripture, and yet for the sake of argument we will assume she was a Type A personality. She was bossy, dominating, impatient, and had a difficult time sitting still.

What do you think is the one characteristic that was the biggest problem for Martha? Most of you would probably answer: "Difficulty in sitting and quietly relaxing or reflecting." In this story Martha obviously has trouble doing this. This is what distinguishes her from her sister Mary. Mary was able to sit at Jesus' feet and quietly listen to his wisdom, while Martha felt she needed to busy herself with the task of being a hostess. Sitting still and relaxing is certainly a big problem for Martha, yet I wonder if even Martha was able to sit and quietly relax and reflect on occasion, especially if all her chores were done. Everyone runs out of gas at some point, even the Marthas of this world. Even people who suffer from ADHD will run out of steam and sit still on occasion. If you do have difficulty sitting and quietly relaxing or reflecting, I would encourage you to set aside a portion of your day to sit still, meditate, pray, read, do yoga or stretching exercises, or just make yourself sit in a corner like you used to have to do in elementary school.

Still, I don't think this was Martha's biggest problem. I believe her biggest problem was that she had a propensity to become irritated by the action of Mary because Mary did not conform to her sense of propriety or correctness (the fifth item in the above list). This is why Jesus criticized Martha. He didn't criticize her for being hyperactive. Hyperactive people can't help themselves. Instead, Jesus criticized Martha because she was irritated with Mary's behavior. This is the point I feel most commentators miss. The real lesson of this story is that we should be very careful, if not reluctant, to criticize and judge others whose behavior does not fit our understanding of propriety or correctness.

Sometimes, of course, we have to be critical of other people's behavior, especially if they are hurting themselves or other people. Being a nonjudgmental person does not mean that we can never judge the actions of another human being. However, it does mean that we should exercise caution and restraint before we criticize and judge, making sure that we are not just trying to make everyone conform to our way of thinking or our way of living.

For further insight into this story, notice the social roles Mary and Martha are playing. Martha represents the traditional female role of subservience. She is the stereotypical submissive woman in a male-dominated culture. Since she has a Type A personality she is able to play that role very well. There's nothing better (for men) than a Type A woman who can't seem to sit still and who loves to serve other people. You can get a lot of mileage out of a person like that. In contrast to Martha, Mary plays a very non-traditional role for a female in that culture. Sitting at the table in fellowship with a bunch of men and listening to a rabbi was probably the most radical thing a woman could do in first-century Palestine. Therefore, this isn't a story about studying vs. serving as much as it is about traditional social roles vs. non-traditional social roles.

This story reminds me of Thanksgiving holidays at my childhood home in West Texas. The Dallas Cowboys, as you know, play every Thanksgiving, so for Cowboys fans, Thanksgiving means more than just turkey and dressing. It means eating turkey and dressing while the game is on—at least for the men. The women in my family cooked, served, and cleaned, while the men ate, ate more, unbuttoned their pants, watched the game, and slept. And then there was Aunt Bobbie. (The name has been changed to protect the guilty.) For some reason, either because she had a male name, or didn't like to help in the kitchen, Bobbie always found a way to sit and watch the game with the men. Did the men care? Heck no. Did the other women care if Bobbie watched the game? Heck yes. Some of the women in my family, much like Martha, had a propensity to become irritated by Bobbie's actions because she did not conform to their sense of propriety or correctness. To say it with a Victorian flare, she was not a "proper" lady. Aunt Bobbie was willing to shed her traditional female role and sit at the feet of Tom Landry, Roger Staubach, and Tony Dorsett, and learn some football. Of course, not all the women in my family would openly express their criticism of Aunt Bobbie. Looking back, I realize that only the women who stayed busy the entire day were the ones who were openly critical. Not only could they not sit down and quietly relax and reflect on the beauty and grace of Roger Staubach, they thought it was improper for any woman to do so. This is classic Type A behavior.

Most people are willing to live and let live, within reason. Type A people, in contrast, are determined to make sure that everyone does what they are "supposed" to do. In the movie, *Anchorman*, Will Ferrell plays the role of a very successful television news anchorman. The movie is a comical satire of the 1970s when women were starting to break through into traditional male jobs. In this story, a woman, played by Christina Applegate, becomes the first female news anchor in America. Of course, she has to put up with a lot of resistance and male chauvinism. Think about any scenario where people behave or play roles that do not fit the cultural stereotypes and you will find others (Type A personalities) who can't stand it. In our lifetime, think of the criticism leveled against mixed race marriages, male nurses and teachers, female ministers and soldiers, gay Republicans, and gun-toting Democrats. I'm being a little humorous, and yet any time people like Mary break out of their stereotypical roles, there is always another Type A person like Martha, ready and willing to criticize and judge.

My advice to Type A Christians, whoever you are, is this: serve Christ in the best way you know how, and allow others to do the same in the best way they know how. Allow others to come to their own conclusions about what it means to be a Christian. Allow others to find their own way, follow their own bliss, and seek their own path. If they come to the conclusion that watching the Dallas Cowboys is more important than washing dishes, so be it.

Luke 11:1–13

He was praying in a certain place, and after he had finished, one of his disciples said to him, "Lord, teach us to pray, as John taught his disciples." He said to them, "When you pray, say: Father, hallowed be your name. Your kingdom come. Give us each day our daily bread. And forgive us our sins, for we ourselves forgive everyone indebted to us. And do not bring us to the time of trial." And he said to them, "Suppose one of you has a friend, and you go to him at midnight and say to him, 'Friend, lend me three loaves of bread; for a friend of mine has arrived, and I have nothing to set before him.' And he answers from within, 'Do not bother me; the door has already been locked, and my children are with me in bed; I cannot get up and give you anything.' I tell you, even though he will not get up and give him anything because he is his friend, at least because of his persistence he will get up and give him whatever he needs. So I say to you, Ask, and it will be given you; search, and you will find; knock, and the door will be opened for you. For everyone who asks receives, and everyone who searches finds, and for everyone who knocks, the door will be opened.

TALK TO THE AIR

WHAT ARE WE TO make of the strange act of prayer? I say "strange" because if an alien from another world observed human beings for very long it would notice some people seemingly talking to the air in all sorts of funny-looking postures. It would observe Christians with their heads bowed and eyes closed or arms raised and eyes open, Muslims on their knees and faces to the ground, and Buddhists in a lotus position (a position my body simply refuses to take). The alien would also discover that many of us have very strong beliefs about the efficacy of prayer. Some of us sincerely believe in answered prayers if not outright miracles. Even if we don't believe in outright miracles we still believe that prayer is beneficial for us. For some of us, prayer is like punting in a football game. When all else fails, pray. Like punting, we usually don't score (unless the opponent fumbles the catch and we recover it and run it into the end zone), and yet a good punt may give us better field position. At the very least, we believe that prayer puts us in better field position with the Creator of the universe.

Jesus' disciples knew that prayer was very important. One day, while they were watching him pray, they asked him, "Lord, teach us to pray, as John taught his disciples." We can surmise that John the Baptist must have given a lot of attention to the spiritual discipline of prayer. I can relate to the disciples' frustration and ignorance about prayer. This is hard for a minister to admit, but I don't know how to pray either. In public I fumble around hoping to find the right words. I want to make sure that my theology is sound, that my prayer is not too long or too short, or that it sounds sincere, and so forth. And I never know whether to sound like I'm speaking casually to another person or if I should use a lot of religious terminology like "thee" and "thou." And for what should I pray? Should I pray for my own needs, or just the needs of others? Does prayer even work, I ask myself. I'm sure many of you have had the same struggles. Prayer, of course, implies that there is someone who hears the prayer. For the sake of argument, and because most people who are reading this book are prone to think there might be a deity or some kind of cosmic force or power that can actually hear our prayers, we'll just go with that.

Jesus obliges his curious disciples by offering a sample prayer, what we Protestants call the "Lord's Prayer" and Catholics call the "Our Father." Luke's version of this prayer is briefer than the one we find in Matthew and the *Didache*, an early Christian document. In fact, the version of the prayer we use in worship is a combination of Matthew and the *Didache*. Luke's version is more of a *Reader's Digest* version, yet it still offers us a glimpse of how Jesus might have understood the nature of prayer.

The first thing we notice about this prayer is its simplicity. Jesus does not use the fancy and formal language of the temple; he uses the language of the people. He even uses the word *Abba*, a word that means something more akin to Daddy or Papa than the more formal Father. Just like infants today often utter the words "dada" or "papa," *Abba* would be something even an infant could say. So, the Lord's Prayer, in all its various forms, is meant to be a simple prayer. Speaking of simplicity, the best prayer I ever heard came from the lips of a Little League baseball player. I also shared this in my book, *Big Jesus*. Years ago, I was attending my little brother's game. I was standing near the dugout when I heard the coach ask if anyone would like to offer a prayer before the game began. A big kid named Shane volunteered. As far as I knew he never attended church and he had a reputation as a ruffian and a bully of sorts. So I suspected that we were in for a real treat. His prayer was this: "Dear Lord, thank you for *everything*. Amen." Best prayer I ever heard. Simple and to the point.

The second thing we notice about the Lord's Prayer is that it is very idealistic if not totally impractical. It encourages us to pray for things that seem beyond the realm of possibility. It is utopian in its scope: bread or sustenance for everyone, forgiveness of sin and debts for everyone, and the complete avoidance of temptation—totally idealistic and impractical. If Jesus had offered a more practical prayer, it would have read this way: "Give those of us who work hard each day our daily bread. And if we are good enough forgive us our sins, for we ourselves forgive some who are indebted to us, as long as they don't owe us a lot of money. And since thdre is no way to help us avoid all temptation, make sure that, well, we get some really good ones." The Lord's Prayer teaches us, in contrast, that prayer *should* be idealistic and impractical. We should pray not for those things we can expect, but for those things for which we hope. If we are going to pray we might as well push the envelope. To use a poker analogy, we might as well go "all in."

Finally, the Lord's Prayer teaches us to be persistent. Jesus said, "When you pray, say . . ." In other words, repetition. Continue to pray for those things that seem beyond the realm of possibility (i.e. idealistic and impractical). Be persistent. Jesus then tells a nice little story about persistence. A man is traveling and finds himself in need of bread. He stops at a friend's house but the friend has nothing to share with him. So the friend goes to his neighbor's house. It's the middle of the night. The neighbor is reluctant to open the door, and yet, as Jesus says, if the friend persists, the neighbor will eventually open his door and give them bread.

Let me interject with a theological footnote here. I don't think we should be persistent with our prayers because we think God is either deaf or stubborn. God doesn't need a hearing aid. I think we should be persistent with our prayers because it keeps us focused on the big picture. Persistent prayer helps us to maintain focus on our hopes and dreams for a better world. And if we do that we might actually accompany our prayers with action, don't you think?

My favorite example of persistence comes from the world of sales. No one is more persistent than a salesperson, which, in some ways, is what we are as disciples of Jesus (without the commission). Salespeople often have to convince people they need something they don't think they need. Christians are called to do the same with the Gospel. Jesus tells his followers they need to keep asking, seeking, and knocking. I love this characterization of persistent prayer because it reminds us that we are on a journey. And what's the first thing we do before we embark on a journey? We *ask* for directions. Now we know why women are more spiritual than men. All kidding aside—I mean some kidding aside—Jesus understood that asking is the most basic form of prayer. It gives us spiritual direction. Which way should we go? What should be our hopes and dreams? What should be our goals for a better world? How do we bring about the kingdom of God on earth as it is in heaven? One reason many of us have difficulty sustaining a persistent prayer life is because we have given up on the inquisitive side of our faith. Perhaps the questions ceased to be asked years ago after Confirmation class. Perhaps the curiosity lapsed when church became nothing more than a Sunday ritual. No matter the reason, if we want direction in our spiritual journeys we should take Jesus' advice and ask.

After we ask for directions, the *search* is on. Jesus said, "Seek, and you will find." One of my favorite descriptions of religious people in general is the word "seeker." It implies that we are on a search, and that we are open and flexible to what lies ahead in our spiritual journey. Searching, of course, implies persistence. Because I have only lived in St. Louis for a short while, I am still in a search mode. I can find almost everything I need in my immediate neighborhood, yet if I venture beyond that I am instantly in a search mode. I'm wearing out my GPS. Occasionally I get lost or turned around, and yet I have found that persistence pays off. We don't usually think of prayer as an act of seeking, but it is. Prayer, at its core, is a search for the mysterious, hidden God. Not only do we search our own hearts for an authentic expression of our hopes and dreams for a better world, we also search for the mind and will of God. And because we are never certain about any of this, we continue to search. That's why spirituality is more of a journey than a destination. The journey versus destination analogy might be the biggest difference between mainline progressive Christianity (emphasis on the spiritual journey) and conservative evangelical Christianity (emphasis on the spiritual destination). I choose the former because I'm not ready to get there yet.

However, there are times in our spiritual journeys when we feel that we have arrived, that we have *found* a level of certainty about things, a measure of confidence. We feel that we have come to a door of destination. We have asked for directions, we have searched, and now we *knock* on that door. In other words, prayer is not always just an open-ended, inquisitive, searching exercise that all too often results in frustration. At times, persistent, simple, idealistic, inquisitive, searching prayers can put us on the precipice of what I call an "open door" moment. If I were a mystic I could better explain what this open door is all about. If I knew how to pray as well as I should, I could elaborate more effectively on the results of persistent prayer, the kind of prayer Jesus is talking about here. But I can't. So, keep reading.

(LUKE) CHAPTER 11 BANKRUPTCY

I am the last person in the world that should be offering advice about money matters, although I am an expert at being in debt. Try going to college for thirteen years and raising three children without any financial support. You will dig yourself a financial hole deeper than Saddam Hussein's spider hole. Financial debt is a huge problem in this country, which you wouldn't think possible in a nation as prosperous as ours. The biggest evidence of our national plague of debt is the number of bankruptcies that are filed each and every year.

Do you remember the prosperous 1990s? From 1994 to 1998, the number of personal bankruptcy filings increased seventy-nine percent. There was a slight decrease in 1999, and yet in the following decade bankruptcy filings increased significantly. Since 1994, personal bankruptcies have increased ninety-eight percent. We don't even have to include Donald Trump's bankruptcies in this analysis to make it true. Middle-class families are one layoff or health problem away from financial destitution, including bankruptcy or homelessness. Without a doubt, the widespread use of credit cards has contributed enormously to the increase in personal bankruptcy filings during the last couple of decades. Since the mid-1990s there has been a dramatic increase in credit card delinquencies along with the increase in personal bankruptcy filings. All of this, despite the fact that the US economy was as strong as it has ever been . . . until 2008. At a time when per capita income was rising, household borrowing grew at an even faster pace. And when people borrow too much, they put themselves in danger of having to file for bankruptcy. Who's to blame for this, credit card companies or the people who use them? Some blame credit card default rates on lenders, arguing that lenient standards have allowed consumers to borrow more than they can repay. A survey by the Federal Reserve Board found that eighty-eight percent of respondents agreed that "credit card companies make too much credit available to most people." On the other hand, some people blame borrowers for spending beyond their means. Ninety percent of those who responded to that survey agreed that "overspending is the fault of consumers." In other words, most people blame *both* the credit card companies and the credit card users.[1]

It's easy to blame the borrowers, or credit card users, for overextending themselves financially. One man said to his overextended friend, "Tell me, how did you get into such destitute circumstances?" The friend said, "Well, when I had the world by the tail, I let go to reach for the moon." So, yes, those of us who have allowed ourselves to get overextended need to point the finger at ourselves first. However, the credit card companies are to blame as well, because they make going into debt so easy, and they wouldn't be doing it unless they were making tons of money. We are living in a prosperous time and place, and yet we need to realize that our prosperity has very little to do with how much money we have saved. It has more to do with how much money we spend. Money has almost become an abstract concept because of the increasing use of electronic transactions and credit cards. John Lukacs, in his book, *At the End of an Age,* says that, among other things, we are nearing the end of the age of money.[2] Credit is becoming more important than actual ownership of money or assets. Potential to make money is more important than actual income. This is all fine and good for people like Donald Trump who can be in debt one day and a billionaire the next. For most of us, however, this age of plastic money prosperity has become a debt trap.

So guess what many people in our society today have in common with the vast majority of people in Jesus' day? We are in debt. In our day the poor are not as much in debt as the middle-class because the poor do not have as much access to credit as middle-class people do. It's not the poor who are filing for bankruptcy. It's the middle-class. Nevertheless, in Jesus' day, the ones who were in debt were the poor. When Jesus traveled throughout the countryside preaching and teaching his primary audience was the poor, or the peasant class.

One day one of his peasant disciples asked him how to pray. The Lord's Prayer is a product of Jesus' answer. When we read, pray, or sing the Lord's Prayer, we should do so as if we are first-century peasants who are poor and hungry. Reading the Lord's Prayer in the context of peasant life provides new insight into the meaning of the prayer. "Give us this day our daily bread." Bread, or enough food, was always an issue in the peasant class. "Forgive us our debts, as we forgive our debtors." Being in debt was a constant fact of life for these peasants.

1. Hindenach, Jeff. "Who Is to Blame for the Nation's Crippling Credit Card Debt?" https://www.huffingtonpost.com/jeff-hindenach/who-is-to-blame-for-the-n_b_3288815.html.

2. "At the End of an Age Summary." https://www.enotes.com/topics/end-an-age.

Of course, as you know, when Christians from various traditions come together and pray the Lord's Prayer, there is always a hesitation because we are not always sure whether to say "debts," "trespasses," or even "sins." Part of the reason for the confusion is different English translations of the Gospel texts. Confusion also lies in the fact that there are three versions of the Lord's Prayer in early Christianity. Matthew and Luke each have one, as does the *Didache*, written around the year 100. In wording that is almost identical, Matthew and the *Didache* both use the word "debt": "And forgive us our *debts*, as we also have forgiven our *debtors*." Luke's version is different. Luke curiously uses the word "sins" in the first half and "debts" in the second half: "And forgive us our sins, for we ourselves forgive everyone indebted to us." Whether Christians use Matthew's "debts," Luke's "sins," or the mysterious word "trespasses," we have most commonly understood the true meaning to be "sins": just as God forgives our sins, so we should forgive those who sin against us.

This is a good teaching, and the world is better when it is observed. And yet scholars generally agree that what we find in Luke's version of the Lord's Prayer, at least in the first part of the prayer, is a spiritualizing of the notion of debt. In the first century, the word "debt" was often used as a metaphor for sin. One can be in debt financially and one can be in debt in terms of sin. This is why the early Christians began to see Jesus' death on the cross as "paying the debt of our sins." Nevertheless, when Jesus used the word "debt," there is every reason to think that he had the financial meaning in mind. For these poor and hungry peasants, a word of hope about financial debt would have had much more relevance than a word of hope about their debt of sin. Along with bread, debt was the primary survival issue in peasant life. John Kloppenborg writes, "Bread and debt were, quite simply, the two most immediate problems facing the Galilean peasant . . . Alleviation of these two anxieties were the most obvious benefits of God's reign." Indebtedness could lead to the loss of one's land, if one still owned some. Indebtedness could mean descending from the peasant class to the even more destitute life of a tenant farmer or day laborer. Finally, indebtedness could cause the peasant and their families to be sold into indentured labor. If they had had a color-coded warning system for indebtedness like we have had for terrorism, their warning system would have always been on the most severe level. There was a constant threat of indebtedness.

So here comes this Galilean peasant preacher telling the rest of the peasants that he has good news for the poor, that they should pray for the forgiveness of their debt (even as they should forgive their debtors). Wouldn't the people have thought him to be crazy? Not necessarily, because when these peasants heard a word of hope concerning their debt they would have automatically thought about the Hebrew Scripture's notion of a Sabbatical Year or the Year of Jubilee. The Sabbatical Year occurred every seven years and the Year of Jubilee was supposed to occur ever fifty years. Three things were expected during the Sabbatical Year: land was given a vacation (crops were not to be planted or harvested); people who had been sold into indentured labor because of their debts were released; and all debts were erased. At every fiftieth year, the Year of Jubilee, the ownership of land was supposed to be returned to the owners who held it at the beginning of the fifty-year period. When Jesus taught the people to pray, "Forgive us our debts as we forgive our debtors," they would have understood that Jesus was talking about the Sabbatical Year and the Year of Jubilee. From everything I've read, it is doubtful whether the Sabbatical Year and the Year of Jubilee were observed very often, if at all, in Israel's history. Even if they were never practiced, however, they were important symbols of economic justice in Jewish life. I'm sure the political and religious leaders did not appreciate Jesus stirring up people for economic justice.

What does all this mean for us? Well, in our debt-ridden society I think it means that Christianity is as much about forgiveness of literal debt as it is forgiveness of sin. Obviously, in an economic system like ours, forgiving people's debt is not going to happen, although I do think Christians should be raising ethical questions about all the debt individuals and nations find themselves in. We should be asking some hard questions about how credit card companies operate, about how interest rates drain income primarily from the poor and middle class, and about how wealthy nations keep poor nations in debt. The Lord's Prayer teaches us that God's kingdom is as much about practical material and economic matters as it is about spiritual matters.

As we continue our quest for such spiritual things as forgiveness and spirituality, we must also be concerned about things that affect people's day-to day-lives: jobs, fairness in pay, consumerism, and the economy. When we pray the Lord's Prayer each and every Sunday, we need to be aware that our religious faith is not just something that pertains to the inner person. It also pertains to the outer realm of human existence. It teaches us that God is not just concerned with *moral* bankruptcy. God is also concerned with *financial* bankruptcy. God is concerned about the whole person: spiritual, emotional, mental, physical, and yes, financial. So let us lead people to chapter 11—not a chapter 11 bankruptcy which only reorganizes our debt—but chapter 11 of the Gospel of Luke, for there the still speaking Jesus offers real words of hope.

Luke 12:13–31

Someone in the crowd said to him, "Teacher, tell my brother to divide the family inheritance with me." But he said to him, "Friend, who set me to be a judge or arbitrator over you?" And he said to them, "Take care! Be on your guard against all kinds of greed; for one's life does not consist in the abundance of possessions." Then he told them a parable: "The land of a rich man produced abundantly. And he thought to himself, 'What should I do, for I have no place to store my crops?' Then he said, 'I will do this: I will pull down my barns and build larger ones, and there I will store all my grain and my goods. And I will say to my soul, Soul, you have ample goods laid up for many years; relax, eat, drink, be merry.' But God said to him, 'You fool! This very night your life is being demanded of you. And the things you have prepared, whose will they be?' So it is with those who store up treasures for themselves but are not rich toward God." He said to his disciples, "Therefore I tell you, do not worry about your life, what you will eat, or about your body, what you will wear. For life is more than food, and the body more than clothing. Consider the ravens: they neither sow nor reap, they have neither storehouse nor barn, and yet God feeds them. Of how much more value are you than the birds! And can any of you by worrying add a single hour to your span of life? If then you are not able to do so small a thing as that, why do you worry about the rest? Consider the lilies, how they grow: they neither toil nor spin; yet I tell you, even Solomon in all his glory was not clothed like one of these. But if God so clothes the grass of the field, which is alive today and tomorrow is thrown into the oven, how much more will he clothe you—you of little faith! And do not keep striving for what you are to eat and what you are to drink, and do not keep worrying. For it is the nations of the world that strive after all these things, and your Father knows that you need them. Instead, strive for his kingdom, and these things will be given to you as well."

THE DAIRY QUEEN BARN

WE WANT THINGS TO be fair, do we not? Not long ago, there was a lot of discussion about the "Fairness Doctrine." In simple terms, the Fairness Doctrine says that broadcasters cannot present only one side of the ideological divide that exists in America between liberals and conservatives. Typically, the group that doesn't feel their voice is being heard enough on public airwaves will claim things are not fair. For example, FOX News can claim they are *"fair* and balanced" because when they began they felt that a conservative slant on the news was underrepresented on television. Now, however, after years of conservative dominance, especially on the radio, liberal commentators are appealing to the Fairness Doctrine for more fairness and balance.

Those who feel cheated will always claim that things are unfair. Such was the case with the man who approached Jesus one day and asked him, "Teacher, tell my brother to divide the family inheritance with me." The man must have assumed Jesus was a rabbi because settling disputes was something rabbis did in that day. We don't know all the details about this dispute, yet it is probable that this man was the younger brother of an older sibling who had inherited the family fortune. The eldest son was due two-thirds of the family inheritance, although he apparently had taken all of it for himself, leaving the younger brother high and dry.

The younger sibling has a legitimate gripe. Fairness and the laws at that time demanded that the younger son get his fair share. (Sorry, ladies, there was nothing fair about any of this for you.) Jesus, however, was not as sympathetic to him as one might expect. Jesus understood that underneath the younger sibling's cry for fairness was a subtle form of good old-fashioned greed. When you think about it, fairness and greed are often two sides of the same coin. When a child cries, "That's not fair!" the child is usually only concerned about getting his or her fair share.

This passage in Luke 12 is one of the most insightful of all the accounts we have of Jesus' teachings. Jesus was one smart dude. The notion that our desire for fairness is often a subtle form of greed is hard for us to accept because it seems to fly in the face of conventional wisdom. After all, fairness is good. But Jesus knew the human heart. He knew that greed is like a cancer that can begin on a very small scale and grow and grow until it completely overwhelms a person's soul. As Ralph Waldo Emerson said, "Want is a growing giant whom the cost of Have was never large enough to cover."

Greed is something that is not always easy to detect because all of us are greedy to one degree or another. We all want things, desire things, covet things. Unless you're living naked in a cave, you want to have some possessions. Even folks who live a simple life have possessions. Not to brag, but I once made an attempt at simple living. A few weeks before I moved to Louisville, Kentucky, I held a yard sale for the first time in my life. I sold enough stuff to fill up a small house. I knew that I was moving to a smaller house with virtually no storage, so to be honest, I was forced to downsize. Still, I like to think that I was being spiritual. And yet even my yard sale, in retrospect, was a subtle exercise in greed. Although I didn't charge much for my stuff, I was still partly motivated by dollar signs. Greed, in other words, is not something we can easily shed like a snake sheds its skin. It's not a stain we can remove from the human condition very easily. Jesus knew that, and so he focused a great deal of his teachings on what we call "stewardship," which is the discipline of managing our resources in an appropriate manner. Stewardship is the practice of overcoming our greed. It is the practice of acknowledging our greed and making a concerted effort to overcome it.

Jesus' response to the young man who wanted his brother to be fair to him is one of the best stewardship lessons in the entire Bible. Luke 12:13–21 is a passage that is rich in meaning, pardon the pun. Jesus tells the man: "Take care! Be on your guard against all kinds of greed." Jesus knew that greed is ubiquitous, and yet not always obvious. Greed may be obvious in the wealthy, those who can't seem to get enough, although oftentimes the wealthy practice generosity in an effort to offset their desire for more. Greed may be just as present in what Benjamin Franklin called "the middling class," or those who want to be the upper class (as Franklin did). Sometimes, however, their desire to get ahead is more about peace of mind and college tuition for their children than greed. Greed may also be present in the poor, who want to be middle class; still, it is difficult, if not disingenuous, to call someone greedy if they have very little wealth or possessions to begin with. That's like calling a minority group "racist" when they don't actually have the power to be racist. Despite the fact that racist whites often call blacks racist, African-Americans, by definition, cannot be racist. Racism implies the power to oppress a minority group. Not even President Obama had the power to be racist, although he has a great jump shot.

The presence of greed is not always easy to determine in individual cases, and yet if we look at the total picture we know it's there. To give one glaring example: Did you know that more storage sheds are being sold than ever before? This is at a time when there is already more storage in houses than we have ever seen. We've got extra stuff inside and extra stuff outside. We fill our closets, attics, basements, garages, and storage sheds with things that we may never use again. To use the wisdom of Jeff Foxworthy: if your backyard is full of storage sheds, you might be greedy. To use the wisdom of Jesus: "Life does not consist in the abundance of possessions."

From my perspective this oft-quoted verse has a double meaning depending on which word is emphasized, "abundance" or "possessions." First of all, we can read it this way: "Life does not consist in the *abundance* of possessions." Possessions are still important. As I said, unless you live naked in a cave you will have possessions. It is the *abundance* of possessions that is in question, not the fact that we have them. How much qualifies as abundance? Hold a yard sale. If you sell enough to fill an entire house, and after the sale you still have enough to fill an entire house, then you probably have abundance.

The other way to read this passage is like this: "Life does not consist in the abundance of *possessions*." This implies that life might consist in the abundance of other things, such as love, joy, relationships, or chocolate. Our quality of life is more dependent upon intangibles than tangible, material possessions. Perhaps Jesus was trying to tell the young man that as long as he was running around obsessively trying to find a judge or arbitrator to get his fair share from his older brother, he might be missing out on some of life's intangibles, including perhaps a relationship with his older brother.

Jesus' parable in verses 16–20 also seems to suggest that greed and the hoarding of possessions can make us act a little crazy. A farmer began to do very well. He discovered, however, that he didn't have enough room to store his crops, so he decides to build bigger barns. At first this seems to be economically prudent. If you need more storage for your grain, then you should obviously build more storage because you don't want your crops to go to waste before you can take them to market. That's being smart. But that's not exactly what the man did. He built bigger barns to store his grain and other goods to keep for himself. He said he wanted to store up these goods so that he could "relax, eat, drink, and be merry," what I call "Dairy Queen living." (Dairy Queen's motto used to be "eat, drink, and be merry." Now their motto is "eat, drink, and sound like an idiot while drinking a cup of coffee with fellow idiots in the morning." Most people at the so-called Wisdom Tables don't sound "merry" to me.) The man let his greed go to his head. How could he possibly use all that grain for himself? Wouldn't it go bad? Wouldn't it be economically wiser to take his extra crops to market? There's just something about greed that can take over our brains and make us crazy. It's like having Mad Cow Disease, the kind William Shatner had on *Boston Legal*.

Toward the end of this parable, God gets into the act. God tells the man, "You fool! This very night your life is being demanded of you. And the things you have prepared, whose will they be?" Here's what's interesting about that question: Apparently the farmer had so alienated himself from his loved ones (if he even had loved ones to begin with), that there is no one to claim his estate once he dies. He has no heir. How lonely his greed had made him. Have you ever known families that were torn apart because of greed after a patriarch or matriarch dies? This is exactly what Jesus is trying to say to the young man who came to him to settle a financial dispute with his brother. Don't be so possessive of what you think is yours or else you risk alienating yourself from your loved ones. If the older brother wants to act greedy and possessive, that's his problem. But you, little brother, should cut that cancer out of your life right now.

The final point Jesus makes with this parable is that greed also alienates us from God. Greed is not just an economic problem. At heart it is a spiritual problem. We tend to separate issues of wealth and poverty from religion and spirituality, yet Jesus did not. Some would argue that how we view and handle our possessions is a close barometer of our spirituality. Perhaps we all need to hang a sign on our bathroom mirrors so we can read it each morning, a sign that says, "We can't take it with us." Ironically, we can take our mirrors with us. And yet, alas, they do invisible spirits no good, so don't bother.

THE GREED GENE

Although greed is not a crime in our society, and it is usually only chastised in its most extreme forms, we need to be reminded that despite what Gordon Gecko proclaimed in the movie *Wall Street* (20th Century Fox, 1987), greed is *not* good. Although in many ways greed is the fuel that runs our economy, we should agree with Erich Fromm, who famously said, "Greed is a bottomless pit which exhausts the person in an endless effort to satisfy the need without ever reaching satisfaction."[1] Typically, when preachers talk about greed they address it from a spiritual angle, and yet I would like to address it from a scientific if not biological angle. I'm not sure we can locate it, but I'm convinced there must be a "greed gene."

---

1. Fromm, *Escape from Freedom*, 121.

To illustrate this, I will begin with a monkey story. Have you ever heard how monkeys are captured so that they can spend the rest of their lives in zoos? A shining metallic object is placed in a long-necked jar tied to a tree. As monkeys swing through the trees, their eyes catch the reflection of the sun on the shining object. Reaching into the jar poses no problem to them, yet when they try to bring their closed fists through the narrow openings, they can't make it. To gain freedom, all the monkeys need to do is to let go of the worthless object. Instead, the monkeys sit by the jar holding onto the object until their captors come to take them away. This is also how we catch children's hands in cookie jars, especially those with fat hands.

What this illustrates is that greed is a natural phenomenon. All animals exhibit greed because out in the wild, greed is necessary for survival. They have to be greedy in order to eat and procreate. They are in competition with one another for survival. Darwin's "survival of the fittest" really means "survival of the greediest." And if our closest biological relatives—the primates from the ape family—exhibit such blatant greed in nature, then it stands to reason that we humans also possess the greed gene. Primates are naturally greedy and we share well over 90 percent of our DNA makeup with our primate cousins. I think we can draw our own conclusions from that.

We can also refer to this as a "hoarding instinct." This is a basic instinct that we find in all animals. Stephen Vander Wall wrote the definite book on this called, *Food Hoarding in Animals*. He notes that animals hoard food in order to survive. The classic example is the squirrel hiding nuts for the winter. However, they aren't the only hoarders out there. Wildcats often bury small prey, such as birds. Moles store up earthworms in mounds. Foxes store eggs or bones in shallow holes. Mice scatter and hoard seeds and nuts in underground nests. And if animals hoard, you can bet that people do as well, and I'm not just talking about people who suffer from an extreme compulsive hoarding disorder, the kind of people we saw on that television show a few years ago.

Many people hoard things out of what they believe is necessity. We often call this a "Depression era mentality," which, of course, developed during and after the Great Depression. We all have known people in our families that accumulate and keep things because of a hidden fear that it will all someday go away. That "tight" uncle you have, or your sister who is "frugal"—they might just be showing signs of a Depression era mentality. Of course, being frugal is not always the same as hoarding, and hoarding is not always the same as being greedy, and yet we are talking about the same family of human traits—some extreme and some not. I assume we all fall on the spectrum at some point or another. As I previously noted, we are all greedy to one degree or another (even if we aren't particularly frugal and even if we don't hoard things).

So is greed a product of nature or nurture? Do we learn it, sometimes for very practical reasons (like mere survival), or do we inherit it? Is it possible that there is a genetic component to this? Are we born with a "greed gene"?

The income for identical twins has a higher correlation than income for fraternal twins. In other words, there seems to be a genetic component at play here. It is quite possible that a tendency to be greedy is inherited (which is why identical twins are more likely than fraternal twins to have the same income potential).[2]

So what does all this mean? I believe this gives us an insight into greed as a natural phenomenon. And yet that's not really the problem. The problem is why do we see greed in the human species exhibited at extreme levels? If greed evolved through the various animal species as a survival technique, then why did it evolve into a human tendency to do more than just survive? Note that the main character in Jesus' parable in Luke 12 is a rich man who had already produced abundantly. He is already rich; he is in no danger of not surviving. And yet, it's not enough. It's never enough. This reminds me of John D. Rockefeller's response to a reporter's question, who asked, "How much money does it take to satisfy a person?" The billionaire snapped back, "Always a little more!"

This is the greed gene gone awry. Perhaps it's a mutation of the greed gene, a mutation that may have become the norm in the human species. The rich farmer in Jesus' parable had an interesting dilemma. He had too many crops and not enough storage. So he decided to build bigger barns. Who could argue against that strategy? That's just common sense, right? Furthermore, there is no indication that the farmer is a bad man, that he is cheating anyone, or breaking any laws. Greed is not against the law. Nevertheless, according to Jesus' parable, God does not have a favorable impression of this rich farmer, to say the least.

Why do you think Jesus is telling a story about a rich and greedy farmer to what is most certainly a crowd of poor peasants? Isn't he preaching to the choir, so to speak? Wouldn't there have been a lot of "Amens!" coming from the crowd of listeners? No, and I'll tell you why. Poor people are just as greedy as rich people. That's right. I said something politically incorrect. The difference is that rich people have more opportunities to be greedy. We could find any number of random poor people on the streets, give them a

---

2. Caplan, Bryan. "Is Greed in the Genes?" https://www.econlib.org/archives/2009/03/is_greed_in_the.html.

winning lottery ticket, and then sit back and watch in amazement as the greed gene takes over their minds and bodies . . . and their souls. By the way, as a critic of greed, Jesus would never be selected as an economic advisor for any Western government—conservative or liberal—because our economic systems are largely fueled by human greed. Greed is what compels people to get educated, earn more money, and buy more things. Let's just be frank about that.

We also have to be frank about the fact that since greed is a natural part of our humanity, just as it is for monkeys and squirrels, it's not going anywhere. We can detest it when we see a CEO making four hundred times the amount an employee makes working in the same company. We can rail against it when we see personal yachts over five hundred feet long. We can decry the growing accumulation of wealth in the hands of the notorious one percent while the middle class continues to disappear. And yet at the end of the day, all of us will desire to have more tomorrow than we have today. We would all jump at the chance to build bigger barns.

Along the way, however, we need to be a little more evolved than monkeys and educate ourselves about the economic injustices that are an unfortunate part of the fabric of our way of life. Awareness breeds action, and action breeds change. And even if we are influenced by a greed gene, perhaps we can do our best to allow our other genes a chance to grow and prosper and bring a sense of balance to our lives. We don't have to let our unevolved animalistic side get the better of our more evolved spiritual side. So, let go of the shining object (or the cookie). Set yourselves free.

THE BIRDHOUSE BARN

A Sermon Preached at the 50th Anniversary of St. Andrew United Church of Christ, Louisville, Kentucky

Fifty years ago, a group of people gathered together by Reverend Gilbert Bumb met for worship for the first time in an old farmhouse on this very spot. At that time they had no guarantee that their little evangelical and reformed mission church would thrive or even survive. But it did. And so after fifty years we, the heirs of that small gathering of people can say to one another, "I've found you tried and true!" It stands to reason, after all, that in the span of fifty years a congregation will have to endure many so-called trials and tribulations, tests and temptations. You name it and I bet St. Andrew has had to endure it.

However, this morning I would like to focus on one specific thing that every church at every time and place has had to overcome. This is a constant, never-ending trial by fire, a test of its metal and merit, a temptation that, if not overcome, can completely overwhelm the spiritual health of a congregation. I'm talking about the temptation to *worry about the future*. It's one thing to focus on the future, to plan for the future, which we are currently doing. It's altogether a different thing, however, to *worry* about the future.

This is exactly the point Jesus is making in Luke 12 when he tells his listeners not to worry about the future, instead trust that the God who takes care of even the ravens and the lilies has provided a world of abundance for us as well. Jesus is speaking to a crowd of people when someone says to him, "Teacher, tell my brother to divide the family inheritance with me." In that time and place the oldest male offspring in a family usually inherited most, if not all, of the inheritance. This didn't always set well with everyone, especially the younger siblings. We can assume, then, that a younger brother has approached Jesus for help in this matter. He is worried about his future, particularly his financial future. Jesus refuses to help, possibly because he doesn't have the qualifications to be an arbitrator. His degree at the University of Phoenix wasn't cutting it.

So, he tells a parable in order to convince his questioner and all his listeners that our trust in God's goodness should keep us from worrying about the future. The parable is about a prosperous farmer who discovers that he doesn't have enough storage for all the grain he is suddenly producing. Therefore, he pulls down his barns and builds bigger ones. Now he assumes he can take it easy because his future is secure. The deity in this parable, however, criticizes this man for storing up treasures for himself rather than being "rich toward God."

One thing we have to take into consideration when we read this account is that Jesus is talking primarily to peasants, people who have absolutely no opportunities to store up anything at all. Since there is no way to help them economically, Jesus tries to help them psychologically. He tells them they are not to worry about such things as food and clothing, that is, whether they will have a secure future. Listen to some of the language he uses, keeping in mind that these are words directed at poverty-stricken peasants: "Therefore I tell you, do not worry about your life, what you will eat, or about your body, what you will wear." "Can any of you by worrying add a single hour to your span of life? If then you are not able to do so small a thing as that, why do you worry about the rest?" "And do not keep striving for what you are to eat and what you are to drink, and do not keep worrying." He's giving very practical advice to these peasants: You can't change your economic condition, so why worry about it?

And yet in the midst of this advice Jesus tries to comfort them with a little God-talk. He is being very pastoral. He compares the value of his listeners to that of the ravens and the lilies which represent nature as a whole. He makes the point that God provides more than adequately for them, so why wouldn't God provide for human beings? Therefore, don't succumb to the temptation to worry excessively about the future. It will only give you gray hair and ulcers. Nice comforting words for a crowd of peasants.

While these words may not have as much of an emotional impact on us as they did on Jesus' original audience, I think we can see why this text was chosen for the very first worship service on this property back in 1959. I'm sure Reverend Bumb knew that the future of this nascent group was on everyone's mind. Meeting in an old farmhouse (and barn), they couldn't have felt totally secure about whether this mission church would succeed or not. I can see how Jesus' words about the ravens would have connected with a group of worshipers who had not yet built a church: "Consider the ravens: they neither sow nor reap, they have neither storehouse nor barn, and yet God feeds them."

I can also imagine Reverend Bumb thinking that even if this new church has to continue meeting in an old farmhouse, or a barn, or even outdoors, things will be okay. The kingdom of God will go on regardless. As Jesus said, "Strive for (God's) kingdom and these things will be given to you as well." And they were. In a few short years they were able to build a beautiful sanctuary, which . . . closely resembles a birdhouse. In 1999, you were blessed with another addition, this time the people of St. Matthew UCC, who decided to leave their building to those who are engaged in other types of ministry and become part of this congregation. And then earlier this decade you were able to add new space, a majestic gathering area, and a multi-use Education Building/Fellowship Hall/gymnasium/kitchen. You certainly now have a lot of storage space. The difference between now and fifty years ago is that, like the wealthy farmer in Jesus' parable, you have managed to pull down the old barn and build a larger one.

Nevertheless, as Jesus would have guessed, we continue to worry about the future. We may differ with our predecessors in that materially speaking we have more, yet we are similar in that our future existence as a congregation is thought to be in jeopardy (due to financial constraints). We are not the only religious body to worry about its future. I had a conversation the other day with some other UCC ministers in our association. One of them asked if we thought the United Church of Christ will still be here fifty years from now. We all decided there is a good chance it will not exist in its present form. Because of the diminishing size of all mainline denominations, it is entirely likely they will all eventually merge into one. We also agreed that we can't worry about this. I made the comment that whether the United Church of Christ continues to exist as a denomination or not, the kingdom of God will continue in some form or fashion . . . which brings us back to what Jesus said in Luke 12.

Rather than worrying about the future of the institutional church, we should focus on the kingdom of God. "Seek first the kingdom of God," as the old King James Version says. As we contemplate the next fifty years of this congregation, our best approach is not to seek the expansion of St. Andrew United Church of Christ per se, but the expansion of the kingdom of God. And know that the two are not always the same.

So, what is this kingdom of God? First of all, many people are uncomfortable with the phrase itself because it sounds so patriarchal. And yet this is the phrase used by Jesus, a phrase that is both theological and political at the same time. For Jesus, the kingdom of God—the empire of God, if you will—is what contradicts, critiques, and counteracts *our* empires, especially when they are oppressive (as the kingdoms of Herod and Caesar were in Jesus' day). The best definition of the kingdom of God I have ever heard or read comes from the pen of John Dominic Crossan in his book, *Jesus: A Revolutionary Biography*. He writes, "The Kingdom of God is what the world would be if God were directly and immediately in charge."[3] You may have your own vision about what that world would be like, and yet according to Crossan it is a world where "the overpowering action of God" moves "to restore justice and peace to an earth ravished by injustice and oppression."

Admittedly, that is a lofty goal; still, it is what we are to strive for. The church just happens to be an institution that enables us to imagine and envision freely and fully what that might look like and to do our best to flesh it out. So, at its best, the church is the institution that inspires and empowers us to help God's empire on earth come to fruition. In many Christians' minds, however, the church is *equivalent* to the kingdom of God. This is where we would be mistaken. The "kingdom of God" is not a synonym for the church. The kingdom overlaps and yet is separate from the church. It is also much, much broader.

The point I am trying to make, as carefully as I possibly can (not wanting to be misunderstood), is that even *if* St. Andrew doesn't make it another fifty years, the kingdom of God will continue to be a reality in the here and now and that which we await more fully in the future. While St. Andrew is here we will certainly do our best to contribute to this reality. But this congregation, like all congregations, is a means to an end, not an end itself. The "end" is the kingdom of God, as Jesus understood that term. We are not

---

3. Crossan, *Jesus*, 55.

called to build up St. Andrew. We are called to build up the kingdom of God, with a little help from God, of course!

As Alfred E. Neumann used to say on the cover of *MAD Magazine:* "What me worry?" What if St. Andrew the institution didn't live to see another year, another decade, or another half century? What would happen? I can tell you what would happen. A little St. Andrew DNA would spread throughout the body of Christ in Louisville, Kentucky. You all would scatter out among the churches of this community like wildflowers in a field of planted crops. You would be like leaven in the bread of other congregations. You would be the jalapeno peppers in their nachos. There are worse things that can happen than a church not surviving.

Although Reverend Bumb and some of you worked really hard to start this church fifty years ago, I'm sure that the words of Jesus in Luke 12 were a great comfort to him. He knew that whether they succeeded or not the kingdom of God would continue. And as we embark on a second fifty years, we should bear in mind the same truth. Strive for God's kingdom, what the world would be if God were directly and immediately in charge. And if we continue to keep that as our goal, then fifty years from now our successors will look back and say, "Those people were tried and true."

Luke 12:32–34

Do not be afraid, little flock, for it is your Father's good pleasure to give you the kingdom. Sell your possessions, and give alms. Make purses for yourselves that do not wear out, an unfailing treasure in heaven, where no thief comes near and no moth destroys. For where your treasure is, there your heart will be also.

TREASURE HUNT

I LOVE A GOOD scavenger hunt, although now I guess they are sort of old school. The "in" thing to do a few years ago was the *Pokemon Go* game for smartphones. This is the game that had thousands of millennials walking through neighborhoods seeking to "spot" one of the many Pokemon characters from their childhood. Even before there were scavenger hunts and *Pokemon Go*, however, there were treasure hunts. Jesus said, "For where your treasure is, there your heart will be also." Let's go on a treasure hunt, shall we?

Let me be clear about a few things, however. Jesus wasn't talking about the kind of treasure hunt that pirates dream about. He wasn't talking about the kind of treasure hunt that excites those who scour backyards and playgrounds with metal detectors. And he wasn't talking about following a rainbow to find a pot of gold either. He was talking about the kind of treasure hunt that our faith inspires and demands.

Before we begin this hunt, let's talk about that word "treasure." The origin of the word "treasure" is interesting. A few hundred years ago the word "treasure" replaced the Old English word "goldhord," from which we get our modern word "hoard." Thus the two words "treasure" and "hoard" are historically related to one another. Today, one of the words—"treasure"—has a mostly positive image, while the other word—"hoard"—has a very negative image. These two word siblings have the same parent, although they have grown up and gone in two different directions. The same thing happens to human children. I work as a pastor and my brother works in a casino. Other than that we're almost twins.

So, let's go on a treasure hunt; not a hoarding hunt. But what should we treasure?

Possibilities might include such things as God's forgiveness, mercy, compassion, and justice. These things are certainly worth hunting. A problem occurs, however, when the entire goal of one's religion is to find these things for ourselves. This is an age-old problem in all the world's religions. We are notoriously self-centered when it comes to religion. We go on treasure hunts primarily for ourselves. We are self-centered rather than other-centered. Perhaps we should seek these things for others, including the oppressed, the poor, the orphans and widows, etc.

Another possible goal of our spiritual treasure hunt could be faith. Faith is not necessarily something we can hoard for ourselves, and yet it is something we can hunt and seek, much like a buried treasure. Because that's where it is, buried deep within each one of us. Faith is not easily definable, although the writer of Hebrews did manage to come up with what is probably the best known definition of faith in all of religion: "Now faith is the assurance of things hoped for, the conviction of things not seen." Notice the key words in this definition: assurance, hope, and conviction. These are not bad things to hunt for. In spiritual terms, these things would fill up our treasure chests rather quickly. We could do worse spending our entire lives on a treasure hunt for faith, exploring where that might take us. It won't take us to the end of rainbows, yet it will give our lives more meaning and purpose.

All of these things—forgiveness, mercy, compassion, justice, and faith—are worthy goals of a spiritual treasure hunt. But what was Jesus searching for? That's a good question. It's easy to see what he didn't treasure. He tells his followers to sell their possessions—so he wasn't a materialistic person. He wasn't a hoarder. In fact, he likely died with no possessions whatsoever, not even the clothes he had been wearing. He didn't treasure material possessions; instead he treasured people. I think we can say he was always on a treasure hunt for people who had eyes to see and ears to hear. He was always searching for a receptive audience. This is where his heart was.

In the above passage, Jesus twice uses the word "treasure." The first one reads: "Make purses for yourselves that do not wear out, an unfailing treasure in heaven, where no thief comes near and no moth destroys." He's speaking literally and metaphorically here. Literally, he is celebrating the art of making your own stuff, like purses and clothing, which is a sign of *not* being materialistic. Metaphorically, he is suggesting that we should treasure things that are more permanent and lasting, things that truly make a difference in the world. Then Jesus famously says, "For where your treasure is, there your heart will be also." As we continue on our spiritual treasure hunts in our own lives, these are the words we should have imprinted in our minds at all times. Jesus is telling us to follow our hearts; however, we first need to make sure our hearts are in the right place.

So what do we treasure? Where are our spiritual treasure hunts taking us? Not long ago my wife and I were driving through Kentucky where we noticed that the world's largest yard sale—the Highway 127 yard sale—was about to begin. This annual yard sale runs all the way from Michigan to Alabama. Every year thousands of people stop along this large stretch of highway, sorting through boxes and bins, clothes racks and tables, no doubt looking for that one special item that has been eluding them their entire lives. And to think, the treasure they might find was someone else's trash. As we embark on our own treasure hunts, albeit of a more spiritual nature, let's make sure we are searching for treasure and not trash. Let us learn to treasure others as much as we treasure ourselves.

Luke 13:1–9

At that very time there were some present who told him about the Galileans whose blood Pilate had mingled with their sacrifices. He asked them, "Do you think that because these Galileans suffered in this way they were worse sinners than all other Galileans? No, I tell you; but unless you repent, you will all perish as they did. Or those eighteen who were killed when the tower of Siloam fell on them—do you think that they were worse offenders than all the others living in Jerusalem? No, I tell you; but unless you repent, you will all perish just as they did." Then he told this parable: "A man had a fig tree planted in his vineyard; and he came looking for fruit on it and found none. So he said to the gardener, 'See here! For three years I have come looking for fruit on this fig tree, and still I find none. Cut it down! Why should it be wasting the soil?' He replied, 'Sir, let it alone for one more year, until I dig around it and put manure on it. If it bears fruit next year, well and good; but if not, you can cut it down.'"

A CALL TO FERTILIZE

WE ALL HAVE BIASES. For example, politically-minded people often interpret events through their own partisan biases. Biases are also evident in the reading and interpretation of Scripture. There is much interpretive bias involved when people try to explain the parable of the barren fig tree in Luke 13. One reason for the wide variety of interpretations is that the parable raises a lot of questions for the reader. Allegorically speaking, what or who does the vineyard, the fig tree, the owner of the vineyard, and the gardener represent? Isn't both the owner of the vineyard and the gardener flawed? Neither one seems to know much about farming in general, or caring for a fig tree in particular. The owner does not seem to know that the only way to get rid of unwanted fig trees is to uproot them, not cut them down because then they will simply sprout right back. And why didn't the gardener dig around the tree and manure it in the three previous years if he thought that such treatment was helpful for fig trees? Or had he, and it just didn't work? And why is there a fig tree in a vineyard to begin with? Doesn't it occupy space and drain off the resources of the land? Or was it deliberately planted there as a trellis for supporting the vines, and if so, why would it matter if it bears fruit or not? Is the reference to putting manure on the tree an insult to someone? And what is Jesus trying to say by not telling us the ultimate fate of the tree? Is this parable about God's judgment, God's mercy, or both? Does it teach that all who do not repent will perish, or is it trying to say that God gives people multiple chances to repent? Is it trying to say that under the rule of God there is always hope regardless of how barren things seem, or that hope eventually fades away?

Do you see how difficult interpreting a parable can be? Surely, the original hearers of this parable, who viewed life in terms of God's blessings and curses, heard it one way. They believed that if you obey—if you are fruitful—God will bless you, and if you disobey God—if you are unfruitful—God will judge or curse you. The preceding verses tell us that Jesus' audience assumed that some Galileans who were killed by Pilate were judged by God, as well as eighteen Jews who were killed when the tower of Siloam fell on them. They would have interpreted Jesus' parable as saying that those people had not been fruitful, so they were punished by God. They were cut down. And yet you and I do not generally view life in such simple black and white terms. We know that bad things happen to good people (not just bad people), and good things often happen to bad people. As Jesus said in Matthew 5:45, we believe God "makes his sun rise on the evil and on the good, and sends rain on the righteous and on the unrighteous."

As twenty-first century Americans, we have our own interpretive biases. We read the parable of the barren fig tree in our own settings. Let me offer some possible examples:

Imagine that you are a tree doctor. Obviously, you would become bewildered as you read this parable. You would ask questions I raised earlier: Why does the gardener wait until the fourth year to try to save the tree? If the tree serves as a trellis, why does it matter whether it bears fruit or not? A tree doctor would simply wonder if maybe Jesus was trying to be funny.

Imagine that you are a couple who can't have children. If you are a woman who has what the Bible calls a "barren womb," you will probably become a little emotional reading this parable. You may feel devalued if you are not able to biologically bear fruit.

Imagine that you are a couple with three sons or three daughters. You want desperately to have a child of the other gender, but you are not sure you want to add another mouth to feed. What do you do? Do you try to be fruitful again or do you voluntarily become sterile? Notice that the parable doesn't say whether the tree was cut down or not, so the couple is not given clear guidance.

Imagine that you are a war-time president. The war is constantly on your mind. You want to keep fertilizing the situation to try and save it. You feel it would be wrong to cut and run as your opponents want you to do. If you're the president you may read this parable and say to yourself, "One more year; one more chance." If you are opposed to the war you may read this parable and say, "It's time to cut the tree down because it's never going to bear fruit."

Imagine that you are anyone who needs another chance. You made a mistake and cost your employer a lot of money. You abused your spouse or were unfaithful. You took a test at school and failed. You struck out the last three times you went to bat and your coach wants to bench you. If you are someone who needs a second, third, or fourth chance, you might read this parable and hope, like the gardener, that you get one more chance.

Imagine that you are a three-time loser. You have received your third felony conviction and now, because of "three strikes you're out," you're going away for a long time. You might read this parable and plead with the judge, "If you let me go through a rehabilitation program (i.e. "put manure on it"), then I'll forsake my criminal ways (i.e. "bear fruit"). But if I mess up again you can lock me up and throw away the key (i.e. "cut it down"). Fortunately, the "three strikes" policy struck out.

Imagine that you are someone who has had multiple unsuccessful marriages. You might read this parable thinking that you might give it one more attempt—this time with a little more preparation and nurturing of the relationship before you tie the knot. There is always hope that you might find the right person the next time around. This reminds me of a gentleman who had been very unhappy in marriage. His wife died and after that he married again. Samuel Johnson said of this man: "His conduct was the triumph of hope over experience." That seems to be the conduct of the gardener in Jesus' parable. There is very little reason to think that the tree will bear fruit after three years of unfruitfulness.

Imagine that you are Congress. Do we give it another chance or do we "cut it down" (i.e. "drain the swamp")?

Imagine that you are someone who needs another medical opinion. You are seriously ill and your doctor tells you there is no hope. Do you seek the opinion of another doctor, or two, or three? This parable might speak to you in a very grave situation like that.

Imagine that you are a salesperson. Salespeople are trained to not accept the first few "No"s. Years ago I attended a two-week sales training conference and that's exactly what I was taught. I was so brainwashed that for several months I would get ill in my stomach if I heard a negative comment. The gardener in Jesus' parable was a salesperson. His job was to sell the idea to the owner of the vineyard that the tree was worth saving. This, then, is a parable about persuasion. At least, that's one interpretation.

So how do we interpret the parable of the barren fig tree? It really depends on who you are and where you are on life's journey. You may need the hope of God's mercy, or, for reasons I could never fathom, you may want to be threatened with God's judgment. You may be seeking hope that something good is going to come out of a bad situation, or you may need to awaken to the fact that nothing good will come out of it. You may need another chance at your job or your love life, or you may need to come to the realization that another chance won't do you any good. You may need another opinion from a doctor, another verdict from a judge, another opportunity to take a test, or another moment to try to persuade. Or you may come to the conclusion that nothing you do will bring about a different conclusion.

In the final analysis, we don't know whether the tree in Jesus' parable was cut down or not. Life remains a mystery. It's not carved in stone. There is always hope and there are always moments when hope fades away. Ironically, if not comically, all we can really do is apply as much manure as we possibly can to our situation, and see what happens.

A STAY OF EXECUTION

As I said, there are many ways to interpret the parable of the barren fig tree. It speaks to many issues, including capital punishment. This is one of the most complex and controversial issues in our society today. As a student of ethics in the late 80s and 90s, this was one of my favorite topics to research and write about. It has also become one of my favorite book and movie genres. Among my favorites are: Truman Capote's *In Cold Blood*, *Dead Man Walking* with Susan Sarandon and Sean Penn, *The Green Mile* with Tom Hanks, *The Life of David Gale* with Kevin Spacey, and *Monster*, a true story starring Charlize Theron who won an Oscar playing a prostitute who becomes a serial killer and winds up on death row. Of course, let's not forget Mel Gibson's *The Passion of the Christ*. I don't know how many people would include *The Passion* as a movie about capital punishment but on some level that's exactly what it is. No, I didn't really like *The Passion of the Christ*, mainly because of theological problems I see in the movie and the fact that Mel Gibson is rather low on my list of favorite celebrities. I was so unenthused about the movie that I brought a large popcorn and fountain drink into the theater. Apparently the evangelicals surrounding me did not find munching on popcorn while Jesus was getting whacked a proper use of my time.

The question of whether or not governments should have the power and authority to put people to death is fascinating to me. There are so many angles from which to approach this issue: justice, mercy, revenge, forgiveness, power, grace, etc. Still, as interesting as the issue of whether or not the government should have power over whether people live or die, the issue of whether or not God has power over whether people live or die in an eternal sense is even more provocative an issue. Do we deserve capital punishment in a spiritual sense because of our crimes, i.e. our sins?

In Luke 13, Jesus speaks to this very issue, yet in an ambiguous way. One day some people told Jesus about a tragic event that had just happened: Pontius Pilate had some Galileans murdered while they were worshiping. (For anyone who thinks after watching Mel Gibson's movie that Pilate was not that bad of a fellow think again. Historical evidence suggests Pilate was extremely brutal and wouldn't have batted an eye about putting Jesus to death. Gibson prefers the anti-Semitic approach: blame the Jews for Jesus' death because, you know, Mel thinks Jews have cooties.) Jesus uses this occasion to make a theological point. People in that day assumed that if something terrible happened to them, they must have been so sinful they deserved it. The people talking to Jesus believed that God punished those Galileans because they were more sinful than other Galileans. Jesus rightly criticizes that type of thinking and then makes a very curious comment to the crowd: "Unless you repent, you will all perish as they did."

He then reminds them of another incident, when eighteen people were killed when the tower of Siloam in Jerusalem fell on them. Once again, the people would have concluded that those eighteen people must have deserved this. And yet Jesus asks, "Do you think that they were worse offenders (sinners) than all the others living in Jerusalem? No, I tell you; but unless you repent, you will all perish just as they did." What is Jesus saying here? He is not willing to distinguish between those who deserve punishment from God and those who do not. He basically puts all of humanity in the same boat. He levels the playing field. We are all guilty, he seems to be saying, and in need of repentance. Just because one person suffers and another doesn't has no relationship to the depth of sin in either one of their lives.

This is an example of Jesus criticizing the popular theology of that day, which was that God blesses the obedient and curses the disobedient. The assumption would have been that those Galileans and people from Jerusalem who died tragically had been disobedient to God. The same logic would conclude that those who died on 9/11, for example, were cursed for being disobedient to God. This doesn't make any sense. Jesus is severely critical of this type of theology. And so should we be.

After Jesus baffles his audience with his views, he takes the opportunity—as he often did—to teach with a parable—the parable of the barren fig tree. This parable is not as well-known as some of his others, but I believe it is one of the most insightful of all Jesus' parables. The fig tree was a familiar metaphor of Israel's spiritual condition. A fruitful fig tree was a sign of God's blessing and a barren fig tree was a sign of God's cursing. Again, notice how Jesus manages to criticize this type of thinking with the parable. The listeners would expect the parable to end with the man saying, "Cut it down! Why should it be wasting the soil?" The fig tree is barren because it is cursed, so just cut it down. However, Jesus added a little glimpse of God's grace by having the gardener talk the owner of the vineyard into giving it one more year to bear fruit. This is possibly a parable about God's grace. Coming after his discussion about whether those people who died were worse sinners than everyone else, Jesus is saying that God's grace—not condemnation, not death—extends to even the worst of sinners, represented by the barren fig tree.

Many people read this parable and interpret it to mean that God's grace is limited. After all, the owner of the vineyard is giving the gardener just one more year to make the fig tree fruitful. But Jesus' listeners would have heard something different. They would have heard Jesus say that God's grace is unlimited. Here's why: Because three years had elapsed and this fig tree did not bear any fruit, it was hopelessly barren. In addition to that, a fig tree absorbs a very large amount of nourishment and therefore deprives the surrounding vines of their needed sustenance. Furthermore, fig trees do not normally need the kind of care offered by the gardener in Jesus' parable. So the gardener is going out of his way to do something very unusual: care for a hopelessly barren fig tree that, for all practical purposes, should be cut down.

This is why Jesus' listeners would have found this parable to be so utterly startling: the owner of the vineyard actually gives the gardener permission to take care of this hopelessly barren fig tree for another year. This makes no practical sense. The implication is this: when the owner comes back next year he knows there will be no change in the fig tree—it will still be hopelessly barren—and yet the same scenario will occur. The gardener will ask to tend the fig tree and the owner will give the okay. There's no reason to think he won't. This is a parable about God's unlimited, unconditional, and unmerited grace.

To make the point even stronger let's be creative for a moment and retell the parable of the barren fig tree, this time using the language of courtroom justice rather than the language of agriculture. This is not meant to accurately reflect our criminal justice system. Nevertheless, I think you'll get the point:

> A judge had a death row inmate brought before him to see if the prisoner had made any progress with good behavior, and yet he could tell that the prisoner was still unrepentant. So he said to the prisoner's lawyer, "Look, for three years I have given this prisoner a stay of execution, but I don't believe he has made any progress in his behavior. He hasn't repented for his crime. So now I sentence him to death. Why should we waste any more time, money, and prison space on him when the prisons are so overcrowded?" The lawyer replied, "Your honor, let's give him one more year and see if I can get him the help he needs to become repentant and begin to show good behavior. If he makes any improvement by next year, then you can give him another stay of execution, but if he is still unrepentant for his crimes, then you can sentence him to death."

Like the fig tree, this criminal will possibly make no improvement. He's been on death row for three years and is still not repentant. Practical wisdom suggests that his death sentence needs to be carried out in order to make room for other prisoners. However, the judge allows the lawyer to keep working with the hopelessly hardened criminal, knowing full well that he will make no improvement whatsoever.

The parable of the barren fig tree—like the parable of the condemned criminal—has a very clear message to those who have ears to hear: God's grace is unlimited. Jesus' audience believed that God's grace depends upon repentance, obedience, and righteousness. God blesses the obedient and curses the disobedient. God gives the death penalty to those who don't do right, or as many Christians today think, believe right, and gives life to those who do and think right. Jesus, however, wants us to have a radically different view of God. According to Jesus, God is so impractical that even those who deserve capital punishment won't get it. We have been given a permanent stay of execution.

Luke 13:10–17

Now he was teaching in one of the synagogues on the Sabbath. And just then there appeared a woman with a spirit that had crippled her for eighteen years. She was bent over and was quite unable to stand up straight. When Jesus saw her, he called her over and said, "Woman, you are set free from your ailment." When he laid his hands on her, immediately she stood up straight and began praising God. But the leader of the synagogue, indignant because Jesus had cured on the Sabbath, kept saying to the crowd, "There are six days on which work ought to be done; come on those days and be cured, and not on the Sabbath day." But the Lord answered him and said, "You hypocrites! Does not each of you on the Sabbath untie his ox or his donkey from the manger, and lead it away to give it water? And ought not this woman, a daughter of Abraham whom Satan bound for eighteen long years, be set free from this bondage on the Sabbath day?" When he said this, all his opponents were put to shame; and the entire crowd was rejoicing at all the wonderful things that he was doing.

THE ILLUSION OF HOLINESS

SOMEONE ONCE ASKED STANLEY Hauerwas, the noted theologian who uses rather salty language in his lectures, if he is a Christian. Hauerwas responded, "No, and I don't know anyone who is." As I noted in my previous book, *Big Jesus*, I don't remember where I heard or read that statement. It better be true, by golly.

So what is a Christian anyway? I could offer some pat answers that you might receive at just about every other church in town, but I don't want to insult your intelligence. My general answer is that a Christian is, by definition, a follower of Christ. My more specific answer is that a Christian is someone whose concern for compassion outweighs their concern for holiness. To put it another way: For Christians, compassion trumps holiness. (Please excuse my use of the word "trump.") Jesus spent his entire ministry—albeit a short one—helping people move beyond holiness (which is an illusion) to compassion. This took a lot of work because holiness was extremely important to his religion.

Marcus Borg said, "No aspect of the quest for holiness was so publicly visible to the non-Jewish world as the observance of the sabbath."[1] And, he argues, their observance of the Sabbath was the most visible aspect of this quest. The command to observe the Sabbath is the only one of the Ten Commandments explicitly linked to holiness. Exodus 20:8–11 reads: "Remember the Sabbath day, to keep it holy. Six days you shall labor, and do all your work; but the seventh day is a Sabbath to the Lord your God; in it you shall do no work . . . for in six days the Lord made heaven and earth, the sea, and all that is in them, and rested the seventh day; therefore the Lord blessed the Sabbath day and hallowed it."

Observance of the Sabbath was crucial for the life of their community. Multiple laws about the Sabbath were developed and instituted. For the Pharisees—the religious party in Israel most devoted to the concept of holiness—precise observance of the Sabbath was that which most separated the Pharisees from ordinary Jews. Observance of the Sabbath was the one thing that most distinguished a "true Jew" from those who had become disloyal to God. They believed, in fact, that observance of the Sabbath guaranteed the survival of Israel in a hostile world and that all major calamities in their history occurred when they neglected the Sabbath. There was nothing more important for the Jewish people than the Sabbath.

Enter Jesus. Controversy between Jesus and his opponents concerning the Sabbath is illustrated in all of the Gospels. Jesus apparently chose the Sabbath as an issue over which to do battle. One reason we know this is because Jesus, not the afflicted, always took the initiative in healings on the Sabbath. The afflicted usually expected to wait until the Sabbath was over. Also, Jesus' Sabbath healings never involved cases in which there was danger to life. The healings could have waited another day.

In the above story from Luke 13, Jesus is teaching on the Sabbath when a woman appears in the crowd who is crippled. Luke writes, "She was bent

---

1. Borg, *Conflict, Holiness and Politics*, 156.

over and was quite unable to stand up straight." This is not a life-threatening illness. She has been afflicted for eighteen years. Surely her healing can be stalled for another day or two. Nevertheless, Jesus takes the initiative, calls her over to him and says, "Woman, you are set free from your ailment." He lays his hands on her and according to the story she is healed.

If most of us saw something so remarkable, we would respond much differently than the leader of the synagogue who witnessed this extraordinary event. He became "indignant because Jesus had cured on the Sabbath." Harkening back to the Ten Commandments he argues, "There are six days on which work ought to be done; come on those days and be cured, and not on the Sabbath day." By the way, for those of you who have gotten caught up in all the frenzy about the Ten Commandments in recent years, wanting it posted in courthouses and other public places, please note that Jesus himself may not have been a big fan of the Ten Commandments. It certainly wasn't his priority.

The point of Luke's story is that the leader of the synagogue is more concerned about holiness—observance of the Sabbath—than compassion for this poor crippled woman. Jesus finds the leader's attitude completely unacceptable. Jesus responds as he often does in the face of religious idiocy. Knowing that many, if not most of the people in the synagogue that day, agree with the leader, he says to the crowd, "You hypocrites!" and then proceeds to suggest that people (other than maybe Michael Vick) often show more compassion to animals than human beings: "Does not each of you on the Sabbath untie his ox or his donkey from the manger, and lead it away to give it water?" (Yes, Jesus occasionally used *ad hominem* attacks. Sometimes name-calling is divine.) The key word here is "untie" because it suggests that they would untie an animal for the sake of its health, yet they wouldn't allow this woman to be untied from her physical bondage (at least not on the Sabbath).

This story is not unique in the Gospel accounts. We see this same pattern over and over again. Jesus initiates acts of compassion on a holy day, the Sabbath, even though the religious elites in that day interpreted Sabbath laws as prohibiting such acts. Jesus, however, believed that compassion trumps the illusion of holiness. We see this as well in his acts of table fellowship. Jesus supped with just about anyone. (The only exception, not mentioned in the Bible, was people who ate with their mouths open. Jesus couldn't stomach that.) And in that time and place—as is true for most times and places—eating with the wrong crowd was considered unholy. The religion of Jesus' day was largely based on purity codes, and one of the ways a person could become impure, unclean, or unholy was to eat with sinners, gentiles, or other despicable characters. And yet, as I said, Jesus was more concerned with showing compassion than casting the illusion of holiness.

Does this sort of thing still occur in our time and place? That is, are we still tempted to maintain the illusion of purity or holiness at the expense of being compassionate human beings? I believe we are. Examples are a dime a dozen. Not long ago, a United Church of Christ congregation in my city voted to leave the denomination presumably because of the UCC's welcoming stance toward the LGBT community. I am fully aware that people have mixed feelings about this issue, yet at the risk of sounding too judgmental I would suggest that congregations who leave the United Church of Christ because of this issue are more concerned about the illusion of holiness than the gospel's admonition to show compassion.

This sort of thing, of course, doesn't just happen in the United Church of Christ. I read once that a Texas megachurch canceled a veteran's memorial service after learning the deceased was gay. The Reverend Gary Simons of High Point Church initially approved the service to honor Cecil Sinclair, who served in the first Gulf War and died, at age 46, following heart surgery. Twenty-four hours before the service, however, Reverend Simons changed his mind after learning of Sinclair's sexuality. The decision was "not based on hatred, not based on discrimination, but based on principle," Simons said. "It's not that we didn't love the family." No, my response is that Reverend Simons loved his illusion of holiness more than his call as a Christian to show compassion.

I'll offer another example. One night my stepson and I ventured down to the theater to watch the musical, *Hairspray*. The movie is set in the early 1960s when the issue of racial segregation and integration was on everyone's mind (and apparently lots of hair spray was on everyone's head). A young white girl loves to dance, and even though she is overweight she manages to become part of a local televised dance program in Baltimore, Maryland, learning all the new rock-and-roll dances that were emerging in the early 1960s. All of the dancers are white except on one show called "Negro Day," when a group of African-American youths take to the floor. I couldn't help but think of the symbolism of this event. The white kids are given a "day of rest," a Sabbath, while the dance floor is inhabited by the "wild gyrations" of the black kids. One of the songs used for the white kids contained the words "good white kids," implying that the black kids were not good, i.e. not holy. The young overweight white girl—herself an outcast, i.e. unholy— eventually befriends the black dancers and seeks to integrate the program. Why not have white and black dancers together on every show, she argues. This is a story, then, about a young girl who shows compassion toward the black community. Until the end, however, she is thwarted by the studio manager's concern for the appearance or illusion of purity and holiness, which she felt interracial dancing would endanger. The movie ends, of course, with black and white kids together on the dance floor. Institutional holiness, which is always just an illusion, is pushed aside in favor of compassion and the healing of relations between the white and black communities of 1960s Baltimore.

So when do Christians become Christian? I wish I could offer you a magic formula, a simple three-step program, or a quick and easy prayer that would morph each one of us into holy saints. But I can't. All I can do is suggest what I think Jesus would say. I believe he would say that Christians become Christian when a concern for compassion outweighs or trumps a concern for holiness, which is always an illusion.

WHEN SOMETHIN' JUST AIN'T RIGHT

How many of us actually follow our consciences? I guess that could be a good or bad thing. Mark Twain tells a story that illustrates how precarious it is to rely on one's conscience. He once stole a watermelon from a cart when the owner was not looking. He carried the melon to a secret spot, sat down, and was just about to bite into the melon when he realized that he should not do that. It just wasn't right. So, he got up, took the watermelon back, replaced it on the cart, and took a ripe one.

Most of the time following our conscience is a good thing. The dictionary defines conscience as "the inner sense of what is right or wrong in one's conduct or motives, impelling one toward right action." No one really knows where the human conscience is located or how it developed in human beings in the first place, and yet it does seem to be the one thing that distinguishes us from the rest of the animal kingdom. Theologically, we could argue that God created the human conscience, our sense of right and wrong. One of my favorite quotes I memorized years ago goes like this: "The human conscience is the playground where God and humanity meet." So, whether we explain our moral compass—our conscience—biologically, psychologically, or theologically, we should give thanks to God for its existence, and pray that more people learn to follow the dictates of their conscience.

One of the first people to popularize the notion of a human conscience was an eighteenth-century English bishop, Joseph Butler. Bishop Butler tried to answer questions like: Why be moral? Which morality should we follow? Even though he was a Christian bishop, he concluded that morality is a matter of following human nature. There is a hierarchy of sources of moral authority, including what we learn from our parents and our religion, although at the top of the hierarchy is the natural human conscience. It's where the "buck stops" (to quote Harry Truman). Of course, Butler was a theologian, so he sometimes refers to the conscience as the "voice of God," yet for the most part he viewed the human conscience as a natural part of human existence that could be explained apart from God. It is that which we must follow, regardless of what any other source of moral authority suggests.

What happens, then, when our conscience tells us something other than what the laws of the land or the laws of our religion tell us? Should we follow our conscience or follow the laws and rules of society and religion? Fortunately, we are not presented with this dilemma very often. In fact, it may be possible to live one's entire life without having to make a crucial choice between law and conscience. Nevertheless, we need to realize that almost anyone who has ever helped make the world a better place to live in had to make that choice, sometimes by paying for it with their own lives. Jesus, of course, is a perfect example. He followed his conscience rather than mindlessly following some of the more oppressive, if not stupid, laws of his society.

At very crucial times in his ministry Jesus practiced what we might call "religious disobedience." We could also call it "civil disobedience," yet in truth they were one and the same in Jesus' place and time. The laws of his religion and the laws of Jewish society were one and the same. There was no separation of religion and government in his time and place, what we refer to as "separation of church and state." Their society was theocratic rather than democratic. Other than the laws that came from the occupying power, Rome, their laws stemmed from the Jewish religion. Curiously, Jesus never seemed to fight against the Roman laws. He even supported paying taxes to Rome with his famous statement, "Render unto Caesar the things that are Caesar's, and unto God the things that are God's." For the most part I don't believe Jesus had many qualms about the laws of his religion. And yet on the rare occasion when he was forced to choose between the Jewish laws and the dictates of his conscience, Jesus chose the latter.

The most famous example occurred when he entered the temple court and overturned the moneychanger's tables and let loose some of the animals used for sacrificial purposes. Jewish law allowed the temple to exploit people financially; Jesus, however, had a problem with it. Other than that, perhaps the most important dispute between the conscience of Jesus and first-century Jewish law related to the observance of the Sabbath. There were many laws regulating activity on the Sabbath. For example, Deuteronomy 5:13 and Exodus 20:9–10 prohibited work on the Sabbath. In Jesus' day there was a lot of debate about what constituted work and what didn't. So when this woman who had been crippled for eighteen years comes to Jesus for a healing touch while he was teaching on the Sabbath, he rightly understands that healing her is not work, it's an act of humanity. It's an act of following one's conscience. Even though the leader of the synagogue was upset with Jesus for healing on the Sabbath, Jesus decides to follow his conscience rather than a stupid law.

This wasn't the only time he ran into trouble over this issue. In Luke's Gospel alone, we read of a time when Jesus and his disciples were criticized for plucking heads of grain in a field, which was perfectly legal for hungry people to do, although the Pharisees thought it broke the laws against working on the Sabbath. On another occasion he healed a withered hand, even though the scribes and Pharisees were keeping an eye on him to see whether he would heal on the Sabbath or not. Finally, Luke records another instance where Jesus heals a man with dropsy on the Sabbath and found himself in trouble once again. In every instance he was criticized for doing "work" on the Sabbath, and in every instance he put the needs of people before a strict interpretation of the law.

On a very important level, however, the spirit of the law against working on the Sabbath was actually very wise and practical. We know today that if people do not get a break from their labor they will experience burnout. Many countries around the world have less than a forty-hour workweek because they believe a well-rested worker can actually accomplish better work. Years ago, when I worked for my parents, I tried to explain to them that if I worked fewer hours yet was paid for working forty hours I would actually do better work. They wisely didn't believe me.

The old "blue laws" were the result of American Christians trying to be faithful to the biblical principle of resting on the Sabbath. According to God, I mean Google, the term "blue laws" was originally applied to the seventeenth-century laws of the theocratic New Haven colony; they were called "blue laws" after the blue paper on which they were printed. And to think, I thought they were called blue laws because they made bar-hoppers sad. Of course, in a capitalist system like ours the government is never going to be very successful in telling people they can't work on a certain day. I imagine that Jesus would not support blue laws in our society today, yet he would support the notion that human beings should have a day (or two) of rest.

Still, having a day or two of rest should not be an excuse for not showing care and concern for other human beings, people who are hungry or hurting. Jesus was wise enough to see how the blue laws of his day could become so legalistic that people could actually suffer as a result. So, according to the biblical record, Jesus followed his conscience rather than the dictates of the law and practiced religious disobedience, what we today would call civil disobedience. In some ways, we have Jesus to thank for the rich tradition of civil disobedience practiced by people from many and varied cultures throughout history. The phrase "civil disobedience," incidentally, was coined by an American writer, Henry David Thoreau, the author of *Walden*. His most famous essay is called "Civil Disobedience." It was written after he was put in jail overnight for refusing to pay his poll tax, although his real crime was protesting slavery and the Mexican War. (Yeah, that's a real crime right there.) Someone paid the tax for him, after which he sat down and wrote "Civil Disobedience," a document that influenced both Gandhi and Martin Luther King Jr. Jesus could have written the most famous sentence in this essay: "Must the citizen ever for a moment, or in the least degree, resign his conscience to the legislator? Why has every man a conscience, then? I think that we should be men first, and subject afterward. It is not desirable to cultivate a respect for the law, so much as for the right. The only obligation which I have a right to assume is to do at any time what I think is right."[2]

As I mentioned above, for most of us there are not many occasions when we will need to practice civil disobedience. We should thank God that we live in a society where opportunities for civil disobedience are few and far between. However, we still need to realize how important civil disobedience has been, especially in recent history. Aside from the example of Gandhi and King, civil disobedience was practiced (effectively) in the 1940s by the Danish resistance, in the 1950s by people who opposed McCarthyism, in the 1960s in the struggle against South African apartheid, and in the 1970s by a generation of anti-war activists. And then there were the Dixie Chicks and Colin Kaepernick. Whether we agree with all the reasons people have practiced civil disobedience or not, we must realize that we are talking about something practiced and perfected by Jesus himself. I would never argue that you and I should go out and look for a reason to follow our conscience against unjust laws, but if your conscience tells you that somethin' just ain't right, then muster the courage to follow your conscience. If you don't trust your conscience, then I recommend reading the Gospels carefully and following Jesus' conscience. You could do worse.

RULES THAT FREE

Why do we humans have so many stupid laws or rules anyway? Do you know it is illegal in St. Louis to sit on the curb of any city street and drink beer from a bucket? Why? Wouldn't it be handy to have a bucket available

---

2. Thoreau, Henry David. "On the Duty of Civil Disobedience." http://www.gutenberg.org/files/71/71-h/71-h.htm.

after drinking too much beer? Sometimes rules are cut and dried, and can't be bent or broken. Other rules, however, are not so cut and dried and require some interpretation. Because of that, people will disagree about how to interpret the rule.

A good example of this is the Second Amendment in our Bill of Rights, which was adopted on December 15, 1791. You know, when everyone was walking around with AK-47s, AR-15s and other weapons of mass destruction. The Second Amendment reads: "A well-regulated Militia, being necessary to the security of a free State, the right of the people to keep and bear Arms, shall not be infringed." Unless you are so anti-gun that you think we should go door to door and confiscate every single weapon in America (even hunting rifles and shotguns), or you are so in love with guns that you think everyone, regardless of age, mental capacity, or criminal tendencies should own an arsenal of weapons, you probably understand that the Second Amendment is very much open to interpretation. The latter group is most accurately called "ammo-sexuals." Years ago, while attending graduate school at Baylor University, I wrote a paper on the ethical issues surrounding gun ownership and the Second Amendment, and my research led me to conclude that almost everyone interprets the Second Amendment based on feelings, not facts. This is true about most controversial ethical issues, so I wasn't surprised.

The Bill of Rights is the collective name for the first ten amendments to the United States Constitution. It is an interesting list to read because either they are somewhat outdated (like the Third Amendment about the quartering of soldiers) or they are very much open to interpretation in our modern context (such as the First Amendment's clause on religion or the Second Amendment about guns).Very little in the Bill of Rights is cut and dried.

The same could be said for another "list of ten" that we find in the Bible: the Ten Commandments. It is interesting that in our Judeo-Christian-dominated culture we put so much emphasis on the Ten Commandments, even as we realize they are somewhat dated or even irrelevant. For example, how are we supposed to take seriously the first commandment, which states, "You shall have no other gods before me"? I don't know anyone who even believes in the existence of other gods, much less putting those other gods before the one true God. And then there's the fourth commandment to "remember the Sabbath, to keep it holy." What should we make of this rule? We all agree with the notion of a Sabbath. But what does it really mean?

People had—and still have—different interpretations and applications of the Sabbath commandment. Even today, Jewish people disagree about how to observe the Sabbath. One of the issues, for example, is whether a Jew can drive to the synagogue on a Sabbath. Orthodox Jews say no,

Conservative Jews say maybe, and Reform Jews say yes. Well, that's clear, right?

A more ancient example of the problem of interpreting the Sabbath law is found in Luke 13. One Sabbath day, Jesus was teaching in the synagogue, as was his custom. A woman was in attendance who was severely crippled. She was unable to stand up straight. That in itself is not unusual. Even today, with our advanced medical knowledge, many people can't stand up straight. Imagine living in a time before back surgery and chiropractors were available. So Jesus said to her, "Woman, you are set free from your ailment." Then he laid his hands on her—a common method for a mystic healer in the ancient world (and even today in some circles). Luke claims that she "immediately stood up and began praising God."

This is good news, right? Well, not so fast. Apparently, in the opinion of the leader of the synagogue, you know, one of those control freak pastor types, it was not okay to heal on the Sabbath. For the leader of the synagogue, whose job it was to keep things orderly and running smoothly, he must have felt like things were getting out of control. What was happening was too exciting, too out of the ordinary, for a typical Sabbath day. He apparently had to state his case, repetitively, to the unconvinced crowd. He says, "There are six days on which work ought to be done; come on those days and be cured, and not on the Sabbath day."

In other words, if you want to be cured, lady, make an appointment. The interesting thing about this story is that the leader of the synagogue is interpreting healing as work. I guess it is work if you're a modern health care provider who has regular office hours. But for Jesus this really isn't work. This is ministry.

Other than healing the sick, another thing Jesus was very good at was spotting hypocrisy. His rebuttal to the leader of the synagogue, in earshot of the crowd, was that people take care of their animals on the Sabbath, so why not take care of people on the Sabbath? No offense to PETA, but aren't people more valuable than animals?

After appealing to logic, Jesus appeals to their emotions. Remember, in the audience are Jewish people who remembered that their ancestors were once upon a time in bondage to Pharaoh in Egypt. So, he says to the synagogue leader, "And ought not this woman, a daughter of Abraham (that is, a Jew) whom Satan bound for eighteen long years, be set free from this bondage on the Sabbath day?"

Here's what he was getting at: the Ten Commandments, including the Sabbath rule, were originally written in response to the Israelites' experience in Egypt. There they were, slaves who worked every single day, all day long, producing more and more bricks for Pharaoh. Imagine how former slaves would have originally heard these words: "Remember the Sabbath day, and keep it holy. Six days you shall labor and do all your work. But the seventh day is a Sabbath to the Lord your God; you shall not do any work—you, your son or your daughter, your male or female slave, your livestock, or the alien resident in your towns." In other words, take a day off.

The Sabbath law, then, is not a law that constrains. It's a law that frees. When Jesus pointed this out, his opponents, including people in the audience who were supporting the leader of the synagogue, were "put to shame" and everyone else started cheering. Jesus had taken a rule—to keep the Sabbath—and interpreted it in a way that was freeing, not constraining.

I realize that some rules, maybe even most rules, in a society have a constraining purpose, and usually for good reasons. However, in a religious context, rules that free us are much preferable to rules that constrain us. Yet, for some reason we prefer even our religious rules and laws to be constraining rather than freeing. Think about the way the third commandment has been interpreted and utilized in our own culture. We tend to associate the Sabbath commandment with "Don't do this on Sunday rules," although the original Sabbath was Friday at sundown to Saturday at sundown, but why quibble over details?

My wife and I were on vacation and were seeking a restaurant for lunch in Roswell, New Mexico on a Sunday afternoon. I was struck by how few places were open. It was like the old blue laws were still in effect. I thought I was back in the 1940s (and not just because that's when the little green aliens crashed their spacecraft near Roswell). Years ago, Walter Brueggeman, the UCC Old Testament scholar, said this about American Sabbath observance: "It is unfortunate that in U.S. society, largely out of a misunderstood Puritan heritage, Sabbath has gotten enmeshed in legalism and moralism and blue laws and life-denying practices that contradict the freedom-bestowing intention of Sabbath. Such distortions, moreover, have led to endlessly wearying quarrels about 'Sunday activities' such as attending movies and card-playing and, currently in my state of Georgia, purchasing liquor on Sunday."[3]

The Sabbath, says Brueggeman, is "freedom-bestowing." Tell that to the leader of the synagogue in Luke's Gospel. For Jesus, it is a rule that frees rather than constrains. Today, our historical setting is different, yet the message is the same: take time to rest from your frantic need to produce. Take a breather. And if someone needs a little help, help them. This ain't rocket science.

---

3. Bogle, Laura. "A Wholehearted Sabbath." https://www.questformeaning.org/quest-article/a-wholehearted-sabbath/.

Luke 13:31–35

At that very hour some Pharisees came and said to him, "Get away from here, for Herod wants to kill you." He said to them, "Go and tell that fox for me, 'Listen, I am casting out demons and performing cures today and tomorrow, and on the third day I finish my work. Yet today, tomorrow, and the next day I must be on my way, because it is impossible for a prophet to be killed outside of Jerusalem.' Jerusalem, Jerusalem, the city that kills the prophets and stones those who are sent to it! How often have I desired to gather your children together as a hen gathers her brood under her wings, and you were not willing! See, your house is left to you. And I tell you, you will not see me until the time comes when you say, 'Blessed is the one who comes in the name of the Lord.'"

THE TRUSTEE, THE LEFT TACKLE, AND THE MOTHER HEN

WE HAVE CONVINCED OURSELVES that we serve God and humanity, and sometimes we do. We have plugged into a local church, serve on ministry teams, sing in the choir, give to charity, reach out to the community, and invite others to join us. We are fairly adept at serving God in many and diverse ways. We could say that we are trustees in God's realm. We do our best to manage or take care of the church, and to take care of our fellow parishioners, neighbors, community, and even the earth. God can trust us to continue to serve.

But do we trust God to serve *us*? Do we experience God as a trustee of our souls, so to speak? We are told that God has a purpose for our lives, yet we may not be inclined to fulfill this purpose because we may not trust that God has our best interests at heart. Maybe we don't trust that we can decipher what God's purpose for us is, or whether God even has a purpose for us. Maybe we don't really trust that God is working in and through us at all. This lack of trust in God that plagues all of us on some level is reflected in the classic humorous anecdote about the man who fell off a cliff. At the last moment as he fell, he managed to grab hold of a shrubby bush. As he dangled in space, he was filled with terror and called out toward heaven, "Is there anyone up there?" A calm, powerful voice came out of the sky, "Yes, there is." The man pleaded, "Can you help me? Can you help me?" The calm voice replied, "Yes, I can. Simply let loose of the bush, and everything will turn out fine." There was a tense pause, then the man yelled, "Is there anyone else up there?"

In some ways, this is what you and I go through every single day. Life is full of moments when we feel as if we are falling off a cliff and we do our best to save ourselves. We grab hold of whatever we can, yet we fear letting go and letting God protect us, shield us, guard us, preserve us, and defend us. To use a football analogy, we have a difficult time trusting God to block for us.

The movie *The Blind Side* (Warner Bros. Pictures, 2009) starring Oscar-winner Sandra Bullock, is a true story about a young African-American teenager who was living on the streets in Memphis, Tennessee. He was taken into the home of a wealthy white family, nurtured by them, and became a star football player in the National Football League. While in high school he took an IQ test, scoring low in all categories except one: He was in the 98th percentile in "protective instincts." That can happen to a person living on the streets. The movie's title is a football phrase referring to a left offensive tackle that must protect a right-handed quarterback from pass rushers on his blind side.

Are we willing to trust God to block for us, to protect our blind side? To use a classic religious term, are we willing to have "blind faith" or trust in God? Do we trust God's protective instincts? Do we have, as John Wesley, the founder of Methodism, said, a "disposition of the heart" that trusts God's grace?

If you struggle with your trust in God, just know that you are not alone. The inhabitants of the ancient city of Jerusalem beat us to the punch. In Luke 13:31–35 we find Jesus, speaking for God as prophets do, saying this about the people of Jerusalem, "How often have I desired to gather your children together as a hen gathers her brood under her wings, and you were not willing." As a city, as a cultural center, as the epicenter of a religion,

Jerusalem was not able to trust God. They were not able to trust that God is their mother hen, that God is their left tackle, that God is their trustee.

One day some Pharisees warn Jesus of a threat from the Jewish king, Herod Antipas. This is ironic, because in other places in the Gospels the Pharisees are pictured as antagonistic toward Jesus. Nevertheless, there were obviously some Pharisees who were concerned about his well-being. Herod wants to kill Jesus. This is not an idle threat because this is the same Herod who killed John the Baptist. And yet Jesus shows a lot of courage. Although he refers to God as a mother hen, Jesus is no chicken. He calls Herod a "fox." I couldn't help but be reminded of the old fox in the henhouse analogy. In rural America and on the American frontier, where people raised chickens for sustenance, several American proverbs arose, such as "Don't put the fox to guard the henhouse," "The sleeping fox catches no chickens," and "When the fox dies, fowls do not mourn."

While the prospect of foxes killing chickens has always been a real problem for chicken farmers, we have learned to utilize these animals as metaphors for certain kinds of people. The "fox" is a dangerous and destructive, yet sly and clever person. The chicken is innocent, unaware of the devious, devouring behavior of the fox. And the mother hen is someone who wants to protect her baby chicks from the fox. Jesus wants to protect the innocent and unaware people of Jerusalem from corrupt government and religious institutions that do not have the best interests of the people in mind. The fox is in the henhouse and he wants to be the mother hen.

Jesus is no ordinary chicken. He tells the Pharisees to give a message to Herod that he will continue his ministry of proclaiming the presence of God's realm, which consists of healing and liberation. Mother hen stuff. Jesus believed his ministry contrasted with the oppression of both Caesar and Herod's governments and the temple religion in Jerusalem. These were the foxes that were devouring the people. Because Jesus' mother hen ministry was such a contrast to these foxes, he knew his life was in danger, yet he was willing to go to the henhouse, to Jerusalem. "I must be on my way," he says.

All throughout its history, any time anyone (namely, the Hebrew prophets) journeyed to Jerusalem to try to turn people's trust away from corrupt religious and political institutions and toward trust in God, they were either run off or killed. As Jesus said: "Jerusalem, Jerusalem, the city that kills the prophets and stones those who are sent to it!" When he says, "Jerusalem, Jerusalem" he's not talking about the innocent people who live there. He's talking about the religious and political leaders who are corrupt, oppressive, and murderous. He's talking about those who have the power to do such things, those who are murderous because they have their own interests to protect.

The political and religious leaders in Jerusalem were analogous to Colonel Sanders and KFC. The leaders lived in power and luxury at the expense of the chickens, the people of Jerusalem, and all of Israel. (Please note that I love KFC and have paid homage to Colonel Sanders' grave in Louisville, Kentucky.) Jerusalem had become a domination system. And when you add the extra layer of the Roman Empire on top of the temple religion in Jerusalem, you have multiple foxes feasting on all the chickens all the time.

Jesus wants to be their mother hen, their trustee, their left tackle. Unfortunately, as he says, they were not willing to allow that to happen. The reason they were not willing is because they trusted the powers that were already there, the powers they could see, the powers of Caesar, the powers of Herod, and the powers of the temple. They probably felt they had no other choice. They knew that these powers could make life miserable for them if they looked elsewhere for protection. Imagine living in a neighborhood ruled by a mafia family. Even though the people may not like the mafia, they know they have to pay their dues to the family for protection . . . or else. (Please note that I love the mafia. I don't want them to be mad at me.) That's what the common people of Jerusalem were facing: paying their taxes to Rome and their tithes to the temple . . . or else. These were the only powers they could trust. And then here comes this new prophet, Jesus of Nazareth, telling them to trust him, or better, trust God, although they were not willing. I realize hindsight is twenty-twenty, but they messed up.

NARCISSISM ISN'T NEW

Let me begin here with a definition. "Narcissism" refers to an "inordinate fascination with oneself; excessive self-love; vanity." The word comes from Greek mythology. Narcissus was a youth who fell in love with his own reflection in a pool, and who, after his death, was transformed into the narcissus flower. In our culture, perhaps the antithesis of narcissism is reflected in the cartoon character, Charlie Brown. With whom do you identify the most: someone who falls in love with their own reflection in a pool (like Narcissus or perhaps Lucy), or someone who feels totally inadequate (like Charlie Brown)? I hope its somewhere in between thinking you are nobody to thinking you are the center of the universe.

A recent study reveals that today's college students are more narcissistic and self-centered than previous generations of college students. The lead author of this study, Jean Twenge of San Diego State University, blamed this on what the study called the "self-esteem movement" that emerged in the 1980s, otherwise known as the "Me Generation." According to this study, the effort to build self-confidence has gone too far. Twenge said, "We need to stop endlessly repeating 'You're special' and having children repeat that back. Kids are self-centered enough already."[1]

Like anything else, of course, narcissism can have both positive and negative effects on people. Positively, it can help you meet new people and give you the self-confidence to audition on shows like *American Idol*. But the negatives far outweigh the positives. The study reveals that narcissistic people "are more likely to have romantic relationships that are short-lived, at risk for infidelity, lack emotional warmth, and to exhibit game-playing, dishonesty, and over-controlling and violent behavior." Twenge also said that narcissists "tend to lack empathy, react aggressively to criticism and favor self-promotion over helping others."[2] They examined the responses of 16,475 college students nationwide who completed an evaluation called the Narcissistic Personality Inventory test, which was also given to college students in 1982. The study shows that today's students are 30 percent more narcissistic than they were in 1982.[3] Please don't tell my millennialist offspring I wrote this. I might need them to care for me in my old age.

Even if today's college students or young people are more narcissistic than past generations, I still want to claim that narcissism isn't new. After all, it's been around since Narcissus fell in love with his own reflection in the pool. And in my view, as long as there are politicians there will always be narcissists. (Wouldn't you have to be a little full of yourself to run for public office?) Narcissism will always be alive and well as long as there are politicians, celebrities, preachers, and, well, human beings. Some pundits today argue that Donald Trump is actually the Narcissist-in-Chief. Please don't tell him I repeated that. I actually enjoy my life.

Although today's college students may or may not be more narcissistic than in the past, they didn't invent it. Even Jesus himself had to deal with narcissistic people. Herod is a good example. As noted above, Jesus is on his way to Jerusalem. Along the way he stops in the villages and the countryside to minister to the people. Jesus encountered some Pharisees who warn him that Herod, a Roman puppet ruler of the Jewish people, wants to kill him. This Herod, by the way, is not to be confused with the first Herod, called "the Great," a ruthless man who died in 4 BC, about the time Jesus was born. After Herod the Great died, revolts erupted throughout his kingdom,

---

1. Quenqua, Douglas. "Seeing Narcissists Everywhere." https://www.nytimes.com/2013/08/06/science/seeing-narcissists-everywhere.html.

2. Frank, Natalie. "The Increase in Narcissism in College Students." https://owlcation.com/social-sciences/Increasing-Narcissism-in-College-Students.

3. Frank, Natalie. "The Increase in Narcissism in College Students." https://owlcation.com/social-sciences/Increasing-Narcissism-in-College-Students.

violently suppressed by the Romans. Rome then divided Herod's kingdom into three parts, each ruled by one of his sons. Galilee and trans-Jordanian Perea were assigned to Herod Antipas, the area northeast of the Jordan to Philip, and Judea and Samaria to Archelaus, who ruled from Jerusalem (but was eventually replaced by Roman governors such as Pontius Pilate).

The Herod referred to in Luke 13 is Herod Antipas, the ruler of Galilee, Jesus' homeland. Presumably, Antipas felt threatened by Jesus, who had been gaining wide popularity among the Galilean peasants. This is the same Herod, by the way, who had John the Baptist executed for criticizing him for marrying his brother's wife. Herod Antipas was not exactly a good man. As noted above, Jesus calls him a "fox," which is a first-century equivalent of a "skunk." I don't think there is any question that Herod Antipas was what we now call narcissistic. After all, he was a politician (although not an elected one). He certainly reacted aggressively to John the Baptist's criticism of him. He tweeted incessantly about it. He was over-controlling, exhibited violent behavior, lacked empathy for his subjects, and favored self-promotion over helping others. Jesus had his hands full with this man.

All of us know narcissistic people. They are the ones who constantly talk about themselves and who don't react very well to criticism. However, narcissism is not just a disorder exhibited in the lives of certain individuals. It can also be a cultural phenomenon. Such was the case, I believe, with the city of Jerusalem in the first century. Jerusalem was a narcissistic city (and still might be, by the way). In this episode, Jesus is on his way to Jerusalem where he will eventually meet his death. It was such a violent city that Jesus could claim, "It is impossible for a prophet to be killed outside of Jerusalem." In other words, if a prophet like Jesus is going to be murdered, it will be in Jerusalem because it was a city that didn't like criticism.

And prophets were known for dishing out criticism. Jesus said, "Jerusalem, Jerusalem, the city that kills the prophets and stones those who are sent to it!" I'm sure this pissed them off. Like Washington, DC today, Jerusalem was a self-absorbed, power-hungry city. The first thing Jesus did when he came to Jerusalem at the beginning of his last week on earth was to enter the temple, turn over the money-changers' tables, and chase away people and animals. He focused much of his teachings, including his parables, on criticism of the temple religion in Jerusalem and the Roman government that ruled the area from Jerusalem. And apparently they didn't take kindly to his criticism.

Other than being violent and not taking criticism very well, another sign of narcissism is being over-controlling and unwilling to allow others to help. Jesus addressed this when he says about Jerusalem, "How often have I desired to gather your children together as a hen gathers her brood under her wings, and you were not willing!" Jerusalem is a beautiful city. It's a sacred place to the three major monotheistic religions in the world. It's full of history. Yet even today it is also full of itself. When I was there about thirty years ago I passed a shop one day walking down the streets of Jerusalem. A T-shirt in the window showed a picture of an army tank and a caption which read, "Don't worry, America, Israel's on your side." As I said, the city is a little too full of itself.

We should all look inside ourselves for signs of narcissism. We will find them because we are human, and humans are naturally self-absorbed. We should look for signs of narcissistic behavior, such as short-lived romantic relationships, infidelity, a lack of emotional warmth, playing games with other people, dishonesty, over-controlling and violent behavior, a lack of empathy, aggressive reactions to criticism, and favoring self-promotion over helping others. I'm not saying we should eliminate so many of our narcissistic tendencies that we become like Charlie Brown. But if we can minimize our Lucy-like characteristics, then we'll be okay. After all, as the old self-esteem book says, "I'm okay. You're okay." Just don't go repeating that to your children.

Luke 14:1–14

On one occasion when Jesus was going to the house of a leader of the Pharisees to eat a meal on the sabbath, they were watching him closely. Just then, in front of him, there was a man who had dropsy. And Jesus asked the lawyers and Pharisees, "Is it lawful to cure people on the sabbath, or not?" But they were silent. So Jesus took him and healed him, and sent him away. Then he said to them, "If one of you has a child or an ox that has fallen into a well, will you not immediately pull it out on a sabbath day?" And they could not reply to this. When he noticed how the guests chose the places of honor, he told them a parable. "When you are invited by someone to a wedding banquet, do not sit down at the place of honor, in case someone more distinguished than you has been invited by your host; and the host who invited both of you may come and say to you, 'Give this person your place,' and then in disgrace you would start to take the lowest place. But when you are invited, go and sit down at the lowest place, so that when your host comes, he may say to you, 'Friend, move up higher'; then you will be honored in the presence of all who sit at the table with you. For all who exalt themselves will be humbled, and those who humble themselves will be exalted." He said also to the one who had invited him, "When you give a luncheon or a dinner, do not invite your friends or your brothers or your relatives or rich neighbors, in case they may invite you in return, and you would be repaid. But when you give a banquet, invite the poor, the crippled, the lame, and the blind. And you will be blessed, because they cannot repay you, for you will be repaid at the resurrection of the righteous."

SNOBS, SOCIAL LADDERS, AND SOCIETY PAGES

I'M NOT SURE THERE have been very many societies in the history of humanity that compare with the British in terms of sheer snobbery, and yet the British didn't invent snobbery. It's been around forever. Even Jesus had to put up with an occasional upstart. This may be an unfair assessment, but the Pharisees come across in the Gospels as the biggest snobs of first-century Palestine. They certainly loved to throw exclusive dinner parties.

One day Jesus found himself on a Pharisee's guest list. He was invited for two reasons. First, he had acquired status. He was no longer just the lowly carpenter's son from upper Galilee. He was now a well-known rabbi, sage, and healer. He was renowned, and to have a successful dinner party, one must invite those whose presence can put your party on the society page of the local newspaper. The second reason he was invited, however, was so the Pharisees and other religious leaders could keep an eye on him. They were beginning to be very uncomfortable with his popularity, if not downright envious.

Just then an uninvited man with dropsy approaches Jesus. Dropsy is a condition of edema, or retention of bodily fluids, which was perceived as being unclean. On the first-century Jewish social ladder, this man was at the bottom. If the local newspapers found out he was at this party, the party would never make the society page. Much to the chagrin of his hosts, Jesus heals this unclean man. The hosts must have realized that if they made a big deal out of this incident the party will be ruined, so they let it go without saying a word, hoping the party will get back on track. I can imagine the disapproving looks and nods as Jesus ministers to the unclean man. I can also imagine the sighs of relief when the unclean man leaves the party. Now they can get back to the important stuff like finding a good seat, one that was appropriate for the social standing of these Pharisees and lawyers.

Realizing that his hosts are tolerating him, if not trying to be gracious to him, Jesus uses this opportunity as a teaching moment. He first launches into a parable about how people at a dinner party should choose a less esteemed seat so that if the host needs or wants to move them, they are likely to be moved to a better seat. On the other hand, if they choose a highly esteemed location, like the center of the head table, the only direction they can move is to a lesser seat. Jesus intends this parable to illustrate how in the kingdom of God "all who exalt themselves will be humbled, and those who humble themselves will be exalted." He is trying to teach a room full of snobs that they should be humble. Has anyone ever tried to do such a radical thing in the history of humanity?

Again, at least according to Luke's account of this incident, there is no response from the hosts. Are they listening to him or are they merely tolerating him? My guess is that the response is mixed. Jesus is getting through to some of the dinner guests, while others are probably rolling their eyes with contempt for this Galilean peasant-turned-rabbi who has the audacity to tell them where to sit.

What Jesus says next is even more audacious. After he tells a bunch of snobs where to sit at an exclusive dinner party, he then tells them whom they should invite. They must have thought Jesus had been drinking too much wine. What right does he have to criticize their guest list? He should be thankful he's on it. He actually says to them that they should invite people from the lower end of the social ladder to their exclusive parties. Two things are obvious here. First, it ain't gonna happen. Ever. People on the high end of the social ladder in every society that has ever existed have always socialized with others on the high end. When they do rub elbows with those on the lower end of the social ladder we call it charity work. But Jesus isn't talking about charity work. In fact, he's not even talking about real dinner parties. He's talking about the kingdom of God. He is telling this audience of snobs that God's banquet doesn't operate according to the same standards as theirs. Human beings are only fooling themselves if they think the social ladder makes a hill of beans difference in the kingdom of God.

In my denomination, the United Church of Christ, we have tried to put Jesus' understanding of this egalitarian kingdom of God to practice by our observance of the Lord's Supper or communion. We practice open communion because we believe that nothing about a person should bar them from the table. Religious elitists as well as people with dropsy are welcome at our table. The wealthy as well as the poor can come to our banquet. No one is barred from the table based on their race, gender, age, marital status, sexual orientation, theology, clothing, smell, or whether they served in the military or not. In reality, however, if we invite someone to church they will likely have similar demographic characteristics. More than likely they will come from the same rung of the social ladder. And that's okay. Our natural audience will be people in our own social circle. These are the people we know. And yet I encourage us to keep in mind what Jesus is saying here. To be faithful to the gospel of Jesus Christ, we must at least be willing if not proactive in expanding our invitation list to include those who reside at different rungs on the social ladder.

One thing that might be helpful is to realize why human beings reside on their particular rung in the first place. There are reasons why some are at the bottom, some at the top, and some are somewhere in the middle. It's not just a matter of choice or effort. Realizing this makes it easier to accept people who reside at a different rung. Sociologists argue that there are at least seven factors that place us on a particular rung of social life. Some of these are factors we can change or manipulate and some are not.

There are, for example, biological constraints, which includes physical traits, intelligence, energy levels, skin color, gender, and inherited diseases. There are cultural values, which includes whether or not hard work is valued or ridiculed. There is the factor of personal motivation, which includes the amount of personal gumption, drive, and sheer persistence. There exist community assets—it makes a big difference whether your community has good schools, jobs, hospitals, and other cultural opportunities. Family stability is also a factor. Many people come from emotionally disturbed or dysfunctional families that can create lifelong problems. Some people benefit from financial inheritance, what we might call the "silver spoon" syndrome. And last but certainly not least is the notion of "chance." We can't overlook the factors of good or bad luck. Some people find themselves in the right place at the right time; others are in the wrong place at the wrong time.

What these factors help us realize is that snobbery is based on ignorance. In an award-winning book called, *The Upside Down Kingdom,* the author Donald Kraybill, says, "A realistic grasp of how we arrive at different rungs on the social ladder wipes away arrogance and propels the people of God toward sympathetic understanding."[1] Knowing all this helps us to be "woke."

A LINE IN THE SAND

Jesus was able to erase barriers between folks while, at the same time, drawing a line in the sand. In Luke 14, he draws a very clear line between compassion and legalism. As noted above, Jesus is invited to a dinner party at the home of a Pharisee. It was the Sabbath day and so the Pharisee and his friends have invited him there to keep an eye on him. While there, he heals a man with dropsy, or swelling. The compassionate act of healing on the Sabbath is a very clear line in the sand for Jesus. This was no gray area for him. This was not an occasion for compromise. We are either willing or not willing to sidestep a worthless rule that claims one can't heal on the Sabbath. For Jesus, compassion and legalism are two very different options. One needs to choose one side of the line or the other.

When we say, "Rules are made to be broken," what we mean is that sometimes compassion calls us to break a rule. Generally speaking, compassion is the primary reason to break a rule. In this story we have to read

1. Kraybill, *Upside-Down Kingdom,* 249.

between the lines—pun intended—to see how Jesus is drawing a line in the sand between compassion and legalism. Jesus tells a parable about a wedding banquet. He tells his listeners not to invite friends, relatives, or rich neighbors because there is nothing noteworthy about that. Instead we are to invite those who can't repay us: the poor and the physically challenged. I admit that most of us are rarely, if ever, going to take this advice in a literal way. When we invite people who are poor or physically challenged to our homes, they are usually our friends or relatives.

So, what's Jesus getting at? Here's where we have to read between the lines: In ancient Jewish society, to allow such "unclean" people in your home would make you unclean as well. By that, I don't mean physically unclean or dirty; I mean religiously dirty. To be religiously unclean meant to be impure or unholy. Why were the poor and physically handicapped considered religiously unclean? Because people believed they were that way because God was punishing them for their sins.

I know . . . that's stupid, right? But that was the theology of the day, and from that theology developed a lot of crazy rules about staying away from the unclean. Obviously, a Pharisee is not going to invite unclean people to his house for a party because the name "Pharisee" means "separate one," meaning separate from the unclean, impure, and unholy masses of people out there. A Pharisee was the last person to host an inclusive party. So, here's what Jesus was doing: He was drawing a line in the sand between a set of worthless purity laws (legalism) and the one thing that supersedes all laws: compassion.

Luke 14:25–33

Now large crowds were travelling with him; and he turned and said to them, "Whoever comes to me and does not hate father and mother, wife and children, brothers and sisters, yes, and even life itself, cannot be my disciple. Whoever does not carry the cross and follow me cannot be my disciple. For which of you, intending to build a tower, does not first sit down and estimate the cost, to see whether he has enough to complete it? Otherwise, when he has laid a foundation and is not able to finish, all who see it will begin to ridicule him, saying, "This fellow began to build and was not able to finish." Or what king, going out to wage war against another king, will not sit down first and consider whether he is able with ten thousand to oppose the one who comes against him with twenty thousand? If he cannot, then, while the other is still far away, he sends a delegation and asks for the terms of peace. So therefore, none of you can become my disciple if you do not give up all your possessions.

DISCIPLESHIP AT WARP SPEED

WE SEEM TO BE on the cusp of discovering something really interesting in terms of the possibility of life elsewhere in the universe. Not long ago we detected the possibility of an earth-like planet in a solar system near to us, and shortly after that scientists detected a possible signal of some kind coming from outer space. The results of these findings are still in dispute; however, these kinds of discoveries are generating a lot of excitement in the field of astronomy.

Despite what I saw while visiting Roswell, New Mexico, I do not believe that we have ever been visited by aliens. I believe the distance between the stars is simply too great for space travel to occur in a timely fashion. I am convinced the answer to the Fermi Paradox[1] is that, even if there is intelligent life elsewhere in the universe, they are too few and too far away for contact. And yet, for those of us who grew up watching *Star Trek,* we have been conditioned to believe space travel between solar systems with habitable planets is possible because of one thing: warp drive. For those of you that missed out on the *Star Trek* phenomenon, let me explain. If you were consumed with the *Star Wars* fantasy crap I simply apologize for our failure as a society to steer you in the proper sci-fi direction. In the fictional *Star Trek* universe, warp drive is the method of propulsion that starships and other spacecraft use when they are traveling faster than the speed of light. Impulse drive, on the other hand, is the method they use when they are traveling below the speed of light, although they are still moving very fast.

I would like to apply this notion of warp drive and impulse drive to Christian discipleship. There is, in my opinion, discipleship on impulse drive and discipleship on warp drive. Discipleship on impulse drive is discipleship on cruise control. It's normal, safe, routine, familiar, conventional, and traditional. It's discipleship without having to put a lot of effort into it. Discipleship on warp drive, on the other hand, is not familiar to us. It's not safe or easy. It is contrary to conventional wisdom, tradition, normalcy, and some would even say, sanity.

We see discipleship on warp drive all throughout the Gospels, but rarely is it as obvious as it is in the above story. Luke tells us that Jesus was speaking to a large crowd of wannabe disciples. He begins his talk with a particularly shocking attention-grabbing point. He tells the crowd to hate members of their families. I can envision coffee cups hitting the ground because they cannot believe what they just heard. Hatred of family as a condition of discipleship? Is he being serious? This is almost beyond our ability to understand, so let's put on our "ears to hear." Jesus is not messing around here. He's trying to make disciples who operate on warp drive, not just impulse drive.

If he was operating on impulse drive he would have said, "Folks, don't let your relatives get in the way of your discipleship," which would have been met with a huge collective yawn. How boring. But operating on warp drive he says, "If you don't hate your relatives, you can't be my disciples." If

---

1. The Fermi paradox or Fermi's paradox, named after Enrico Fermi, is the apparent contradiction between high estimates of the probability of the existence of extraterrestrial civilizations, such as in the Drake equation, and the lack of evidence for such civilizations. https://en.wikipedia.org/wiki/Fermi_paradox.

anything, each person standing there would have given serious thought to how their family dynamics affect their relationship to the kingdom of God. Then, as a second condition of discipleship, Jesus says they must be willing to die. He says, "Whoever doesn't carry their own cross and follow me cannot be my disciple." If he had been operating on impulse drive he would have said, "Following me can get kind of tricky at times. People may not always appreciate what you have to say, or what you do. So be careful." Yawn. But Jesus is operating on warp drive. "You have to be willing to die," he says.

Years ago I picked up a young man walking down a rural highway in pouring rain. He gratefully got into my car. We exchanged pleasantries for a few minutes and then he asked, "Are you willing to die for me?" I didn't know what he was getting at, yet I began to suspect that I could possibly be the victim of a homicide in a very short time. So I danced around the question for a few minutes, drove into a crowded parking lot in the nearest town, jumped quickly out of my car with keys in hand, and told him to get out. He did, and then I drove off. I have no idea if he had it in his mind to kill me, but I was not willing to risk it. Hey, don't judge. I was not willing to die for that weirdo; still, I have to wonder if I'm willing to die for something larger than myself, like my faith. I hope I never have to find out.

Jesus then elaborates by giving two illustrations about "counting the cost." First, he asks if a builder would start a building project without being able to pay for it. Then he asks whether a king would go to war without assurances that he has enough soldiers to win. We may think we are willing to engage in warp drive discipleship, and yet have we counted the cost? Do we really know what all it entails? That's what Jesus is trying to communicate to the crowd.

A few years ago, my wife and I decided to go to a tattoo parlor and get "tats." I talked to other people who had tattoos and they assured me that it didn't hurt. So, I analyzed the situation—I counted the cost—and decided I was ready. Now, I have to admit I was not ready for that pain. About halfway through the process I asked the tattoo artist if anyone had ever backed out before the tattoo was completed. He said, "No, and you don't want to be the first." So I endured the pain and got my tattoo. Jesus is telling us not to go into God's tattoo parlor without first counting the cost, without being completely ready to do whatever it takes, to endure whatever pain is necessary. This means, among other things, to be willing to be a family outcast and to be willing to die for a cause greater than yourselves.

Finally, Jesus concludes with another condition for discipleship: giving away all our possessions. This is a coffee-spewing-through-the-nose moment. How could he possibly be serious? Note, however, that most people in the crowd listening to Jesus were peasants. They didn't have a pot to piss in. Seriously, they didn't have toilets. Even today poor people can hear this condition for discipleship more willingly than people with a lot of possessions. Most of us would prefer to "white out" these words from our red-letter Bibles. And yet again, understand what Jesus is doing here. If he had been operating on impulse drive he would have said, "Hey guys, go through your attics, basements, and garages and find a few items for the church rummage sale; then you can be my disciples." Instead he is operating on warp drive, which says, "Give it all up," forcing us to grapple with our own consumerism, greed, and hoarding tendencies. This is a good place to launch if we want to take this discipleship thing seriously.

So, hate your families. Be ready to die. Give away all of your possessions. You know, as Jesus was saying these things, I bet that crowd scattered like roaches when the lights come on. When I read Jesus' words carefully, I have a hard time understanding why anyone would want to be a disciple of Jesus Christ. And let's not be confused: Being a church member is not the same thing as being a disciple of Jesus Christ. Church membership is what we do on impulse drive. Discipleship is what we do on warp drive. Church membership is like a bike ride in the park. Discipleship is like a ride on a roller coaster. Church membership is like a ride on a horse and buggy. Discipleship is like a ride on a spaceship. Discipleship is what we do beyond the speed of light, beyond that which is natural, normal, safe, conventional, familiar, and comfortable. I'm not even sure a seat belt will help.

Luke 15:1–10

Now all the tax collectors and sinners were coming near to listen to him. And the Pharisees and the scribes were grumbling and saying, "This fellow welcomes sinners and eats with them." So he told them this parable: "Which one of you, having a hundred sheep and losing one of them, does not leave the ninety-nine in the wilderness and go after the one that is lost until he finds it? When he has found it, he lays it on his shoulders and rejoices. And when he comes home, he calls together his friends and neighbors, saying to them, 'Rejoice with me, for I have found my sheep that was lost.' Just so, I tell you, there will be more joy in heaven over one sinner who repents than over ninety-nine righteous persons who need no repentance. Or what woman having ten silver coins, if she loses one of them, does not light a lamp, sweep the house, and search carefully until she finds it? When she has found it, she calls together her friends and neighbors, saying, 'Rejoice with me, for I have found the coin that I had lost.' Just so, I tell you, there is joy in the presence of the angels of God over one sinner who repents."

THE DAY JESUS EXAGGERATED

I WOULD LOVE TO be a late-night comedian during a presidential campaign because there is always a constant flow of new material to use. Two words: Donald Trump. Trump was elected while I was writing and editing this book. If my social media feed is any indication of reality (although I do live in a bubble), more people have laughed and cried sequentially and/or simultaneously since Trump's election than at any other time in the history of the United States. Will Rogers once said, "There is no credit to being a comedian, when you have the whole government working for you. All you have to do is report the facts. I don't even have to exaggerate."[1] Presidential candidates exaggerate in two ways. First, they exaggerate about what they will do for the country if elected. Second, they love to exaggerate about how bad their opponents are. Politicians are rarely, if ever, as bad as their opponents make them out to be (and rarely as good as they think they are). Unfortunately, candidates for public office often feel they have to exaggerate in order to get elected.

In some ways, this reminds me of Jesus. Jesus loved to exaggerate. He loved to use an occasional hyperbole, which is an obvious and intentional exaggeration. Let me offer some examples of how Jesus seems to have exaggerated some of his teachings:

> Blessed are the poor.
>
> It is easier for a camel to go through the eye of a needle than for a wealthy person to get into God's kingdom.
>
> God counts all the hairs on my head.
>
> Love your enemies.
>
> Hate your father and mother and sister and brother.
>
> The last will be first and the first last.
>
> Give to everyone who begs from us.

These statements seem to be exaggerated in order to make a point. The same could be said about the parables of the lost sheep and the lost coin.

A shepherd has a hundred sheep in his flock. One of them gets separated from the flock and is lost. The shepherd leaves the ninety-nine sheep behind and goes after the one lost sheep. Literally speaking, this is difficult to imagine happening. A shepherd would never risk leaving ninety-nine sheep behind in order to seek out one lost sheep. The ninety-nine would be in danger of getting lost themselves or attacked by predators. It does not make economic sense for a shepherd to seek after one lost sheep. Not only that, but after he finds the lost sheep he doesn't even return to his flock. Instead he goes home to have a party with his friends and neighbors celebrating the fact that he found the one lost sheep. I doubt if this would have been a good reason to throw a party unless the newly found sheep became the meal. From our perspective, Jesus exaggerates the behavior of the shepherd.

In the parable of the lost coin, Jesus suggests exaggerated behavior on the part of a woman who searches her entire house at night (before

---

1. https://quotes.yourdictionary.com/author/will-rogers/99136.

the advent of electricity) for one coin. She could have waited until morning when there would have been more light. The text says she only had ten coins in all, so we are not surprised that she would want to find the missing coin. But to throw a party because she found her coin is not exactly normal behavior. Of course, people don't really need an excuse to party. Oh, and by the way, she probably used that coin to pay for the party.

Most of Jesus' parables are parables of exaggeration. To understand the meaning of his parables we need to pinpoint the context in which he uttered them. The parables of the lost sheep and lost coin are given in the context of Jesus being criticized for being in table fellowship with sinners. The implication is that sinners, according to Jesus, are "lost." This was a very strange concept to the Pharisees and scribes. To them, sinners were simply unclean, what we might call "bad." They had openly disobeyed or not followed the rabbinical laws closely enough to be considered clean or good. That's why you didn't eat with them. Jesus, however, redefines sinners as people who are lost, not as people who are unclean. To say that something is lost is to imply that it is worth looking for. To the Pharisees and scribes, Jesus' redefinition of the sinners from unclean to lost was an exaggeration of their worth. To the Pharisees and scribes, sinners were not worth looking for, yet Jesus had a different opinion.

If a particular sheep that goes astray from the flock is unclean or unworthy, the shepherd doesn't leave behind ninety-nine clean sheep to go looking for it. On the other hand, if the shepherd values the sheep then he will consider the sheep lost and therefore he will seek to find it. Similarly, if a particular coin is missing from a woman's change purse that is not worth much, the woman is not going to spend any time looking for it. And yet if she values the coin then she will consider the coin lost and therefore she will seek to find it. To say that something is lost is to imply that it is worth looking for.

I have never been very comfortable using the word "lost" to refer to people (as I heard over and over again in my Baptist upbringing). Still, while the theology of my childhood faith may have been a little short on sophistication, thinking of people as lost does not have to be judgmental and condescending because thinking of people as lost implies they are worthy enough to be found. Notice how these parables differ from our typical understanding of lost-ness. We tend to believe that if someone is spiritually lost then that person needs to go looking for God. And yet if the parable of the lost sheep is accurate, then many people who are lost have no idea where to go. The shepherd looks for the sheep; the sheep do not go looking for the shepherd. Boom! There goes evangelicalism . . .

Likewise if the parable of the lost coin gives us any insight into lostness then many people who are lost do nothing at all. A lost coin is not even aware that it is lost. The owner of the coin looks for the coin, not the other way around. A lost sheep is, well, too dumb to notice they are lost. From our limited perspective there is an exaggerated nature to these parables. In our experience *we* are the ones who search for God or spiritual enlightenment. Isn't Jesus exaggerating to suggest that lost sinners do nothing at all? Nothing about these parables matches our experience or knowledge of the world. We don't invite sinners to our dinner tables. (The exception to that rule is holidays, when we feel obligated to invite the black sheep of the family to our family gatherings. Pun not necessarily intended. In fact, the days of utilizing the phrase "black sheep" should be relegated to the dustbin of history, where all subtly racist, politically incorrect statements belong.) Shepherds don't leave ninety-nine sheep behind to search for one. Women don't sweep the entire house at night for one solitary coin. In fact, most Christians do not picture God as a woman in the first place. What was Jesus thinking?

When it comes to the details of many of his parables and short sayings, Jesus seems to be exaggerating, obviously and intentionally, in order to make larger points. However, about his main point, that all God's children are worthy enough to be found, he is not exaggerating. "God's children," for me, is all-inclusive, including John Ritter's "problem child."[2] It is no exaggeration to say that God's love for us is infinite, unconditional, unmerited, and unearned. To be loved and valued by God, we can be as clueless as a lost sheep and as unaware as a lost coin. Jesus didn't have to exaggerate about that, and he didn't.

---

2. John Ritter starred in *Problem Child*, Universal, 1990.

Luke 15:11–32

Then Jesus said, "There was a man who had two sons. The younger of them said to his father, 'Father, give me the share of the property that will belong to me.' So he divided his property between them. A few days later the younger son gathered all he had and traveled to a distant country, and there he squandered his property in dissolute living. When he had spent everything, a severe famine took place throughout that country, and he began to be in need. So he went and hired himself out to one of the citizens of that country, who sent him to his fields to feed the pigs. He would gladly have filled himself with the pods that the pigs were eating; and no one gave him anything. But when he came to himself he said, 'How many of my father's hired hands have bread enough and to spare, but here I am dying of hunger! I will get up and go to my father, and I will say to him, "Father, I have sinned against heaven and before you; I am no longer worthy to be called your son; treat me like one of your hired hands."' So he set off and went to his father. But while he was still far off, his father saw him and was filled with compassion; he ran and put his arms around him and kissed him. Then the son said to him, 'Father, I have sinned against heaven and before you; I am no longer worthy to be called your son.' But the father said to his slaves, 'Quickly, bring out a robe—the best one—and put it on him; put a ring on his finger and sandals on his feet. And get the fatted calf and kill it, and let us eat and celebrate; for this son of mine was dead and is alive again; he was lost and is found!' And they began to celebrate. "Now his elder son was in the field; and when he came and approached the house, he heard music and dancing. He called one of the slaves and asked *what was going on. He replied, 'Your brother has come, and your father has killed the fatted calf, because he has got him back safe and sound.' Then he became angry and refused to go in. His father came out and began to plead with him. But he answered his father, 'Listen! For all these years I have been working like a slave for you, and I have never disobeyed your command; yet you have never given me even a young goat so that I might celebrate with my friends. But when this son of yours came back, who has devoured your property with prostitutes, you killed the fatted calf for him!' Then the father said to him, 'Son, you are always with me, and all that is mine is yours. But we had to celebrate and rejoice, because this brother of yours was dead and has come to life; he was lost and has been found.'"*

LIMBURGER CHEESE ON THE UPPER LIP

Whatever God's grace is, we know it does not guarantee a safe journey through life. Nor does it mean that we will escape mental and emotional anguish. Nevertheless, the most important word in the Christian dictionary is the word "grace." We sing about God's amazing grace through many of our songs and hymns. We talk about God's grace in our responsive readings, our prayers, our sermons, our Sunday school classes, and in our conversations with one another. We reflect on God's grace when we are in need of mercy, love, forgiveness, or an assurance of God's presence. The Christian faith would be meaningless without this strange, incomprehensible notion of God's grace as revealed in Jesus Christ. We could employ all kinds of definitions and theological arguments to help us understand grace, yet I like to use a simple definition: Grace refers to God's unconditional, unlimited, and unmerited gift of love for God's people.

Despite the tragedies and sufferings we inevitably endure, many of us believe that God's grace embraces us like a blanket. God's grace is already here. It's always been here, and it's not going anywhere. It is unshakable, steadfast, constant, and uncompromising. We cannot run and hide from it. We cannot help but be affected by it, even when we are not paying attention to God. And yet there is a catch: We have to own it for ourselves. It is free, in front of us, around us, and within us, but our job is to recognize it and own it.

The notion that grace is free really bothers some people. Our natural inclination is to try and earn it, perhaps because we live in a capitalistic, competitive environment. Nothing is free, even gifts from other people cost them something. And if it's free, how can it be worth anything? We don't like to own things that are cheap or inexpensive. Many people would rather pay more money for the exact same product because it has a designer label on it. We would rather buy the name brand rather than the generic brand of food or medicine because we have been taught to believe "you get what you pay for." We don't even like free advice. We believe free advice isn't trustworthy so we would rather go out and pay for it. Personally, I prefer palm readings to séances and psychic readings, however, my palms are so wrinkled the readers often complain of too much static.

We don't trust anything that is cheap, much less free. And grace just happens to be free. So most of us really don't trust God's grace despite how much we sing about it. We still think we ought to earn it somehow. That would be more American. How many times have we heard preachers complain about "cheap grace"? Cheap grace is the notion that many Christians take advantage of God's grace by not living up to God's standards. (As if anyone actually could.) Again, this is understandable because we do not trust anything that doesn't cost us very much. We would rather pay for it or work for it. If God is going to bestow grace upon us, then by golly we better make sure we are worth it.

Again, somehow, we have to own God's grace. But how do we own something that is free, that is already there? The parable of the Prodigal Son helps us answer that question. A man had two sons. The younger son requested his share of the inheritance and went out and spent it all in dissolute living. The older son stayed at home out of faithfulness to his dad. (If you think I'm getting this story from the Netflix show, *The Ranch*, you've got it backwards.) The younger son soon ran out of money and decided to come back home to his father, whereupon his father met him halfway down the road, welcoming him with open arms and a big celebration. The older son became jealous and angry with his father for lavishing all these gifts on his little brother.

There are many ways to interpret the implication of this parable. Yet I like to think this is a parable about owning God's grace. The younger son was finally able to own God's grace and the older son couldn't. When Jesus told this parable, he was talking with two groups of people: tax collectors and sinners, and Pharisees and scribes. The tax collectors and sinners would have identified themselves with the younger son in the parable and they would have liked the outcome. The Pharisees and scribes would have identified themselves with the older son in the parable and they would not have liked it. In the view of the Pharisees and scribes, the only people who are entitled to God's grace are those who are faithful, righteous, and obedient to God. No one else, especially tax collectors—the epitome of being a traitor to the Jewish people—and sinners—the common people of the land who did not have the knowledge or the means to be righteous—is entitled to God's grace.

From the Pharisees' and scribes' perspective, only they could possibly own God's grace, because only they were faithful and righteous enough to earn it. These religious professionals were the ones who took care of the religious institution of that day. They performed the rituals, recorded the rabbinical laws, obeyed the laws, and did all the necessary religious disciplines such as praying, fasting, and giving alms. There was no doubt in their minds that they deserved God's grace. They found grace the old-fashioned way: they earned it. (If you read this out loud please use a British accent here.) They would never lower themselves and become a common person, living in the far country away from the temple in Jerusalem, rubbing elbows with those who did deplorable things like raise pigs. Perhaps Hillary Clinton was thinking of these folks? Just saying.

Ironically, the tax collectors and sinners would have had the same understanding about who deserved God's grace and who didn't. Both groups would have been waiting for Jesus to say something like, "When the younger son returned from the far country, his father had him arrested and thrown into the eternal fire where there is weeping and gnashing of teeth." Yet to the surprise of all of Jesus' listeners that was not how the story ended. The story ends with the younger unfaithful son owning his father's grace whereas the older faithful son discovered that he had *never* actually owned his father's grace.

Because the older son had not yet discovered how to own God's grace, he became very judgmental of his younger brother, the "sinner." This is a profound truth: when we lack ownership of God's grace in our lives, then we become very judgmental of others who don't practice religion like we do. When we lack ownership of God's grace, we become pathologically judgmental. To be pathologically judgmental means to have an unhealthy compulsion to judge others. This begins with ourselves. When we can't take ownership of God's grace for ourselves, we judge ourselves excessively. We have an unhealthy compulsion to judge ourselves. And this judgment of one's self is projected onto others. My favorite saying about judgmental people is this: "If a man has limburger cheese on his upper lip, he thinks the whole world smells." When we think badly of ourselves, we will think badly of others.

And yet when we come to the conclusion that God's grace is free and accessible for everyone, then, and only then, can we stop judging other people and even more importantly stop judging ourselves. Ownership of God's grace gives us the healthy compulsion to stop judging ourselves and others. God's grace allows us to love our neighbor as we love ourselves. It's a beautiful thing. The older son in the parable represents people who smell limburger cheese on their upper lip because they haven't learned to stop judging themselves. On the other hand, after the younger son hits rock bottom with his own self-judging, he learns to wash off the limburger cheese from his upper lip. The younger son represents those who have taken ownership of God's free and unlimited grace by first loving themselves and then, in turn, loving others. It's a beautiful thing.

TIME FOR DESSERT

"Amazing grace, how sweet the sound . . ." So begins one of the most beloved hymns of all time. The author of these words was the eighteenth-century slave trader, John Newton. On May 10, 1748, on a voyage home, he was attempting to steer his ship through a violent storm when he experienced what he was to refer to later as his "great deliverance." He recorded in his journal that when all seemed lost and the ship would surely sink, he prayed, "Lord, have mercy upon us." Later in his cabin he reflected on what he had said and began to believe that God's grace had begun to work in his life. He continued in the slave trade for a time after this conversion experience; however, he saw to it that the slaves under his care were treated humanely.

He later decided to become a minister. His church in Olney became so crowded during services that it had to be enlarged. In 1767 he became friends with the poet, William Cowper. Together they wrote many hymns, including, "Amazing Grace." In 1780 Newton left Olney to become rector of St. Mary Woolnoth. He continued to draw large audiences, among them William Wilberforce, who would one day become a leader in the campaign for the abolition of slavery in Great Britain.[1]

The hymn, "Amazing Grace," is, of course, about grace, a word or concept that remains difficult for people to grasp. My dictionary has nineteen entries under the word "grace," showing how expansive, if not vague, the word really is. Again, for our purposes, the word refers to the freely given, unmerited favor, love, and mercy of God. The word "grace" is mentioned six times in the hymn, all of them occurring in verses 1, 2, and 4. It is unusual

---

1. Rogers, Al. "Amazing Grace: The Story of John Newton." https://www.anointed-links.com/amazing_grace.html.

that one word would be used so many times in one hymn. Either Newton was not a very good poet and couldn't think of very many synonyms for the word "grace," or he felt it was really important to focus almost exclusively on that one word. So what exactly was he trying to say?

Grace sounds sweet—"Amazing grace! How sweet the sound"

This is a good place to begin. The word certainly sounds good (or "sweet"). A couple of people I know have named their daughters Grace, probably because the word has a really nice feel to it. This reminds me of our response to something someone says to us, like "Let's go for a walk in the park," and we say, "Sounds good." We haven't had the experience yet, but we anticipate that we will like it. Grace is like that. We may not be able to point to God's grace in a specific way, yet we know that the concept of God's unmerited love and mercy sounds really, really good. Or, as the young people like to say in response to something they like: "Sweet!" Unfortunately, this response is often used in the context of illegal behavior, but oh well.

Grace saves wretches—"That saved a wretch like me"

This is obviously an autobiographical comment. As a former slave trader, Newton knew that his life had been wretched. He had hit rock bottom. To be "wretched" means to live in very unfortunate conditions or circumstances, to be pitiable. I believe Newton here is comparing his former life to that of the slaves who lived in extremely wretched conditions. The prodigal son in Jesus' parable was also a wretch in that he had left his father's comfortable home with his inheritance and squandered it all on dissolute living. His life became so pitiful that he decided to come back to his father's home even as a hired hand. And yet when he came home his father met him halfway and threw a big party for him. The prodigal son was saved from his wretchedness. That's what grace does.

Grace strengthens our spiritual well-being—
"I once was lost but now am found, was blind but now I see"

Again, this is an autobiographical statement. As a slave trader, Newton was spiritually "lost" and "blind." He had lost his humanity, and yet as a Christian he was spiritually "found." He was also blind to the plight of the African slaves, but God's grace had opened his eyes to their plight. Ironically, in his later years he actually became physically blind, yet he always believed that God's grace had given him spiritual sight. By the way, the phrase, "I once was lost but now am found" from "Amazing Grace," gains its inspiration from the end of the parable of the prodigal son. The prodigal son was literally lost in a distant country, but at the end of the parable the father tells the eldest son, "He [the younger brother] was lost and has been found."

The phrase, "was blind but now I see," also has its roots in other parts of the New Testament, particularly in stories like the one from John 9. Here a formerly blind man is trying to convince Jesus' critics that Jesus indeed healed his blindness. He said to them, "I do not know whether he [Jesus] is a sinner. One thing I do know, that though I was blind, now I see." God's grace strengthens our spiritual well-being by reversing our spiritual fortunes. Lost-ness becomes found-ness. Blindness becomes sight.

Grace schools us in fear—"Twas grace that taught my heart to fear, and grace my fears relieved"

There are two kinds of fear: healthy and unhealthy. Newton experienced God's grace as that which helped him to learn the difference between the two. "Twas grace that taught my heart to fear" refers to a healthy fear. Healthy fear is necessary for survival. Think of the fear induced by the lurking presence of a predator. Think of the fear of bodily harm or even death when we put ourselves in a dangerous situation. As a seafarer, Newton understood very well that it is sensible to fear such things as violent storms on the high seas. I'm not even sure if we really need God's grace to teach us that. Even the presence of unhealthy or unnecessary fear could result in God's grace working in our lives. If you or I felt like we were suffering from unnecessary or unhealthy phobias, we might go to a professional to receive therapeutic or medicinal help. These fears are symptoms of larger problems. And yet for Newton the only resource he had at that time in history was a simple, humble reliance upon God's grace. Grace, for many people in history, has been good therapy. At the very least, we today should try it as a supplement. Big Pharma should pay attention to this because at least grace doesn't come with a long list of possible side effects.

Grace starts with belief—
"How precious did that grace appear the hour I first believed"

Theologically speaking, God's grace is always operating in our lives, whether we believe it, perceive it, experience it, or not. Yet Newton wisely understood that sometimes we have to put our faith in something before we can recognize its benefits. As someone once said, "Some things must be believed before they can be seen." Of course, believing in grace is one thing; understanding it is another. Grace may be the most misunderstood and least applied doctrine in the Christian faith. Most people put requirements or restrictions on God's grace, which completely nullifies the very concept of grace. No matter how much lip service we give to God's grace, we still manage to criticize, judge, or condemn ourselves and others. That is, we still manage to act ungraceful to ourselves and others. In our heart of hearts we just never quite grow enough in our spiritual wisdom to consider that God's grace is as advertised: free, unmerited, and unconditional. We like the sweet sound of it, yet it rarely satisfies our spiritual sweet tooth. Maybe we just need to trust it a little more.

Grace shields us from spiritual pitfalls—
"Thru many dangers, toils and snares, I have already come; 'tis grace hath brought me safe thus far"

For Newton, this aspect of God's grace was not just a spiritual promise; it was a physical promise. After he had become a minister and his feet were securely planted on British soil, he looked back on his life and recognized that God had led him through some extremely difficult and dangerous times. The same could be said about the prodigal son, as he could no doubt look back and recognize that God's grace had kept him "safe and secure from all alarms." Have you ever looked back and reflected on where you've been, the stupid and dangerous things you've done, and thought, "God must have been looking out for me"? Whether God shields us from physical pitfalls—dangers, toils and snares—I don't know—and yet maybe we can make the case that God's grace shields us from spiritual pitfalls. We'll let that stand as a debatable point.

Grace secures our spiritual journeys—
"And grace will lead me home"

For Newton, "home" was more than just a metaphor. He really felt like God had led him back to Great Britain to pursue the ministry. For the prodigal son in Jesus' parable, his father's home was his literal destination after squandering his inheritance. Most of us, of course, already have a literal home, so the issue for us is more about our spiritual home. Has God led us to a good place in our souls? Are we spiritually secure? Are we comfortable in communion with one another? Does the house of God we frequent feel like a home to us? If it does then maybe God's grace has been working in our lives.

As Christians, we will always struggle with the notion of God's grace. We will struggle with its meaning and its application in our lives. We will struggle with the implication that God intervenes in our lives. Unlike John Newton, we may never experience God's grace to the point where we can write a song about it. Unlike Jesus, we may never invent a parable about it. We may never progress beyond the notion that it just sounds really sweet. Yet if Newton was right, we should at least try to whisper to ourselves in the quiet moments of our lives that God's grace really is amazing. And maybe, just maybe, our spiritual sweet tooth will be satisfied.

Luke 16:1–13

Then Jesus said to the disciples, "There was a rich man who had a manager, and charges were brought to him that this man was squandering his property. So he summoned him and said to him, 'What is this that I hear about you? Give me an accounting of your management, because you cannot be my manager any longer.' Then the manager said to himself, 'What will I do, now that my master is taking the position away from me? I am not strong enough to dig, and I am ashamed to beg. I have decided what to do so that, when I am dismissed as manager, people may welcome me into their homes.' So, summoning his master's debtors one by one, he asked the first, 'How much do you owe my master?' He answered, 'A hundred jugs of olive oil.' He said to him, 'Take your bill, sit down quickly, and make it fifty.' Then he asked another, 'And how much do you owe?' He replied, 'A hundred containers of wheat.' He said to him. 'Take your bill and make it eighty.' And his master commended the dishonest manager because he had acted shrewdly; for the children of this age are more shrewd in dealing with their own generation than are the children of light. And I tell you, make friends for yourselves by means of dishonest wealth so that when it is gone, they may welcome you into the eternal homes."

WHAT DO WE HAVE TO LOSE?

THE MAIN CHARACTER IN this parable seems to be rather immoral, yet I beg to differ. I think he became moral by cheating his boss. At the same time, he solved his problem. Here's what happened:

A rich man has a great deal of property. So many people are farming on his property that he needs a manager. Eventually someone brings charges against the manager that he is mismanaging the property. The property owner, of course, wants to get to the bottom of it, so he asks the manager to turn in his books, to show him he's doing a good job. The manager is understandably fearful that he will be fired. He says he is "not strong enough to dig" and is "ashamed to beg." He says that because a person who loses a job in that first-century economy can only resort to two things: doing work no one else wants to do, like digging graves (which makes a person religiously unclean and thus immortal), or begging. There are no other career opportunities for scandalized property managers in first-century Palestine.

So he comes up with a plan. He will go to all the people who are working the land he is managing and subtract from their lease agreements what he feels they are being overcharged. Of course they are ecstatic. They must think the landlord has suddenly become fair and generous. This puts the landowner in a bit of a bind. He can go back to the people who are working on his land and tell them the manager made a mistake, and that they owe what they previously owed. If he does that, however, the people will see him as greedy and nasty. He can also cut his losses and just fire his manager, yet if he does that he will now be firing a very popular manager, which will also make him look bad. Or he can just go to the manager and say, "Good job. Now, don't do that again." Which is exactly what he does.

Most commentators refer to the manager here as at least ethically suspicious, but I think he was being extraordinarily ethical. I think he thought to himself, "What do I have to lose? I will do what is right and, in the process, make my boss do the right thing." He did, and it worked. The reason we automatically assume he was being unethical, however, is because he was clever. Cleverness is probably the biggest asset of people in the world of crime. Drug dealers, mobsters, bank robbers, to name a few, have been some of the cleverest people that have ever lived. (At least until they got caught.) I think we tend to associate cleverness and shrewdness with people who may not be the most morally upright people around. There's just something about an act of cleverness that we don't quite trust. And yet the parable of the shrewd manager in Luke 16 suggests that Jesus saw cleverness as a virtue.

Cleverness doesn't have to be a tool only for the immoral. By commending the cleverness of an immoral person, Jesus is not commending the fact that he is immoral. Instead, he wants the "children of light" to be just as clever, just as shrewd, just as intelligent, and just as witty as those who use these things for immoral gain. Cleverness is morally neutral. In and of itself, it is not right or wrong. It depends how you use it. We often see people using something for bad that could be used for good. People can use something that is morally neutral for ill or good.

Jesus himself was a very clever person. Of course, he didn't use his cleverness for bad, but for good. For example, he had a clever way of answering people's questions with another question. This would cause the other person to understand more clearly what their motives really were. His parables and short sayings are extremely clever because they are so provocative. They make us think. And anyone who can make people think is certainly using the tool of cleverness. Jesus also employed witticisms that would create a response in his listeners. You can't ignore the things he said.

His acts and deeds were just as clever. What we often call "miracles" were certainly clever deeds even if they weren't actual miracles. Take for example the feeding of the five thousand. Rather than a miracle, many commentators have noted that his true genius was getting people to share what they had with others so that everyone was fed.

Unfortunately, we don't use the tools of cleverness, shrewdness, intelligence, and wit as well in our spiritual lives as we do in our life "out there." We tend to think that we should use one set of tools, like cleverness, in the secular part of our lives, yet we should give these things up in the sacred part of our lives. The message of the parable of the shrewd manager is that there is not a separate set of virtues for the sacred and the secular. Followers of Christ should employ all the tools available to us in all aspects of our lives, including bringing Jesus' vision of the realm of God to the world. If that means we should be as clever as we can, then we should do so. We should be shrewd, intelligent, creative, and astute. We need to use all the resources available to us so that those who do not experience the love of God are not left out simply because we refuse to use our minds and ingenuity to reach them. If the shrewd manager in Jesus' parable can cleverly make their lives a little better, then you and I can cleverly make the world a little better with the message of God's unconditional love.

Luke 16:19–31

There was a rich man who was dressed in purple and fine linen and who feasted sumptuously every day. And at his gate lay a poor man named Lazarus, covered with sores, who longed to satisfy his hunger with what fell from the rich man's table; even the dogs would come and lick his sores. The poor man died and was carried away by the angels to be with Abraham. The rich man also died and was buried. In Hades, where he was being tormented, he looked up and saw Abraham far away with Lazarus by his side. He called out, "Father Abraham, have mercy on me, and send Lazarus to dip the tip of his finger in water and cool my tongue; for I am in agony in these flames." But Abraham said, "Child, remember that during your lifetime you received your good things, and Lazarus in like manner evil things; but now he is comforted here, and you are in agony. Besides all this, between you and us a great chasm has been fixed, so that those who might want to pass from here to you cannot do so, and no one can cross from there to us." He said, "Then, father, I beg you to send him to my father's house— for I have five brothers—that he may warn them, so that they will not also come into this place of torment." Abraham replied, "They have Moses and the prophets; they should listen to them." He said, "No, father Abraham; but if someone goes to them from the dead, they will repent." He said to him, "If they do not listen to Moses and the prophets, neither will they be convinced even if someone rises from the dead."

TOO LATE

This parable speaks to the theme of putting our money where our mouth is, unless, of course, our mouth is in a place that would embarrass our money. Unfortunately, it is about a man who learned this principle too late. In this parable, a beggar named Lazarus hangs out in front of a rich man's gate every day, hoping to get some food, if only crumbs from the rich man's table. As fate would have it, both men die. The angels take the poor man to Abraham. Apparently, in the mythology of Jesus' day, people who died "saw" Abraham; much like Christians today believe they will see Jesus when they die. (If any of this is true, I'm curious about who the heathens will meet.) The rich man, on the other hand, goes to Hades, which is not exactly to be equated with modern notions of hell, but close. Because heaven is up and Hades is down, the rich man looks up and sees Lazarus with Abraham in a much better place. Some versions of this story say Lazarus went to Abraham's "bosom," which is oddly homoerotic.

The rich man is desperate. He wants Abraham to send Lazarus, a man he has ignored all these years, to bring just a fingertip of water to his lips (remember Lazarus had only asked for the crumbs from the rich man's table). But Abraham said to the rich man, "Child, remember that during your lifetime you received your good things, and Lazarus in like manner evil things; but now he is comforted here, and you are in agony." This suggests there is an evening out of things—if you receive good things here, you receive bad things there, and vice versa. Now, don't take this literally. If we took this literally we would all start hoping bad things happen to us in this life, right?

There is also a large chasm between Hades and heaven so that people can't cross it. Not only can the rich man not cross over, neither can Lazarus cross over to help him. This is like a moat at a zoo that keeps the crocodiles away from the people, and vice versa. The rich man, knowing he can't be saved, shows a little humanity by asking Abraham to send Lazarus to his five brothers to warn them about their own despicable lifestyles so that they won't end up in Hades with him. Abraham gives a great reply: "Nah, they already have Moses and the prophets—they should just listen to them." "No, Father Abraham," says the rich man, "but if someone goes to them from the dead, they will repent." Well, yes, I guess they would. Who wouldn't? But Abraham says, "No, that wouldn't work either. If they don't listen to Moses and the prophets, they sure ain't listening to someone who rises from the dead." This is obviously a clear nod to Jesus' resurrection. I think I would definitely listen to someone who rose from the dead. But that's just me.

The moral of that story is that if you are blessed with lots of resources in this life, don't wait until the next life to use it for good. It will be too late then. Put your money where your mouth is now. Unless your mouth is in a place where money loses its monetary value, in which case put it somewhere else.

Luke 17:5-10

The apostles said to the Lord, "Increase our faith." The Lord replied, "If you had faith the size of a mustard seed, you could say to this mulberry tree, 'Be uprooted and planted in the sea,' and it would obey you. Who among you would say to your slave who has just come in from plowing or tending sheep in the field, 'Come here at once and take your place at the table'? Would you not rather say to him, 'Prepare supper for me, put on your apron and serve me while I eat and drink; later you may eat and drink'? Do you thank the slave for doing what was commanded? So you also, when you have done all that you were ordered to do, say, 'We are worthless slaves; we have done only what we ought to have done.'"

JESUS, JESUS, QUITE CONTRARY

ARE YOU A CONTRARIAN? I always thought a contrarian was like that argumentative uncle you have to deal with at Thanksgiving, or that conspiracy theorist coworker, or that know-it-all neighbor—you know, anyone who has strong opinions that are contrary to your opinions. Specifically—and I did not know this—a contrarian is an investor who prefers to buy stocks when most people are selling, and vice versa. I find that interesting.

When I think of a contrarian I also think of the nursery rhyme: "Mary, Mary, quite contrary," which likely originated with Mary I of England, i.e. "Bloody Mary," who was, by all accounts, very quite contrary. I also think of the phrase, "Contrary to popular belief," which usually leads to something humorous, like, "Contrary to popular belief, a barrel full of monkeys isn't fun at all, and is in fact quite horrifying."

Christianity is full of contradictions and contrariness. A good example is Jesus himself. We see his contrarian nature close up in the above passage. Here Jesus says two things that are contrary to what most people believe. First, most people believe that we need a large amount of faith in order to do great things. Even the apostles believed this. They begged Jesus, "Increase our faith!" They were reacting to Jesus' radical teaching about forgiveness. Jesus said we need to forgive a person who sins against us every single time they sin against us, even if someone sins against us "seven times a day." Matthew's Jesus says "seventy times" or "seventy times seven." No matter which calculation you use, that's a lot of forgiveness. Most of us are not likely to be so forgiving. The apostles apparently do not believe they have enough faith to forgive someone so easily, so they beg Jesus to increase their faith.

Jesus is a contrarian, however, and perhaps a little frustrated with them, so he informs them that they already have enough faith—they just need to use it. He famously says, "If you had faith the size of a mustard seed (that is, tiny), you could say to this mulberry tree, 'Be uprooted and planted in the sea,' and it would obey you." Contrary to popular belief, we do not need to have a large amount of faith to do great spiritual things like practice unlimited forgiveness. Just exercise the faith you have. It would be too easy and not very clever to say at this point, "size doesn't matter," but apparently it does.

The second contrarian thing he says has to do with slaves coming in from the fields after a long, hard day's work. He notes that if you are a slave-owner you will not ask your slaves to sit down and enjoy a nice meal after they have worked all day. Instead, you will have them wait on you first and then they can enjoy their own meal. This sounds harsh to us because we are not slave-owners. Jesus was not condoning slavery or the mistreatment of slaves here. He is only describing what slaves do, which is work all day.

Likewise, followers of Jesus should do what they ought to do as well, which is work in the fields of God without expecting a reward at the end of the day. We don't work for the reward, he is saying. We work because we are responding to God's love and grace. Unfortunately, I'm pretty sure that if contemporary Christianity ceased with the reward and punishment message, many congregations would literally become the size of mustard seeds. By the way, when someone uses the word "literally" they usually don't mean it in the sense of actually being literal. In this instance, a congregation cannot literally become the size of a mustard seed without changing drastically our definition of a viable congregation. But I digress.

Let's not lose sight of my point, which is that Jesus was quite the contrarian. I'm not saying he was the kind of guy that would argue with a fence post, however, if you ever find yourself in a debate with Jesus, don't be so wooden.

Luke 17:11–19

On the way to Jerusalem Jesus was going through the region between Samaria and Galilee. As he entered a village, ten lepers approached him. Keeping their distance, they called out, saying, "Jesus, Master, have mercy on us!" When he saw them, he said to them, "Go and show yourselves to the priests." And as they went, they were made clean. Then one of them, when he saw that he was healed, turned back, praising God with a loud voice. He prostrated himself at Jesus' feet and thanked him. And he was a Samaritan. Then Jesus asked, "Were not ten made clean? But the other nine, where are they? Was none of them found to return and give praise to God except this foreigner?" Then he said to him, "Get up and go on your way; your faith has made you well."

AN ODE TO CELIO

LET ME TELL YOU about a man named Celio. When I was a boy working in my parents' grocery story in Sterling City, Texas, Celio was a hunched-over elderly gentleman who came in twice a year, each time to buy two bars of soap. I still remember his words as he was leaving the store: "I'm going down to the river to take a bath." He may have been going down to the river to pray as well, yet he respected the grocery store "code" to not discuss politics and religion in such a neutral cultural center as a mom and pop store in a one-horse town. Furthermore, I never learned why he always bought two bars of soap. I can only surmise that he bought a spare in case the first one slipped out of his hands. Because you know what they say: "Don't drop the soap."

Celio was not a frequent bather. After he left, we would spray Lysol all throughout the store because his stench was simply that bad. Road kill smelled like fresh roses next to Celio. As far as we could tell he never changed clothing because he always wore the same old green jacket. Celio was dirty, filthy, and smelly. He must have never heard, or didn't believe, that famous saying that every generation passes on to their children: "Cleanliness is next to godliness." By the way, that's not a Bible verse. I assume that some beleaguered parents invented the saying in order to coerce their children to take a bath. I also assume that we are one of the cleanest cultures that have ever existed (especially since Celio is no longer with us). There are hundreds of products available in your nearest drug store for cleaning not only the human body but floors, toilets, clothing, sinks, furniture, appliances, the air, and even our pets and automobiles. We are nothing if not clean freaks. College students and hitchhikers excluded.

The main reason we are so concerned about cleanliness is obviously related to health concerns. History has taught us the valuable lessons that unsanitary conditions spread germs that can harm people. If you want to know what history has taught us, read Jared Diamond's Pulitzer Prize-winning book *Guns, Germs, and Steel,* where he explains the role germs have had in the destruction of various societies. But hindsight is 20/20. Learning the effects of germs due to unsanitary conditions was a hard lesson for humanity to learn. After the Roman Empire fell we entered into what is now called "The Dark Ages." The folks in that day took a poll to see what they would label their era in history. "Dark Ages" narrowly defeated "Stinky Ages." (That's not true.)

Of course, humanity paid a price for this faith in un-cleanliness. During the Dark Ages, unsanitary behavior led to filth diseases that swept over Europe and Asia, claiming over forty million lives. The phrase "filth diseases," by the way, was coined in 1958 by British physician Charles Murchison "to describe a class of conditions, mostly caused by infectious pathogens that were associated with squalid living conditions."[1] Of course you don't have to be a physician or have a germ phobia to understand that uncleanliness can lead to health problems. Even before science confirmed how unsanitary conditions could harm our health, most people were aware that there are certain health advantages to cleanliness.

There are also social advantages to cleanliness. Aldous Huxley, author of *Brave New World,* wrote an essay called "Hyperion to a Satyr," in which he argues that our perceptions of cleanliness and uncleanliness have helped to

---

1. "Filth Diseases." https://www.encyclopedia.com/education/encyclopedias-almanacs-transcripts-and-maps/filth-diseases.

increase the gap between the different social classes. By the way, a "satyr" in Greek mythology is a lecherous woodland deity represented as a man with a goat's legs, ears, and horns. Presumably, a satyr would be dirty because he lives among the animals. (That's pure speculation.) Cleanliness, according to Huxley, is a mark of upper class citizenship; uncleanliness signifies that someone is of the lower classes. To prove his point, if you saw someone walking toward you with tattered and dirty clothing—someone like Celio— you would automatically assume, rightly or wrongly, that this person was poor and uneducated, would you not?[2] Cleanliness, therefore, not only has health ramifications, but social ramifications.

This was even truer in the culture in which Jesus lived. We can assume that those people were, on the average, far dirtier than we are today. If Jesus returned today in his original state, the B.O. would be noticeable enough to call into question his divine status. (Now, that is true.) Bathing was much more problematic and they didn't exactly have convenient drug stores on every corner with hundreds of cleaning products from which to choose. Staying clean in such a time and place was a monumental task to say the least. Most people were poor, had little access to bathing, had precious few garments to wear, and lived among open sewers. Even the wealthiest, most refined people in that day were dirty compared to twenty-first century Americans. In such a context, where everyone was relatively dirty and smelly, how could you tell who was truly unclean? After all, human beings have a natural tendency to compare themselves to others. I may be dirty and smelly, but I'm not as dirty and smelly as "those people." So who were "those people"?

There were quite a few groups of people who were considered to be unclean in Jesus' day. And when I say "unclean" I mean—because they meant—people who were not only hygienically unclean but religiously unclean as well. One could be unclean literally and religiously. In Stephen Patterson's essay, "Dirt, Shame, and Sin: The Expendable Company of Jesus," he argues that in Jesus' culture, as in most, "there is an explicit connection between being clean and being holy."[3] Cleanliness is next to godliness. This, he says, is why people have traditionally worn their "Sunday best" to go to church and why not too many years ago the Saturday night bath was a weekly ritual in preparation for Sunday worship.

In Jesus' day, the unclean included such dirty people as gentiles, prostitutes, and even tax collectors. They also believed in unclean spirits, which

---

2. "Adolphus Huxley's Hyperion to a Satyr." 123HelpMe.com. https://www.123helpme.com/view.asp?id=32729.

3. Patterson, "Dirt, Shame, and Sin," 207.

required a cleaning of the soul through an exorcism. And yet at the top of the list of the unclean were the lepers. A note of explanation is required here. In the ancient world, leprosy was a name given to various skin diseases such as what we now call psoriasis, eczema, scabies or ringworms. Dandruff probably totally freaked them out too. The assumption was—rightly or wrongly—that people with a skin disease were unclean. As I said, uncleanliness in that day had not only health ramifications—it had social and religious ramifications as well. To be unclean meant that you were not only dirty, you were also unholy. Cleanliness is next to godliness. That was—and still is—the assumption. Presumably, Mr. Clean is our highest high priest.

Jesus, however, had a different assumption. For Jesus, there is just as much truth in the saying, "uncleanliness is next to godliness." Let me explain what I mean by looking more closely at the story of the ten lepers. Jesus enters a border town between Galilee and Samaria. Border towns are often mixed in terms of ethnicity and culture. They tend to be gathering places for social outcasts, people who feel like they don't belong fully to either neighboring culture. In this case, this unnamed village probably consisted of relatively poor Jewish Galileans and Samaritans, people who were considered to be unclean because they were ethnically impure. Ten lepers come near Jesus, yet keep a proper distance. They know there is a social taboo against people with skin diseases coming too close to others. Nevertheless, they beg for mercy. Now, why are they begging for mercy rather than healing? The answer is that they believe religious uncleanliness is more detrimental to them than physical uncleanliness. And to be cured of religious uncleanliness requires mercy rather than a bar of soap or skin ointment, neither of which was at their disposal anyway.

After their cry for mercy, Jesus does something totally unexpected. He tells these lepers to go and show themselves to the local priests. Why doesn't he tell them to go and show themselves to a local physician? Because he understands that they want religious cleanliness or healing even more than physical cleanliness or healing. Luke tells us that, "as they went, they were made clean." Given the context of this phrase we can assume that the lepers now see themselves as religiously clean. This may sound odd to the reader, yet I would argue that their literal skin disease, whatever it is, remains with them, while the disease of their soul, their psyche, is healed by the authoritative words of Jesus. Despite their dirty and diseased appearance, they are now in the good graces of God.

Let's be pragmatic for a moment. God doesn't have a nose or an immune system, so dirty folks are actually no problem for the Woman up the Escalator. (I say "Woman up the Escalator" to give balance to the lame moniker for God found at every McDonald's breakfast table conversation where aging white dudes refer to God as the "Man Upstairs.")

The confusion of this passage lies in verse 15 where Luke writes that one of them, a Samaritan, "saw that he was healed," and most readers assume that this means his skin disease is literally cleared up. However, again, operating within the overall context of this story, we can assume that what the Samaritan experiences is religious cleanliness. One reason he finds more joy in this occasion than the other nine lepers is because he has been cured of multiple impurities: uncleanliness due to his skin disease, due to his ethnicity, and due to his religion. He believes that Jesus heals him on all counts.

Another source of confusion may be verse 19 where Luke quotes Jesus as saying to the Samaritan: "Get up and go on your way; your faith has made you well." Again, readers might assume that the word "well" refers to physical health, yet the word in its original language is closer to the notion of "salvation" or "'wholeness.'" The Samaritan's faith or trust in what Jesus has done for him brings a sense of wholeness to this man, even if his skin disease remains a problem.

Uncleanliness is next to godliness. For Jesus, this is as true as the saying "cleanliness is next to godliness" because of one very important truth about human beings that we see most clearly in the Samaritan: People often have to hit the proverbial "rock bottom" before they can open themselves to the presence, grace, and healing of a loving God. As I said, the Samaritan experienced more joy in his situation than the other nine lepers did because he had more to gain from Jesus' touch of grace. Jesus offered him a sense of "wholeness," from which we derive the word "salvation," and "affirmation," affirming him despite the public perception of his uncleanliness.

Few of us have been where this first-century Samaritan leper was. Yet haven't we all experienced uncleanliness at one point or another? Have you ever had a serious, even contagious, illness? Have you ever been quarantined, even in subtle ways because of your ethnicity or your religious beliefs? Have you ever been considered socially unacceptable because of your job, your meager bank account, your clothing, or the car you drive? Have you ever been scorned for your lifestyle, for wearing tattoos or having a minority sexual orientation? Have you ever been ostracized because you have been in prison or a mental institution? Have you ever been ignored because the gossip mill has uncovered and publicized an indiscretion on your part? If you've never been unclean, then count yourself among the few lucky ones in human history. Hopefully, your cleanliness will not bar you from the kingdom of God.

THE WEAPON OF MASS DETACHMENT

The lepers in this story had been prosecuted to the full extent of the law in first-century Palestine. Because the law found them unclean, they were not allowed to trespass on anyone's property or even walk on the same side of the road as other people. Other than good health the one thing the lepers desperately needed was mercy. Unfortunately, in a religious system that was based on so many oppressive laws, mercy was in short supply. The lepers couldn't even appeal to God for mercy because their religion had usurped the power to withhold and mete out God's mercy. According to their belief system, God could only show mercy on those whom the religious authorities deemed worthy and acceptable.

If you were a leper in first-century Palestine, you had proof on your skin that you were not worthy to receive God's mercy. Religions may not be able to judge a person's heart, yet they sure can judge a person's skin. Leprosy is a word the Bible uses to describe any and all kinds of skin diseases during that time. The accuracy of the diagnosis, however, wasn't important, because anyone who suffered from something so obvious was considered a victim of God's wrath. The writer George Eliot criticized modern humanity by saying, "We hand folks over to God's mercy, and show none ourselves."[4] Nevertheless, despite the shortcomings of our lack of mercy today, it sure beats the first-century version of religion where they wouldn't even hand folks over to God's mercy in the first place. After all, if God had punished them in such an obvious fashion then what gives us the right to ask God to be merciful to them?

What I find interesting about the religious situation in first-century Palestine is that those who needed mercy couldn't get it, whereas those who presumably didn't need mercy had it in spades. It seems to me that a good religion would be one where those who need mercy can get it, and yet their theology—God punishes the evildoer and rewards the righteous—wouldn't allow it. Mercy does not and cannot exist in a law-based religion. So imagine being one of the ten lepers who are walking down the road in a village that borders the provinces of Samaria and Galilee. At least one of them is a Samaritan. Most, if not all, of the rest are Jewish Galileans. In normal circumstances, Samaritans and Galileans wouldn't be in one another's company. Samaritans, simply because of their ethnicity, are unclean. However, since all of the ten have rotten skin they are forced to create their own community. Today we talk about living in bubbles. Can you imagine the insular existence of these lepers? Not to mention the gross bubbles on their skin.

---

4. Eliot, *Adam Bede,* quote in subtitle.

The word gets to these lepers that Jesus of Nazareth is in town. Jesus' reputation precedes him. He is already known as a religious authority that operates outside of the box. They knew that he had had disputes with the religious authorities over issues that pertained to the Jewish purity laws. Jesus had shown mercy to the sick on the Sabbath, to women of ill repute, and even to tax collectors. Perhaps, they must have thought, Jesus will show mercy to them as well. "Jesus, Master, have mercy on us!" they shouted. There was no hesitation on Jesus' part. He knew instinctively that these people were victims, not just of their unfortunate skin disease, but of the oppressive purity laws. He says to them, "Go and show yourselves to the priests."

This is interesting advice because Jesus knew the local priests would never declare these lepers to be clean. They certainly would not do so based on Jesus' authority alone. Is Jesus showing a little moxie at this point? Does he really have the nerve to send these lepers to the priests as if he is thumbing his nose at them and their oppressive purity laws? We don't know if the lepers even made it to the priests' office. The text doesn't tell us. All we know is that "as they went, they were made clean." The story doesn't claim that they were cured of their skin disease. Rather, they found God's mercy through the authority of Jesus. They accepted the fact that they were clean in the eyes of God.

This story represents an ongoing battle between two opposing theologies in that day (as well as our own). The orthodox view at the time was that lepers were among the cursed. They were being punished by God. Therefore, the priests had no choice but to declare them to be unclean. Jesus' theology was very different. He believed that God's rain falls on the just and the unjust alike. In other words, one couldn't judge someone just because they did or did not have a skin disease or some other misfortune. Much like the theological battles that take place today, the two sides in Jesus' day each had their weapon of choice. For the orthodox, God's wrath was their choice. This theological army is perhaps best represented today by the televangelists, who periodically claim that people who are killed or injured in natural disasters are victims of God's wrath because of some "sin" such as tolerance toward homosexuals or support of evolution.

The weapon of God's wrath has been used effectively by Christians for centuries. They have "won" many battles with it. I once had a professor who told us that Christians have used the doctrine of hell like the Crusaders used the sword. Any time we can scare people into believing and acting a certain way by threatening the wrath of God then we have chosen to fight alongside those who, in the first century, declared the lepers to be unclean. The weapon of God's wrath and judgment is rooted in prejudice and partiality. It divides and conquers. It divides people into good and bad, just and unjust, clean and unclean. The lepers were the losers in this battle between good and evil.

Jesus, however, used a very different weapon. His weapon of choice was mercy. I believe this is the most powerful weapon in the universe. (Unless the Force is with you, then we need to talk.) This weapon has very different results than the weapon of God's wrath. For starters, the weapon of mercy produces no losers. Mercy is not rooted in prejudice and partiality. Mercy doesn't divide people into two neat categories: good and evil, just and unjust, clean and unclean. The weapon of mercy cuts to the heart of every man, woman, and child, telling them that while they are less than perfect, they are more than worthy.

In 2003 we went to war based on faulty information that Saddam Hussein had weapons of mass destruction. The weapon of God's wrath is a weapon of mass destruction because multitudes of people have been victims of this weapon. Jesus' contemporaries did a wonderful job of projecting God's wrath on people like the lepers, the prostitutes, and the tax collectors while they were trying to deflect God's wrath away from themselves. They knew that they could become a victim of friendly fire any day. All they had to do was break a simple purity law.

The weapon of mercy is also a WMD, yet of a different sort. Mercy is a weapon of mass *detachment.* To be detached means to be free from prejudice or partiality. Jesus based his entire mission strategy on the weapon of mass detachment. He was not attached so much to any particular doctrine, code of conduct, or religious ritual that he couldn't show mercy to those who went astray.

Two weapons, then, have dominated the theological wars of Christian history: wrath and mercy. Each elicits a different response. Wrath elicits a response of fear. Mercy elicits a response of thanksgiving. The reason, I think, many Christians utilize the weapon of wrath so much is because it seems to get better results. If Jesus would have pronounced God's wrath on the lepers all ten of them would have responded with fear. Although he used the weapon of mercy, only one of the ten responded with thanksgiving. Perhaps the Samaritan leper who came back to offer thanks felt that he received the most mercy from Jesus simply because he was a Samaritan. The Samaritans deserved only God's wrath. They were ethnically unclean. Not only did this Samaritan have an observable skin disease, he also had the wrong blood. He was the unclean of the unclean. And he was the only leper that offered Jesus thanks.

If only one out of ten of the lepers returned to offer Jesus thanks, how can I possibly claim that mercy is more powerful than wrath? Doesn't history teach us that it's safer and more efficient to use the weapon of God's wrath? Isn't mercy a risky weapon, one that can easily backfire? Yes it is, but isn't it better to have a one-in-ten chance of creating something good and beautiful rather than no chance at all? People respond in kind. If the weapon of wrath is used on them, they are likely to return the same kind of fire. Wrath, judgment, and all similar calibers of weaponry evoke a similar response. Before you know it, we are locked in a vicious cycle, each bullet of wrath eliciting a similar bullet from the other side. By using the weapon of God's wrath there is little chance of creating something as wonderful as a human being giving his or her heart and soul to God.

If the weapon of mercy is used, however, there is a good chance people will ignore us, use us, abuse us, and take advantage of us. Because people are so used to being in the vicious cycle of prejudice and partiality, they don't often trust mercy. Nevertheless, every once in a while someone will accept the mercy that has been fired at them and they will respond in a way that will make the angels sing. Mercy is the most powerful weapon in the universe. It can inspire the afflicted to fall on their knees in praise to God. It can persuade evil men to turn their lives around. As a weapon, mercy may only work about 10 percent of the time, yet that's better than nothing.

LUKE 18:1–8

Then Jesus told them a parable about their need to pray always and not to lose heart. He said, "In a certain city there was a judge who neither feared God nor had respect for people. In that city there was a widow who kept coming to him and saying, 'Grant me justice against my opponent.' For a while he refused; but later he said to himself, 'Though I have no fear of God and no respect for anyone, yet because this widow keeps bothering me, I will grant her justice, so that she may not wear me out by continually coming.'" And the Lord said, "Listen to what the unjust judge says. And will not God grant justice to his chosen ones who cry to him day and night? Will he delay long in helping them? I tell you, he will quickly grant justice to them. And yet, when the Son of Man comes, will he find faith on earth?"

DON'T LOOK A GIFT HORSE IN THE MOUTH

IN THIS PARABLE OF the unjust judge, Jesus seems to encourage us to bug or nag God in prayer. A widow relentlessly pursues justice against her opponent, although we are never told what the opponent did. We can assume that, because she is a defenseless widow, as all widows were in that day, someone is taking advantage of her. It was either a Nigerian prince who wrote her an emotional email or a handsome snake oil salesman. At first the unjust judge refuses to help her, but eventually he gives in because he doesn't want the widow to continue coming to him and wearing him out. He has better things to do. Tee time is at 2:30. He has other cases to resolve. He's more interested in people paying him under the table and other unethical practices that will make him rich. He couldn't care less about this widow woman, and yet to get her out of his hair he brings justice to her situation. (I almost wrote, "He could care less," because that's what all my friends say, and then I point out that it is more accurate to say, "I *couldn't* care less" and usually they respond, "I could care less what you think.")

Jesus then offers the moral to the story: If even an unjust human judge will eventually come around and help someone in need, will not the Almighty Judge do what is right at all times? But we have to keep on keeping on. Jesus suggests that God will answer our prayers if we are persistent. *Does God always answer our prayers if we are persistent?* Some might say, "Yes, but sometimes God answers with a 'no.'" Perhaps it is true that God says "no" to us at times, yet this is merely an assumption on our part. We are assuming that the silent response to our prayers is a "no" when it could just as well be a non-response. Of course, we are also assuming God exists or isn't the kind of God who couldn't care less what we pray. Regardless, if we follow the wisdom of Jesus' parable, we should ignore all the "no"s or non-responses to our prayers and continue to bug God until God says "yes," much like a salesperson ignores the first few "no"s of a prospective customer. I learned to do this long ago in a sales training seminar. This philosophy works fairly well in door-to-door sales, and yet it doesn't work very well in relationships.

There are many types of prayers. There are the traditional prayers of adoration or praise, prayers of thanksgiving, and prayers of confession. Recently there has been a rediscovery of meditation and contemplation, types of prayer that come from the monastic traditions. Yet the type of prayer that seems to be implied in Jesus' parable are prayers of petition. When we pray a prayer of petition, we are asking God for something. Like the widow in the parable, we might ask that God help us not to be a victim of injustice. When we ask God to heal the sick or comfort those who mourn, we are engaging in intercessory prayer, which is a type of petition.

Whether we ask God for something that benefits us or benefits others, prayers of petition are theologically problematic for many modern Christians. For some Christians, asking God for something seems a little silly. In contrast, praising God, offering thanks to God, or confessing our sins in prayer doesn't seem silly. Meditating on God's love or contemplating the presence of God doesn't seem silly. But giving God a verbal wishlist as if God is a heavenly Santa Claus who will give you what you pray for if you are good enough or persistent enough seems a little silly. Although, Santa Claus unequivocally does not seem silly. Santa is real.

Why do many Christians have a problem with prayers of petition? First, if God already knows our needs and wishes, why do we need to persistently nag God about them? Most people believe God is omniscient or all-knowing, that we can't hide anything from God, not even our darkest secrets or our deepest wishes. Most people believe God already knows what we need. If that's true, then what's the point of asking God for something over and over again? Don't we insult God by acting as if God needs to be reminded about these things? Doesn't persistent, nagging prayer imply a senile God? Do we really need to wake up every morning and say, "God, you know that new job I want? When are you going to get it for me? Why do I have to keep reminding you about it?" Obviously, none of us believe God is ignorant or senile, which is why some people have a problem with asking God for things. (Correction: There *is* a theological school of thought that suggests God is ignorant or senile. It is a group of elderly scholars who believe they were made in God's image and well, some of them are ignorant or senile.)

Second, there is the reality of unanswered petitions and intercessory prayers. Let's be honest. I realize honesty is about as popular among confessing Christians as a Hummer is among tree-huggers, so just humor me for a moment. We have all prayed for things that simply did not materialize. I'm sure we have all prayed for someone's healing only to discover that they did not recover from their illness or injury. We have all prayed for world peace, for an end to world hunger, and for a total cure for cancer. If we say that God has simply said "no" to these prayers, then we have to grapple with the reality of a God who doesn't seem to care about people very much.

Should I even say it? It is entirely possible that God doesn't give a hoot about humanity while lavishly offering divine love to penguins. Have you ever seen a starving, injured, sick, mentally ill, or dead penguin? Me neither.

Theologically, many people have difficulty with prayers of petition. Because of that, many people choose not to pray those kinds of prayers. Even when an "asking" prayer seems to work, many people are actually shocked. A minister stopped during his morning walk when he saw a man bending over one of the tires of his car. The rear had been jacked up, and the man was tugging at the tire while muttering profanities. Then he stood up, kicked at the tire, and expressed his feelings at the top of his voice. The minister came over to him and said, "My good man, surely there is no need for such heated profanity. Why don't you calm down and try the power of prayer." The man turned to the preacher and said, "You mean pray about something as mundane as a flat tire? How do I do that?" "Why, I'll show you," said the minister. "It's the simplest thing in the world." The minister raised his eyes to heaven and said, "Our heavenly Father, if it be Thy pleasure, help guide this man to faith and make him aware that all in the universe, from the mightiest star to the tiniest fly, is in Thy hands at all times. Let this man in true contrition of soul find that the removal of this tire is not a hard task for one with faith." As the final syllable fell from his lips, the tire quivered and, of its own accord, plopped off the wheel, made a short spinning clatter on one side, and lay still. The minister stared at it for a moment, then muttered, "Well, I'll be damned." Note: the very same thing happened to me opening a jar of pickles.

Do you see the problem that confronts us? Even when prayer seems to work, we have a hard time believing it. Again, to many modern Christians prayers of petition do not make good theological sense. It seems kind of silly, like a child sitting in Santa's lap asking for a BB gun. Nevertheless, I still believe we can justify prayers of petition for ourselves and others. I still believe there are good reasons to pray for things. Let me offer three good reasons:

First, these prayers feel like a natural way to express our cares and concerns. I've said many times that our prayers are simply an expression of our sincerest hopes and dreams. Just as it is natural for a child to ask for something he or she wants for Christmas or a birthday, so is it natural for people to express their hopes and dreams, cares and concerns, to a higher power. It may not make much theological sense to do so, but it is natural to do so.

Second, there is evidence that prayers for healing *do* have a positive effect on people. I once participated in an academic forum that had studied the connection between health and spirituality. I learned that there is a growing body of research that shows a positive correlation between health and spirituality. The evidence suggests that prayer does have a positive effect on people's health. How we explain this reality is not as important as the reality itself. Marcus Borg, in his book, *The Heart of Christianity*, says, "To refuse to (pray these kinds of prayers) because we can't imagine how they work is an act of intellectual pride."[1] We will probably never know how prayer works, and to what extent prayer works. All we need to know is that prayers never hurt anyone, and sometimes they actually seem to help. The only prayers that seem to hurt people are those that compel your mom to say, "Be careful what you pray for."

Third, regardless of how or when these prayers work, they serve the central purpose of all types of prayer: intimacy with God. Whether we pray verbal prayers of adoration and praise, prayers of thanksgiving, prayers of confession, prayers of petition or intercession, or whether we pray silent prayers of meditation and contemplation, they all have one common goal: intimacy with God. That's reason enough to pray. Jesus concludes the parable of the unjust judge by asking, "When the Son of Man comes, will he find faith on earth?" I think this is what prayer is all about. Prayer is directly linked to faith. We are called to persist in prayer,

---

1. Borg, *Heart of Christianity*, 197.

not because God will finally give up and answer our prayers. We are called to persist in prayer because prayer has a profound effect on our faith. Faith without prayer is dead. (And works. Don't forget works.) Prayer without faith just doesn't happen. So leave this page with one goal in mind, to bug and nag God as much as you can. And if and when one of your prayers seems to be answered someday, don't look a gift horse in the mouth.

Luke 18:9–14

He also told this parable to some who trusted in themselves that they were righteous and regarded others with contempt: "Two men went up to the temple to pray, one a Pharisee and the other a tax collector. The Pharisee, standing by himself, was praying thus, 'God, I thank you that I am not like other people: thieves, rogues, adulterers, or even like this tax collector. I fast twice a week; I give a tenth of all my income.' But the tax collector, standing far off, would not even look up to heaven, but was beating his breast and saying, 'God, be merciful to me, a sinner!' I tell you, this man went down to his home justified rather than the other; for all who exalt themselves will be humbled, but all who humble themselves will be exalted."

MODERATION IN ALL THINGS

MOST OF US WOULD agree that the Protestant Reformation was a moderating influence on Christianity. Martin Luther's 95 theses nailed to the church door at Wittenberg, in which he criticized the sale of indulgences, were statements of religious moderation in the context of what was happening in the church at that time. Today, when we examine the religious landscape, isn't it true that mainline Protestantism is the most moderate form of religious expression, particularly in America? What I mean by "moderate" is that it avoids extremes. Unless we count boredom, then all bets are off. Of course, on occasion mainline Protestants do things that other people would find extreme—such as the former president of the United Church of Christ, John Thomas, getting arrested for protesting the war in Iraq in front of the White House—although it's hard to label something "extreme" when so many Americans agree with a particular action.

On the other hand, religious extremism outside of the mainline church abounds. One thinks of the comments made by Jerry Falwell and Pat Robertson after Hurricane Katrina, blaming the hurricane on specific groups of people Falwell and Robertson didn't like, such as gays and abortionists. I know this question has been asked numerous times: would Falwell, Robertson, and their ilk approve of the abortion of future gay, lesbian, bisexual, and transgender persons? Just asking. Or, going back to 1992 during the Republican National Convention, when Pat Buchanan, a Catholic, declared that there was "a religious war going on in our country for the soul of America." Those are the words of an extremist, and words that made many of the convention-goers very uneasy. I would simply make the observation that most of the religious extremists in America today have very little or no connection to mainline Protestantism or, historically, to the Protestant Reformation. This is why I say that the Reformation and its offspring is a moderating influence on American life, as well as in other countries where Protestantism is present.

Having said that, I have to admit I was struck by the absence of religious moderation in either character in Luke 18:9–14. Both the Pharisee and the tax collector represent religious extremism, yet on different sides of the spectrum. Some people might say the Pharisee had too much religion, whereas the tax collector didn't seem to have enough. Although Jesus obviously favors the tax collector in this parable by claiming that he (not the Pharisee) was "justified" and "exalted," I'm not sure I want to use the tax collector as an appropriate model for my religiosity either. I mean, wouldn't that entail becoming a criminal and stealing from people (even if the New Testament is overstating the thievery of first-century tax collectors)? I struggle enough with whether my current profession is an honest way of making a living, so I don't think I want to take on a profession that many people abhor just so I can walk into a church and fall on my knees and beg for God's mercy. To set the record straight, my profession is an honest one, albeit one that only works one hour per week, or so people tell me.

Jesus' parable seems to be making the case that there are two extremes of religiosity. There is the self-righteous, holier-than-thou, self-imposed sainthood represented by the Pharisee, and there is the repentant, self-deprecating, lower than a worm sinner represented by the tax collector. Jesus' listeners would have had a difficult time discerning who is the hero and who is the villain in this parable. J. Ellsworth Kalas, in an essay titled, "Why Doesn't God Like Religious People?" lays out the dilemma for Jesus' listeners:

On the surface, of course, the people admired the Pharisees. They were in awe of their public righteousness, but they seldom liked them. It's hard to like someone who's always looking at you disapprovingly and perhaps even condescendingly. The tax collectors were no better. They were collaborating with a despised foreign government, that of the Romans. Not only were they collecting taxes—a burdensome calling at best—but also they were violating their ties with their own people and their own religious heritage each day they did so.

If the Pharisee and the tax collector were mascots for first-century sports teams, the people wouldn't root for either team. Interestingly, Jesus favors the tax-collecting sinner over the Pharisaical saint, although I suspect that he is not so much applauding the repentant sinner as he is chastising those who believe they have cornered the market on religious faithfulness, as extremists are known to do.

This parable offers several reasons why we should avoid religious extremism, especially the kind the Pharisee represents, and why we should seek religious moderation. First, religious extremism is characterized by self-righteousness. Luke writes that Jesus told this parable "to some who trusted in themselves that they were righteous." Self-righteousness was just as common in Jesus' day as it is in our own. Who would have thought? A major part of their religion was the "purity codes." The religious elites of that day knew about the codes and followed them (at least in public), and therefore considered themselves to be righteous. The general population, which was largely illiterate, knew very little about the codes and knew they were not following them properly, thus they were in need of God's grace.

This has a parallel in the story of the Protestant Reformation. The early reformers emphasized how inept our attempts at being righteous really are. Luther had a particularly hard struggle with this. We are sinners, they said, and the only thing we can rely upon is God's grace. An early Reformation theme that has continued in evangelical Christianity is that we are saved not by our works but by our faith. In true Reformation Christianity there is no room for self-righteousness, yet that's what happens when religion becomes extreme.

Second, religious extremism is too often contemptuous of others. Luke says that Jesus told this parable to those who were self-righteous and who "regarded others with contempt." This is illustrated very clearly in the Pharisee's prayer: "God, I thank you that I am not like other people: thieves, rogues, adulterers, or even like this tax collector." Even today this is a strong characteristic of extremists. Pat Buchanan's 1992 declaration of a religious war was against, in his words, "radicals and liberals" who were in favor of "radical feminism . . . abortion on demand . . . (and) homosexual rights."[1] (Since then the right has moved on to other issues such as feminism, abortion, and homosexuality. Wait. What?) Extremists need enemies. They are quick to judge and condemn others who they believe do not live up to the "highest standards" of the Christian faith.

Let me offer another example of this kind of extremism. A few years ago, a United Church of Christ congregation in Texas was told it could not participate in an evangelical Christian program that assists children of prisoners because of the church's outspoken gay-friendly stance. The Reverend Dan DeLeon, then pastor of Friends Congregational UCC in College Station, Texas, said he learned that his church was disqualified from Prison Fellowship's Angel Tree program, which encourages churches to buy Christmas presents for the children of inmates. This kind of contemptuousness is what happens when Christians become extreme fanatics in their religious views and practices. Of course, to be fair, the evangelicals may have been afraid that homosexuality is a medical condition that is transferred through the exchange of angel ornaments on trees.

Third, extremist religion often leads to irrational beliefs and practices. We see a hint of this at the end of the Pharisee's prayer where he claims that he fasts "twice a week," and gives "a tenth" of his income. At first glance this sounds really impressive. However, I doubt anyone fasts twice a week and gives a tenth of their income, what we call a "tithe." If they did they would enjoy a thin waistline and emaciated pocketbook. Jesus' listeners would have found this to be impressive as well. Jewish law in that day prescribed only one obligatory fast a year, on the Day of Atonement. And yet people who sought special merit also fasted on Mondays and Thursdays, days that were, coincidentally the main market days in Jerusalem. The fasters would whiten their faces and dress in clothing that would draw attention to themselves. Sounds like poverty-stricken, flamboyant racists to me.

Fasting two days a week seems a little extreme and unnecessary. It's like the Pharisee is trying to earn God's grace by going hungry. Personally, I've never been too sure about what the purpose of fasting is. I sort of like the Islamic view which is that fasting teaches us how the poor and hungry feel, making us better people. Yet somehow I doubt the Pharisee fasted twice a week in order to empathize with the poor and hungry.

As far as the relatively affluent Pharisee's tithing goes, let me just say that it is obviously easier to give a tenth of one's income when one's income is relatively large, just as paying a "flat tax" today would be lighter on the

---

1. Buchanan, Patrick J. "Address to the Republican National Convention." http://www.americanyawp.com/reader/29-the-triumph-of-the-right/pat-buchanan-on-the-culture-war-1992/

wealthy than on the poor. People do not usually give a full ten percent of their income to the church unless their church puts a major guilt trip on them, which is, of course, a characteristic of immoderate, extreme religion. I'm not saying, by the way, that I do not want any of my parishioners to give ten percent of their income to the offering plates. If they choose to do this, however, I just hope that they are rewarding my most excellent sermons and not doing so out of fear of eternal subterranean human barbeque pits. The point is, people who have succumbed to an immoderate, extremist religious faith will often believe and do irrational, impractical things.

All of these criticisms of the Pharisee and the extremist religion he represents are important. The Pharisee was self-righteous, contemptuous of others, and irrational in faith and practice. These are notorious characteristics of extremist religion. So, to borrow a phrase from the Pharisee, "I thank God" that I am part of a tradition that seeks moderation in our religious views and practices. And yet we have to be careful that we don't fall into the trap of thinking of ourselves too highly. After all, Jesus ends the parable by saying, "all who exalt themselves will be humbled, but all who humble themselves will be exalted." As one writer says, "Humility is a humble virtue, so much so that it even doubts its own virtuousness: to pride oneself on one's own humility is to lack it."[2] Which is why I spit on people who tell me I'm humble . . . just to prove them wrong . . . so that I can maintain my humility.

"IN GOD WE TRUST" OR SO SAYS OUR MONEY

When I was a young person I was told to never trust anyone over thirty-five. Funny, now I don't trust anyone *under* thirty-five. I guess one's age has a way of dictating whom we should trust. Nevertheless, who or what should we trust? Obviously, it is important to place our trust in someone or something, else we become totally cynical about life. As relatively prosperous Americans, many of us put our trust in money. We use words such as trust funds and securities. We pay into social security, trusting that by the time we retire there will be a steady paycheck from the government. Although our money says, "In *God* We Trust," I've often wondered if the person who came up with that idea understood the irony. When most Americans get up in the morning they feel much more secure if they've got a savings account with the bank than a "salvation account" with the Lord. I think our money should be more honest and say, "In *Money* We Trust." Why try to hide it?

---

2. Gerhard van Rensburg's blog post: http://neweraleadership.blogspot.com/2008/08/humility-is-virtue-of-man-who-knows-he.html.

Besides money, there are other objects of our trust. In every political season we are asked to vote on the candidates we trust the most (or vote against the ones we trust the least). In order for our personal relationships to be successful there has to be a great deal of trust between friends, lovers, or spouses. We need to feel as if we can trust our neighbors, although most people lock their doors day and night. If you are an athlete you need to trust your teammates. At some time or another, many people will have to trust their pastor. And don't forget the trustees of the church. If you can't trust them, who can you trust? We all feel safer when we can trust our local law enforcement. Finally, if you are a soldier you feel safer if you can trust your fellow soldiers. I've never been in the military, yet I can imagine the trust factor is absolutely crucial.

Our lives depend upon our ability to trust. Our society would literally break down if there wasn't a large degree of trust between people, government, media, schools, businesses, health care institutions, and so forth. Can you imagine having absolutely no trust in any of these institutions? We simply have to trust someone at some time or another, just to get through the day. And we trust people based upon what we need. If we need love, we trust our loved ones. If we need protection, we trust our police force. If we need better health, we trust our health care providers. If we need car repairs, we trust our mechanic.

The parable of the Pharisee and the tax collector tries to answer the question: who should we trust? The two men go into the temple in Jerusalem to pray. Like many people involved in a spiritual quest they are in pursuit of righteousness. (Either that, or the temple was holding an open house that day.) They need assurance that they are considered righteous in the eyes of God. Pursuing righteousness is not the only goal of religion, yet for much of Christian history it has been one of the most important. Perhaps only in recent times has the Christian focus on righteousness begun to fade away, even if just a little. Contemporary (moderate) Christians seem to focus more on the question, "How can I be more loving?" rather than "How can I be more righteous?" because we've learned that the latter often slides into self-righteousness.

The Pharisee and the tax collector are products of their religious environment. They both want assurance from God that they are righteous. But that's where the similarity between the two men ends. The Pharisee, a religious professional who follows all the laws to the letter, trusts *himself* for his righteousness. His prayer—"God, I thank you that I am not like other people: thieves, rogues, adulterers, or even like this tax collector. I fast twice a week; I give a tenth of all my income"—is an indication that he obviously seeks God's stamp of approval for what he has done. Today he would just get a tramp stamp on his lower back and be done with it.

The tax collector, a man who is considered to be one of the worst sinners and a traitor to the Jewish people, understands clearly that he cannot trust himself to be righteous. Instead, he trusts *God* for his righteousness. His prayer is very simple: "God, be merciful to me, a sinner!" The tax collector realizes that the closest he will ever come to being a righteous person is to be a forgiven person.

What I like about this parable is that it clearly points out the two primary choices concerning what you and I can trust: ourselves or God. The Pharisee trusted in himself and the tax collector trusted in God. We can place a lot of trust in other things like money, relationships, politicians, neighbors, clergy, doctors, mechanics, etc., yet when it comes to the question of who we trust in an ultimate way to get through life and do the best we can, our choices narrow down to two: ourselves and God. The parable clearly teaches that God should be the proper focus of our trust. Jesus is obviously criticizing the self-righteousness of the Pharisee and commending the tax collector's reliance on God. He may have wished he had a third choice, but hey, he's the one who told the parable.

This has been a consistent theme in our faith tradition: trust in God. Jeremiah the prophet said, "Blessed are those who trust in the Lord, whose trust is the Lord" (17:7). Teresa of Avila, the sixteenth-century Spanish mystic, said, "God is full of compassion, and never fails those who are afflicted and despised, if they trust in him alone." The witness of our faith tradition is that we need to be able to trust that God can sustain us, protect us, and watch over us. From childhood we are taught to trust God.

But let's be frank, shall we? (If your name already is Frank you can be Fred or someone else.) As we seek to place our trust in God for our well-being and righteousness, we also can't help but place trust in ourselves. The only problem with the Pharisee, who was no doubt a good person, was that he placed too much trust in himself. He had an exaggerated view of his own goodness. Because of that he didn't feel the need to trust in God or anyone else. He only felt the need to get God's approval as well as the approval of others. The tax collector, on the other hand, began with the proper placement of trust in God, yet at some point he was going to have to get off of his knees and learn to trust himself as well. As the old saying goes, "God helps those who help themselves." Someone said this quote is found in the Ayn Rand Bible Version (ARBV), although I am skeptical. Nevertheless, I believe a healthy and balanced spirituality involves trusting God, ourselves, and others.

The flip side of this parable in Luke 18 is that sometimes trusting in God means to trust in ourselves and other people a little more. Sometimes trusting in ourselves and others *is* trusting in God. Our money tells us, "In God We Trust." That's obviously more of a goal than a reality. If there were more room on our paper money, it should say, "In God we trust, but sometimes trusting God means learning to trust ourselves, our loved ones, our politicians, our school teachers, our community leaders, our teammates, and, yes, even our money." Learning to trust at all is the key to our ability to trust in God.

Luke 19:1–10

He entered Jericho and was passing through it. A man was there named Zacchaeus; he was a chief tax collector and was rich. He was trying to see who Jesus was, but on account of the crowd he could not, because he was short in stature. So he ran ahead and climbed a sycamore tree to see him, because he was going to pass that way. When Jesus came to the place, he looked up and said to him, "Zacchaeus, hurry and come down; for I must stay at your house today." So he hurried down and was happy to welcome him. All who saw it began to grumble and said, "He has gone to be the guest of one who is a sinner." Zacchaeus stood there and said to the Lord, "Look half of my possessions, Lord, I will give to the poor; and if I have defrauded anyone of anything, I will pay back four times as much." Then Jesus said to him, "Today salvation has come to this house, because he too is a son of Abraham. For the Son of Man came to seek out and to save the lost."

PAYBACK IS HEAVEN

WE USUALLY MAKE APOLOGIES when we want to rather than when those whom we have offended need it. It takes a while for us to get to a point where we can right the wrongs we do to others. We either have to build up our courage or swallow our pride, admitting our wrongdoing before we are able to right the wrongs we have committed against others.

In the early 1960s, Ray Charles refused to perform before a segregated audience in Georgia, provoking the state to bar him from performing there ever again. However, in 1979 the state of Georgia offered Charles an official apology and even adopted his song, "Georgia on My Mind" as their state song. Sometimes it takes a while to offer an apology, to make right a previous wrong. There are many songs about Georgia that are worthy of state song status; however, ever since the devil went down to Georgia, no one is interested any longer.

There is an old expression: "Payback is hell." This refers to a victim warning their victimizer that if they get a chance at revenge there will be hell to pay. Yet what if we are the ones who did something wrong against someone else? What if *we* are the oppressor, the victimizer, or the wrongdoer? Rather than wait for our victims to pay us back with evil, we should pay our victims back with good. In this instance, payback is heaven. When the wrongdoer seeks to make amends, payback can be a redemptive act for both parties. This is what the state of Georgia did in 1979, and it turned out to be a redemptive act for both the state's reputation and for Ray Charles the performer.

This brings us to the story of Zacchaeus, a wee little man who ran a big business in Jericho. Zacchaeus had a Napoleon complex before the Napoleon complex was cool. Jericho at this time was a large city with pools, parks, and typical Greco-Roman buildings. It was a wealthy place. Lots of taxes needed to be collected. Zacchaeus was rich because he was the chief tax collector of the district. This means there was a team of subordinates who collected the taxes for him. Tax collectors and especially the tax bosses, like Zacchaeus, were despised by almost everyone. This was not only because they were Jews working for the Romans but also because they cheated and used force to collect the taxes. They were so despised that the money they collected could not be given for alms because it was considered tainted, or unclean. Likewise, eating and associating with tax collectors would contaminate the righteous. Perhaps the people gave Zacchaeus his name out of contempt, because his name means "the righteous." He was considered anything but righteous. Yet Jesus has lunch with him, probably in one of the largest, most decadent mansions in Jericho. Of course, being a little guy he may have just lived in one of those very fancy tiny homes.

Oh, to be a fly on the wall. We don't know the details of their conversation, and yet a miracle soon happens. No, a mountain didn't move. Instead, Jesus moves Zacchaeus. He responds to Jesus by saying, "Look, half of my possessions, Lord, I will give to the poor; and if I have defrauded anyone of anything, I will pay back four times as much." We are not told if Zacchaeus actually carried through with this promise, yet if he did his bank account probably suffered significantly. Depending on how much he actually paid back to the people, it may have been emptied. Or he may have remained a rich man. In any case Jesus affirms his action. By the grace of God, a rich man walked through the eye of the needle. Which is fairly easy if one is not riding a camel.

What Zacchaeus did was an attempt to follow the laws of his people. Exodus 22:1 states, "If a man shall steal an ox or a sheep or kill it or steal it, he shall restore five oxen for an ox and four sheep for a sheep." Zacchaeus knew that paying back people he had wronged required paying back with interest. We find this same principle in other Old Testament passages. Leviticus 6:2–6 says, "When any of you sin and commit a trespass against the Lord by deceiving a neighbor in a matter of a deposit or a pledge, or by robbery, or if you have defrauded a neighbor . . . when you have sinned and realize your guilt . . . you shall repay the principal amount and shall add one-fifth to it." It is clear from the Law that when something is stolen, obtained by deceit, or through intentional or unintentional misdeeds, repayment with interest must be made in order to restore the wholeness of the community. And that's what Zacchaeus was attempting to do. Somehow Jesus had convinced him that in order to begin a new life, in order to find peace of mind, in order to find redemption, he needed to pay back what he owed (plus some). Jesus says to him, "Today salvation has come to this house."

Aside from the redemptive value of paying people back for the wrongs we have committed against them, there are a couple of other points I believe this story is trying to make. First, an apology needs teeth. An apology often needs to be more than just words. Ray Charles didn't just receive a verbal apology from the state of Georgia. By adopting his song as the official state song, the state's apology actually meant something. If Zacchaeus had only told Jesus, "You know, Lord, I sure am sorry about how I've run my business. I'll try to do better in the future," he would not have found the new life, the peace of mind, and the redemption that comes with a meaningful apology, an apology with teeth. However, he may have received an upgrade from the Better Business Bureau.

This story also reveals how difficult it is to apologize, make amends, or pay back those whom we have wronged, because if we have wronged people in the past it is very likely that they will not trust us to make things right. Notice that the only thing that happens between the time Zacchaeus welcomes Jesus and the time Zacchaeus makes amends is the grumbling of those who didn't want Jesus to associate with Zacchaeus. There is no way the people would trust Zacchaeus to make good on his promises. People will naturally be skeptical when former oppressors seek to right the wrongs they have committed against others. A spouse wants to make amends with their wife or husband for having wronged them in the past, but the wife or husband is skeptical that the spouse has really changed. A businessperson, like Zacchaeus, wants to offer restitution for a faulty or overpriced product, yet the public cynically thinks that the businessperson is just trying to save the business. A government wants to make reparations for past injustices against a particular group of people, yet the former victims and outside observers are suspicious that this government is just trying to look good in the eyes of the world.

Speaking of the latter, there has been a lot of talk in recent years about making reparations toward people wronged in the past by our government. For example, many people believe significant reparations should be made to the descendants of African-American slaves. The argument goes this way: Enormous wealth was created—either directly or indirectly—by the forced labor of enslaved Africans. The wealth did not go to them, but to white persons, and this wealth has been passed down generation after generation by white Americans to their descendants, while most persons of African descent have had little to pass down to their heirs. Certainly, an apology for slavery is an absolute must (which has already happened). However, as many people argue, shouldn't we follow up an apology with reparations, as without that, our apology is nothing more than hollow words?

On a smaller scale, we have made successful reparations to people we have wronged in the past. Our government paid out more than $1.6 billion to more than 82,250 persons of Japanese ancestry who were unconstitutionally interned during World War II, each receiving $20,000. How we pay back people we have wronged will remain a very controversial issue, yet from the standpoint of a Christian ethic we need to do what we can. In addition to the descendants of African-American slaves and Japanese-Americans who were interned during World War II, we need to continue to think about appropriate ways to apologize to Native Americans, who were overrun, slaughtered, and had their land stolen from them by European settlers. Seriously, we could make fewer bombs, require a fairer tax system, and sell a heck of a lot of Girl Scout cookies to produce an ethical reparations program.

The story of Zacchaeus suggests that efforts to right wrongs committed against others are worthy goals. If we as individuals have wronged another person, the Christian response is to offer an apology or make amends. If we as a church have taken part in an injustice, the Christian response is to offer restitution of some sort. If we as a nation have sinned against others, the Christian response is to offer an official apology or even reparations if possible. Today God is still speaking to us, encouraging us, when needed, to offer apologies, to make amends, and to repair the damage we have done to others. We shouldn't wait until it is convenient to do so, until we have built up enough courage, until we have sufficiently swallowed our pride, or until we have gained enough credibility. We don't need any more time. Today is a good day to pay back what we owe to others.

Luke 19:29–40

When he had come near Bethphage and Bethany, at the place called the Mount of Olives, he sent two of the disciples, saying, "Go into the village ahead of you, and as you enter it you will find tied there a colt that has never been ridden. Untie it and bring it here. If anyone asks you, 'Why are you untying it? Just say this, 'The Lord needs it.'" So those who were sent departed and found it as he had told them. As they were untying the colt, its owners asked them, "Why are you untying the colt?" They said, "The Lord needs it." Then they brought it to Jesus; and after throwing their cloaks on the colt, they set Jesus on it. As he rode along, people kept spreading their cloaks on the road. As he was now approaching the path down from the Mount of Olives, the whole multitude of the disciples began to praise God joyfully with a loud voice for all the deeds of power that they had seen, saying, "Blessed is the king who comes in the name of the Lord! Peace in heaven, and glory in the highest heaven!" Some of the Pharisees in the crowd said to him, "Teacher, order your disciples to stop." He answered, "I tell you, if these were silent, the stones would shout out."

ON A HORSE WITH NO NAME

Two Kentucky farmers who owned racing stables had developed a keen rivalry. One spring, each of them entered a horse in a local steeplechase. Thinking that a professional rider might help him outdo his friend, one of the farmers hired a seasoned jockey. The two horses were leading the race at the last fence, but it proved too tough for them. Both horses fell, unseating their riders. But this calamity did not stop the professional jockey. He quickly remounted and won the race. Returning triumphant to the paddock, the jockey found the farmer who had hired him fuming with rage. "What's the matter?" the jockey asked. "I won, didn't I?" "Oh, yes," roared the farmer. "You won all right, but you still don't know, do you?" "Know what?" asked the jockey. "You won the race on the wrong horse."

To most observers on that day we call Palm Sunday, Jesus also won the race on the wrong horse. He enters Jerusalem straddling, not a great stallion, but a humble beast—a colt of a donkey. This does not meet general expectations. The Messiah is supposed to be a triumphant leader of the Jews against their oppressors, the Romans. He is anything but.

According to this familiar story, Jesus is on his way to Jerusalem knowing that he is heading into the metaphorical lion's den. He knows he is risking his life going to Jerusalem because he has made many enemies, some Jewish, some Roman. He probably assumes this will be his last stop, and it proves to be exactly that. He comes near a couple of small towns just outside of Jerusalem: Bethphage and Bethany. He sends two of his disciples ahead of him to find a young colt that has never been ridden. We are not to think that somehow Jesus is clairvoyant and knows there is a colt sitting out in plain sight. He simply knows from experience that every town or village is populated with donkeys and colts, a common mode of transportation in that place and time. It would be like telling someone today to go into the next town and find a white Bronco. I am obviously trying to connect the docile donkey to its distant cousin, the wild bronco, however, if you would like to make this about O.J. Simpson's ride or Euro-American players on the Denver Broncos, be my guest.

Jesus tells his disciples to tell the owner of the colt, "The Lord needs it," which is exactly what a soldier would say on behalf of a military officer, or a servant would say on behalf of a king or queen who needed something. This is an official requisition. Someone of importance needs your donkey. The disciples follow Jesus' orders and bring him a colt. Jesus hops on the animal and begins the short journey to the east gate of Jerusalem. No doubt the colt will be returned to its rightful owner later that day.

Now, if all we had was the Gospel according to Luke, we would not be referring to the Sunday on which this story is read as "Palm" Sunday because Luke doesn't mention the spreading of any palms. Perhaps we could call it "Cloak Sunday," yet that doesn't have quite the same ring to it, does it? I would vote for "Ass Sunday," but that sends the wrong message and is grossly misunderstood in the fifth- to eighth-grade crowd. All four of the Gospels present slightly varying descriptions of this story. Matthew is the only one that mentions both a donkey and a colt. He also refers to "branches of the trees." Mark mentions "leafy branches." John has famously given us the "branches of palm trees." And in Luke, the people spread their clothes in Jesus' path but there are no palms or branches of any kind.

Regardless of the props for this scene it appears to be a deliberate and ironic parody of how the real Messiah is supposed to enter Jerusalem in triumph. In fact, this event is often called "the triumphal entry." In reality, it is a parody of triumph. Behind him marches no army, just a handful of illiterate Galilean fishermen, hated tax collectors, and women and children. He possesses no weapons, no throne, and no crown. In no way is he prepared to fulfill the then-popular messianic hopes that God would send a powerful leader who would liberate the nation from Roman oppression.

Nevertheless, the timing of this event is impeccable. It is the Jewish festival of Passover. Jews from all over the region are in Jerusalem, no doubt raising the anxiety level of the Roman soldiers assigned to the city. One can imagine the grimace on their faces as these pilgrims line the street as Jesus makes his way through the east gate, shouting, "King," "Son of David," and "Hosanna!," which means "Save us!" These are politically provocative words, much more combustible than the slogans and signs (often misspelled) seen in recent years at Tea Party gatherings in our own country. No one will be executed because of their pro- or anti-government provocations in America. However, someone will be executed because of this parade recorded in all four Gospels. This is a threat not only to Caesar but to Herod, the Jewish puppet-king, because this scene mimics the entrance of a monarch into a city welcoming his sovereignty.

One thing has become clear: Jesus is dangerously popular with the people. Caesar and Herod are not. The Jesus story is as much political as it is religious or theological. Today, 2,000 years removed from the actual events, we try to practice a religion that is personal and spiritual, whereas the original Jesus movement was more political and practical. Nevertheless, it wasn't political in the sense that it was a movement to replace one political entity with another. It wasn't political in the sense that Jesus was a threat to unseat an incumbent. Rather, it was political in the sense that it criticized the way power is often used and abused in human societies. The Palm Sunday event was a deliberate parody on power.

To appreciate the parody you have to remember the historical context. The Jewish nation had been suffering under the rule of Roman oppression for over a century. Before the Romans, it had been one nasty imperial power after another. Rome was huge; Israel was tiny. The only hope to escape this mess was the promised Messiah. A lot of people expected this national savior to appear any day. Popular opinion imagined what the scene would look like when the Messiah came. He'd march into Jerusalem astride a great stallion, a mighty war horse. He'd be leading a vast army. He'd vanquish the despised Romans. He'd march to his throne and be crowned King of the Jews, usurping the throne of Herod. That was the dream. Well, he was eventually crowned King of the Jews, yet on a cross rather than a throne.

So, this story and the religion it spawned is a parody, a critique of worldly power. And boy, that's a tough one for us. What does this mean for people like me and you who actually have varying degrees of worldly power? On any given Sunday, in any given church, there are people in the pews who have political power, economic power, or power in the media. Because we are Americans we have unparalleled military power. This is what I like (or dislike) about Palm Sunday. It is a bone-crushing criticism of who I am and who you are. It steps on our toes, and it does so with the weight of a young donkey. The implication of this story for us is rather straightforward: We follow Jesus into Jerusalem when we faithfully exercise power not simply for ourselves but for others. We are called to serve not just self but others. We are called to use our intelligence, our cleverness, our influence, our money not just to get ahead but to bless the world. Jesus shows us what kind of power makes the world go 'round by his ride into Jerusalem on the first Palm Sunday.

NO MORE FOOLING AROUND

It seems like just about everyone has a holiday these days. Every New Year's Day, time itself gets a holiday. African-Americans (and supporters) have Martin Luther King Jr. day and Kwanzaa. Lovers get a holiday on Valentine's Day. Presidents—good or bad—have President's Day. Catholics—observant or backslidden—get to drink a lot during Mardi Gras. And the Irish-Catholics get to drink some more on St. Patrick's Day. Holocaust victims, Armenian martyrs, Hiroshima survivors, and our fallen soldiers all have their own memorial days. Administrative assistants even have their own day, a day they get to tell people, "I'm not a secretary, damn it!" Mothers and fathers get to be spoiled by their spouses and children for one day a year. Fireworks manufacturers have been given the gifts of Independence Day and New Year's Eve. Workers get to rest on Labor Day. The Italians get Columbus Day while Native Americans call it Indigenous People's Day. Even the United Nations has a holiday. Turkey-eating carnivores get to enjoy Thanksgiving. And for those who are still suffering we have Human Rights Day and World AIDS Day. The Jews have Rosh Hashanah, Yom Kippur, and Hanukkah. The Muslims have Ramadan. And we Christians get Ash Wednesday, Palm Sunday, Easter, Pentecost, and Christmas, to name a few.

Did I leave anyone out? I can't imagine anyone in this country who isn't able to enjoy at least a few holidays. That person would have to be non-ethnic specific, lonely, unpatriotic, atheistic, unemployed, with no children, and who doesn't believe in calendars or eating meat. If such a person exists, at least they have April Fools' Day. That's right, the holiday for everyone, the holiday that truly leaves no child behind (or adult), the holiday that celebrates nothing more than our shared humanity.

April 1 is the day we celebrate and honor our foolishness. It's the day we poke fun at ourselves, realizing that doing so is good for our mental health. People do a lot of creative things for holidays, and yet none compare to the creativity engineered for April Fools' Day. Perhaps the most famous April Fools' Day hoax occurred in 1957. The BBC television program "Panorama" showed the Swiss harvesting spaghetti from trees. They claimed that the despised pest, the "spaghetti weevil," had been eradicated. A large number of people then contacted the BBC wanting to know how to cultivate their own spaghetti trees. The British are quite adept at fooling people. In 1976, British astronomer Sir Patrick Moore told BBC radio listeners that a unique alignment of two planets would result in an upward gravitational pull making people lighter at precisely 9:47 am that day. He invited his audience to jump in the air at that time and experience "a strange floating sensation." Dozens of listeners phoned in to say the experiment worked.

Of course, when it comes to April Fools' hoaxes, the British don't have anything on us. In 1996, Taco Bell took out a full-page advertisement in the *New York Times* announcing they had purchased the Liberty Bell to "reduce the country's debt" and renamed it the "Taco Liberty Bell." Later that day a White House spokesperson said that Ford had purchased the Lincoln Memorial, so it was now called the "Ford Lincoln Memorial." In 1998, Burger King ran an ad in *USA Today* saying people could get a Whopper for left-handed people whose condiments were designed to drip out of the right side of the burger. Finally (my favorite), in 2005 a news story posted on the official NASA website claimed to have pictures of water on Mars. The website showed pictures of a glass of water on a Mars bar.

April Fools' Day had not yet been envisioned when Jesus rode into Jerusalem on the back of a donkey, yet I would imagine that a lot of people thought he was joking. A lot of people may have thought that he was making an ass out of them, if you know what I mean. As I stated above, this event has been labeled Jesus' triumphal entry into Jerusalem, yet from a practical perspective it was anything but triumphant. By the end of the week Jesus would be betrayed, arrested, interrogated, tortured, and executed. If we ignore what happened the following Sunday we could very well claim that the joke was on him.

The Palm Sunday event had all the makings of a grand hoax. If Jesus had been a jokester his first victims could have been the two disciples he sent ahead to the village to find a young colt. Fortunately, this worked out just fine and the two disciples were able to retrieve the young colt without any problem. But what if this had been a hoax? What if the story had turned out this way: The two disciples found a colt and untied it. The owner came out of his house and asked, "Why are you untying my colt?" And they said, "The Lord needs it." And the owner said, "I don't care who needs it! It's my colt! I'm calling the Roman centurions." The two disciples would have been "punked."

Another possible hoax was the fact that Jesus rode a young donkey. What was that all about? Doesn't that seem a little odd to you? Why not ride a big, black stallion into the city? The fact that he rode anything at all is interesting to me. Why didn't he just walk into town? Was he too tired to walk? Had he sprained his ankle? Did he want to be up higher so people could see him better? Was he doing this because it had been predicted by prophecy? Actually, the answer is none of the above. This was not a fulfillment of a prophecy; it was, rather, a prophetic act. Jesus wasn't trying to fool anyone. He wasn't pulling anyone's leg. He wasn't concocting an elaborate hoax. Entering Jerusalem on the back of a young donkey was a prophetic act. It was deliberate. It was based on a passage in the Old Testament that spoke of a humble king who would enter Jerusalem on the colt of a donkey. According to Zechariah 9:9–10, this future king would be a king of peace who would banish chariots, warhorses, and battle bows from the land and command peace to the nations.

No doubt, many of the people who witnessed this event must have thought Jesus was just fooling around. This is no way to be a king. This is no way to run a kingdom. Yet by riding into Jerusalem on a young donkey Jesus enacted his message. The kingdom of God of which he often spoke was a kingdom of peace, not violence. "Surely you jest!" thought the Pharisees who witnessed this occasion. Luke tells us that some of the Pharisees in the crowd said to him, "Teacher, order your disciples to stop." They thought the hoax had gone too far. They thought he was fooling the people into following him. And they knew that there would be trouble on the horizon if Jesus continued to pull the wool over their eyes.

However, Jesus made it clear to these Pharisees that he wasn't fooling around. This is for real. This is serious business. This is no joke. Jesus looked at the Pharisees and said, "I tell you, if these were silent, the stones would shout out." Literally, of course, the notion of "shouting stones" is laughable, yet his message is clear: the kingdom of God is a kingdom of peace.

Here's my biggest criticism of Christianity throughout the centuries: I don't think we actually believe Jesus. Oh sure, we believe *in him*, which doesn't require much on our part. But we don't really believe him, or at least we don't act like we do. We act like we think he was fooling around, making a joke, creating a grand hoax, pulling the wool over our eyes, pulling our leg. Before Jesus' triumphal entry into Jerusalem on the back of a colt, humanity found it necessary to have imperial power, to brandish weapons, to wear helmets, to march, to beat drums, to stir up dust to frighten one another. Good old saber rattling. And after his triumphal entry, humanity—even Christianity (especially Christianity)—continued to do the same. Jesus clearly gave us a choice between two kingdoms: a kingdom of power and domination or a kingdom of freedom and peace, a kingdom of imperialism or a kingdom of God. Most of us will continue to listen to Jesus, claim we "believe in him," and yet live as if he never climbed on the back of that young colt. Well then, aren't we just fooling around? And I don't mean the kind of fooling around one does in the back of a Bronco.

THE LAST CAMPAIGN STOP

The Palm Sunday story is a great story to read at this time in our history because we recently went through one of the most contentious, colorful, and crazy presidential campaigns in the history of these United States of America. The reason I say this is because the event we call the Palm Sunday story, what some like to call the triumphal entry, was very much a political event. (By the way, where were all the references to the "Trump Entry" into Washington? Is this due to the fact that people fear God's wrath if they link Donald Trump with Jesus Christ even in a humorous way?) The Palm Sunday story is as much a political story as it is a religious story. One of the biggest mistakes we modern Christians make in our attempts to read and interpret the Bible is our reluctance to interpret the biblical stories through a political lens. By that I don't mean *our* political lens. I'm talking about the politics of that time and place.

The Palm Sunday story is not the only story in the four Gospels that is political. The entire gospel story is as much political as it is theological. The gospel, or good news, of Jesus Christ has very definite political roots. Many of the labels applied to Jesus in the Gospel accounts were primarily political labels, such as "Christ," "Lord," "Savior," and "Son of God." Those same titles were applied to Julius Caesar, Caesar Augustus, and later Caesars. To the first-century listener, to hear Jesus called "Lord and Savior" would have sounded politically subversive. It meant that Caesar is *not* Lord and Savior. Or, if he was, then we really missed the boat on that one.

Jesus was ridiculed as the "King of the Jews" at his crucifixion, which suggests that the general public saw him in political terms. Even the words

"Christ" or "Messiah," words that literally mean "an anointed one," were usually applied to kings in Israel's history. When we think of Jesus we really should think in terms of a "Messiah-King."

In that time and place there was no separation of church and state, or to be more accurate, separation of synagogue and state. To label something as political was also, to a large extent, the same thing as labeling something as religious. A Messiah-King occupied a religious office as well as a political office. Therefore, Jesus' triumphal entry through the gates leading into Jerusalem, the center of religious *and* political power in first-century Palestine, was a political event as well as a religious event. It was, if I may use a modern American phrase, a campaign stop.

Jesus' campaign stops rivaled the drama and flair of today's campaign stops. Enormous (read "Yuge") crowds followed Jesus everywhere he went. The pictures prove it. Hecklers and protesters, usually in the form of religious leaders or Roman soldiers, were often there. Violence would occasionally ensue. Remember Peter cutting off the ear of a high priest's servant? Of course, Jesus did not condone the violence. Not once did he ever yell, "Get him out of here!" because he wasn't running for the office of President of the United States unlike *some* people I know. (Actually, just one person I know . . . Actually, I don't really know that one person personally.) Overall, his campaign stops were met with great enthusiasm. On his final campaign stop in Jerusalem, a few days before he was arrested, given a mock trial, and executed, the people lined the road, hailing his arrival: "Blessed is the king who comes in the name of the Lord!"

Jesus was a political as well as a religious figure. And yet what exactly were his political views? What was his "platform"? Does it mirror anyone's platform today? Obviously, I can't answer that because the categories we use today do not translate very well into first-century categories. We would be committing the sin of anachronism, using categories from one era to apply to a person of another era, if we suggested that Jesus' political views mirrored those of any of today's political candidates. Jesus was not, nor could he even consider being, a Democrat, Republican, Libertarian, Independent, socialist, capitalist, or communist. None of these labels apply neatly to Jesus.

Jesus seems to have supported through his teachings a government run by God, the "Kingdom of God," as he called it. Normally we would call this a "theocracy," yet a theocracy is a government run by a particular religion. Jesus didn't seem to be interested in a government run by a particular religion. His view of the Kingdom of God did not incorporate a person or religion in charge, but rather God in charge. Jesus was also a populist, an advocate for social change, and a healer. Perhaps we could say he was in favor of "universal healthcare"—yet it looked nothing like any healthcare system in the world today. It was based on compassion and miracles, not co-pays and medicine. Would he have understood health care to be a "right" or a "privilege"? I believe you know the answer to that one.

Did Jesus see himself as a king? If he did, it was more of an "anti-king." This is hinted at in the Palm Sunday story. Here Jesus rides a young donkey into his Jerusalem campaign stop—something akin to a candidate today coming to Washington, DC. Actually, this is like a five-star general, say, Dwight D. Eisenhower, running for president, arriving at a major campaign stop in a Volkswagen Beetle. Remembering the words of the prophet Zechariah, Jesus chooses to arrive at his final campaign stop on a young donkey because he has a very clear message to send to the world: If Jesus is to be inaugurated as Messiah-King, his platform will be very different than every other candidate for Messiah-King. His platform is based on the principle of *nonviolence*. Can you imagine a five-star general today running for office on a "peace platform"?

Based on what I understand about Jesus I decided to come up with a name for his political party: the "Theocratic Anarchist Peace Party." Does that fit any of our candidates running for office today? Nope. Are any of them committed to absolute nonviolence? Nope. Do any of them envision God as the ultimate king of our country? No, even those who claim to be religious might say this only as a symbolic gesture. Are any of the candidates today recommending anarchy, which is a rejection of hierarchy, which translates into no government whatsoever? No, even those who espouse the principle of small government believe there must be a government of some sort or else there would be total chaos.

Jesus was a nonviolent theocratic anarchist. But he's *our* nonviolent theocratic anarchist. He's *our* Messiah-King, *our* Lord and Savior, *our* Son of God. His political views do not translate very easily into our current political world. Still, we are called to follow him, even into the voting booth. In my opinion, the one thing we should always be focused on in our political action—if we are disciples of Jesus—is nonviolence. Nonviolence was the cornerstone of his political and religious worldview. Yes, some Christians have occasionally used Jesus' prophetic act of turning over the moneychangers' tables and setting sacrificial animals free in the temple to argue that Jesus was violent. Remember, however, that minor property damage in a symbolic act is very different from lethal violence against persons. Jesus never used lethal violence against anyone, and yet, his last campaign stop ended in lethal violence against him. The world always finds a way to kill its peacemakers, which is the ultimate irony.

Luke 20:27–38

Some Sadducees, those who say there is no resurrection, came to him and asked him a question, "Teacher, Moses wrote for us that if a man's brother dies, leaving a wife but no children, the man shall marry the widow and raise up children for his brother. Now there were seven brothers; the first married and died childless; then the second and the third married her, and so in the same way all seven died childless. Finally the woman also died. In the resurrection, therefore, whose wife will the woman be? For the seven had married her." Jesus said to them, "Those who belong to this age marry and are given in marriage; but those who are considered worthy of a place in that age and in the resurrection from the dead neither marry nor are given in marriage. Indeed they cannot die anymore, because they are like angels and are children of God, being children of the resurrection. And the fact that the dead are raised Moses himself showed, in the story about the bush, where he speaks of the Lord as the God of Abraham, the God of Isaac, and the God of Jacob. Now he is God not of the dead, but of the living; for to him all of them are alive."

THE PARABLE OF THE BLACK WIDOW[1]

I AM ALWAYS GLAD when an election season is over. Don't get me wrong. I love politics. I am a borderline political junkie who, after an election, has to go through withdrawals just like a drug addict. However, there are two

---

1. Admittedly "black widow" is a sexist, if not racist, phrase. So, what should we call a tanned couch potato who outlives several spouses? A brown recluse?

reasons I'm glad when they are over. First, I get weary of trying to figure out who is telling the truth and who is not. I get weary of trying to sort through all the rhetoric in order to make an informed decision. I'm not the most cynical person when it comes to politics, yet I have figured out that a lot of the information we receive is not always, shall we say, trustworthy. I made this admittedly not very astute observation before the election of 2016. At least now I know the Russians are responsible for much of our ignorance.

Aside from the half-truths we receive during a campaign, the other reason I am glad when an election is over is that I can finally get back to being a Christian rather than a member of a particular party or a supporter of a particular candidate. I was sidetracked long enough. Now I want to get back on the right track. I want to get back on the train where Jesus of Nazareth is the conductor rather than a candidate. To switch metaphors, I am ready to set sail on a ship captained by Jesus the Christ, not a campaign director. This reminds me of a story:

A young ensign, after nearly completing his first overseas cruise, was given an opportunity to display his capabilities at getting the ship under way. With a stream of commands, he had the decks buzzing with men, and soon the ship was steaming out the channel en route to the States. His efficiency established a new record for getting a destroyer under way, and he was not surprised when a seaman approached him with a message from the captain. He was a bit surprised, though, to find it a radio message and even more surprised to read: "My personal congratulations upon completing your underway preparation exercise according to the book and with amazing speed. In your haste, however, you have overlooked one of the unwritten rules. Make sure the captain is aboard before getting under way."

I can't help but feel that many of us take off during an election season on our particular political trains or ships, yet we leave our conductor or captain behind. The gospel of Jesus Christ is left at the train station or the dock while we go off and romanticize about our political messiahs. To continue with the train metaphor, our Christian faith gets sidetracked in the midst of our feverish enthusiasm for political victories. By the way, I'm not condemning our political involvement at all. Politics is extremely important. It's just that in my post-election reflections I can't help but think we all get sidetracked a little too much.

In Henning Mankell's award-winning book, *Sidetracked* (Ordfront, 1995), Kurt Wallander is called to a nearby field where a young woman has been loitering all day long. He arrives just in time to watch her douse herself in gasoline and set herself aflame. The next day he is called to a beach where Sweden's former Minister of Justice has been beaten to death and scalped. Wallander's job is to catch the killer before he strikes again. But his investigation gets sidetracked all throughout the novel by several things: the threat of impending cutbacks in his department, World Cup Soccer, a long-distance relationship with a murdered policeman's widow, and the image of the young girl who set herself on fire.

This is what happens to us in the midst of an election season. We have a job to do, to live and share the gospel of Jesus Christ, and yet other things have a way of sidetracking us. Metaphorically speaking, we see a young girl setting herself on fire. Whatever issue burns brightest at the moment, that's where we'll be. We are like moths drawn to a flame. Three of the most important issues during recent election seasons have included the economy, war, and cultural values issues. And emails and Russian crap obviously. There is no doubt that many people apply their Christian beliefs to these issues, yet that's not the problem. The problem is that these issues become larger than our Christian identity. We are no longer Christians who have honest differences on war, economics, and cultural issues. We are now identified primarily by how we view these issues. During an election season our primary identity is based on our allegiance to particular political views, not on our allegiance to Jesus Christ. In fact, according to some Christians, unless you agree with them on some of these issues you are not even a Christian. Some of us allow our faith to get sidetracked as we jump on the Republican or Democratic train. Our political identification becomes more important than our religious identification.

I'm always amazed, for example, at how much we focus on economic issues. We are always fixated on our economy especially during an election season. I am reminded of Bill Clinton's mantra during the 1992 campaign: "It's the economy, stupid!" Of course, the economy should be a matter of concern for people of faith. Yet Jesus sums up the problem with focusing so much on the economy: "You can't serve two masters: God and money." I would have written "mammon," but I have no idea what mammon is. We think it means "money" or "greed," but the good folks in the Middle Ages thought it was one of the seven princes of Hell. So, no, I don't serve that dude, even when I get all excited about receiving a paycheck.

As Christians, we should be concerned about the economy, yet we should always remember that we are Christians first, and capitalists or socialists second. Chocolate milk is third. Our primary identification should not be based on our conservative, moderate, or liberal economic views, but on whether or not we are disciples of Jesus Christ.

Another issue that has sidetracked people of faith in recent elections is same-sex marriage. This truly has become the defining issue of our day. In the minds of many Christians, Americans are divided into two distinct groups: those who are against gay marriage and those who support it. I think we all need to take a deep breath and relax. The world did not come to an end when same-sex marriage became the law of the land. California did not fall off into the ocean. Unfortunately, climate change rather than a change in the marriage codes will eventually suck California into the surfers' waves. Still, I have never seen people sidetracked about an issue as much as we are about this one. It is consuming us.

The institution of marriage has seemingly always been a topic of debate and concern. One day a group of aristocratic Jewish priests called Sadducees came to Jesus about a marriage issue in relation to the topic of life after death. The Sadducees based their religious beliefs on the first five books of the Bible, the Torah. The Torah does not teach there is life after death, therefore the Sadducees did not believe in life after death. (They were "sad, you see." I know, that's an oldie, but it's a goody.) They ask Jesus a question in order to trick him. The law stated that if a man dies and leaves his wife childless, then his brother should marry the woman and have children with her. The first child born to this couple would be considered the offspring of the first husband. These Sadducees paint a scenario where brother after brother marries the same woman. They all die leaving her childless. Then the Sadducees ask the question, "Whose wife will she be in the afterlife?" My initial guess is that no one would want to be married to a woman who obviously sucked the life out of her husbands; she might carry that particular skill with her into the afterlife. Again, that sounds sexist, and yet one could say the same thing about a man who goes through wives like a race car goes through tires.

The Sadducees were sidetracked with this absurd question about marriage, yet Jesus sidesteps their question and argues that marriage is not part of the afterlife so it's a moot point. In fact, Jesus' response suggests that he was not a big fan of marriage in the first place, which ought to make us pause before we get too dogmatic about our views on marriage. Getting back to gay marriage, I do think it is an important issue, yet I also think that too many conservative Christians are being consumed by an issue that has very little to do with their own lives, unless they happen to be gay. If this is true then I suggest finding a church that doesn't think you are mammon. My point is that Christians should focus on better ways they can express the love of God than trying to control the lives of people in love. Duh.

There is a punk rock band called "Sidetracked." Their website shows two pilots in an airplane smiling back at the camera while their plane is about to crash with another plane. When I saw that I thought of the church. I wonder if the church often gets so consumed or sidetracked by politics, war, economics, and cultural values issues that we may wind up crashing some day in a field of irrelevance. Because if those things are all we are about, why don't we just pay our tithes and offerings to the Democrats or Republicans? I, for one, am always ready to get back to the real purpose of my existence: To preach and practice the love of God as revealed in Jesus the Christ. I'll continue to vote, support my candidates, and get my political fix on occasion, yet I'll do so as a follower of the One who teaches that God loves me no matter who I vote for, or no matter what my views are. At the same time, I don't assume that just because God loves me I'm not voting like an idiot, but I have to start somewhere.

Luke 21:25–36

"There will be signs in the sun, the moon, and the stars, and on the earth distress among nations confused by the roaring of the sea and the waves. People will faint from fear and foreboding of what is coming upon the world, for the powers of the heavens will be shaken. Then they will see 'the Son of Man coming in a cloud' with power and great glory. Now when these things begin to take place, stand up and raise your heads, because your redemption is drawing near." Then he told them a parable: "Look at the fig tree and all the trees; as soon as they sprout leaves you can see for yourselves and know that summer is already near. So also, when you see these things taking place, you know that the Kingdom of God is near. Truly I tell you, this generation will not pass away until all things have taken place. Heaven and earth will pass away, but my words will not pass away. Be on guard so that your hearts are not weighed down with dissipation and drunkenness and the worries of this life, and that day does not catch you unexpectedly, like a trap. For it will come upon all who live on the face of the whole earth. Be alert at all times, praying that you may have the strength to escape all these things that will take place, and to stand before the Son of Man."

HERE'S YOUR SIGN

ONE OF THE METHODS I have used throughout my career to create some interest in my congregations is utilizing an outdoor sign in unique ways. I have consciously chosen not to use the same old clichés that most churches use, for two reasons. First, I would find that rather boring and unimaginative, and second, most church sign messages are theologically unsound (in my humble opinion). I do this because I know that human beings are by nature sign watchers, and I'm not just talking about church signs. We are fascinated with indications, clues, or hints that something is about to happen.

People love to watch the multitude of television shows that depict criminal investigators gathering information that will point them to the guilty culprit. They are looking for signs that will help them identify this person. Meteorologists are the classic example of sign watchers because they look at weather signs, or indicators, that give them information about possible future weather patterns. In our personal relationships we interpret people's facial expressions or body language as a sign or indication about how they feel or what they are thinking. Athletes try to pick up signs or clues that will help them determine their opponent's next move. On our jobs we try to pick up signs or hints from our bosses about our job performance. Our pets even give us nonverbal signs that they are hungry or need to go outside to relieve themselves. (I have intentionally not mentioned the redneck comedian Bill Engvall's famous quip, "Here's your sign," which is a nod toward stupid people because it's a stupid slogan.)

All of this is part of our day-to-day routine. Yet there is another kind of sign watching that is much more mysterious. Some people look for signs that we call "omens." Those would be the same stupid people targeted in Engvall's comedy routines. Omens are signs or indications that something good or bad is going to happen in the future. They imply that someone can actually know the future. In popular mythology omens are the domain of people like psychics, seers, and astrologers: stupid people who prey on other stupid people. One of my favorite stories about omens concerns Adolph Hitler. Hitler was very much disturbed when a clairvoyant let it be known that she could predict the exact day of the Fuhrer's death. Since her predictions were always based on astrology, and since Hitler himself was a believer in the stars, he sent for the woman. After much divination the woman finally said that the omens indicated no specific date for the passing of the Nazi leader, other than that it would definitely take place on a Jewish holiday. "Which holiday?" Hitler demanded. "I cannot be sure," said the astrologist. "You've got to be sure," Hitler ordered, going off into one of his spastic shrieks. "I demand that you be sure." "What difference does it make?" shrugged the woman. "Any day on which you die will be a Jewish holiday." Hitler was stupid.

The above passage is interesting because Jesus is depicted as someone who believes in omens or "signs of the times," specifically signs that he is about to return. Frankly, I don't believe Jesus is going to come back some day. Certainly there are several biblical passages that talk about his return, although most of these passages, like the one from Luke 21, suggest that Jesus' return was supposed to be in the lifetime of the biblical writers. Verse 32 quotes Jesus as saying, "Truly I tell you, this generation will not pass away until all things have taken place." That's hard to ignore. However, one would have to be stupid in order to interpret it literally, unless, of course, Jesus actually believed this.

This is one of the most controversial topics in New Testament studies. Did Jesus himself believe that he would be coming back (sooner or later)? Did Jesus know the future? With the advent of critical studies of the Bible, many scholars have suggested that Jesus' teachings about his second coming are merely words that reflect the writer's theology, not Jesus'. Nevertheless, for the sake of argument, let's just call a spade a spade and acknowledge that Jesus is at least depicted in Luke's Gospel as someone who believes in omens, or signs, about the future. In verse 25, he says, "There will be signs in the sun, the moon, and the stars." Was Jesus a "space sailor," i.e. an astronaut? If so, and he wasn't privy to GPS, he most likely took advantage of the signs in the sun, moon, and stars. It's probable that Jesus was simply reflecting the beliefs of his time. Ancient human beings relied on watching for signs in the heavens in order to predict future events. I assume this is how the practice of astrology actually began.

For example, the story of the magi following the star to the place where Jesus was born has its roots in the ancient belief that the heavenly bodies could tell us things. In fact, the magi are often referred to as astrologers. The difference between modern and ancient people is that the ancients had little, if any, scientific knowledge about the heavens or space beyond earth's atmosphere. For all they knew eclipses, red moons, and shooting stars were signs that God was trying to communicate with them. How else could they interpret these fantastic events? They assumed God lived in the midst of the sun, moon, and stars because in the ancient mind everything we see in the sky is nearby and close together. Their worldview was about as large as an indoor professional football stadium where the lights in the ceiling are relatively close. (Jerry Jones built AT&T Stadium, home of the Dallas Cowboys, with a retractable roof so that God could watch her football team squander season after season even though they have the best offensive line in the NFL.) The ancients didn't know anything about the great distances between heavenly objects.

Today, however, if we observe a solar eclipse, a comet, a blood red moon, or a falling star, we do so with the knowledge of the immensity of space, and we can give scientific explanations for these events without harboring one single thought that God might be trying to give us a sign. The ancients were also greatly affected by natural phenomena taking place on the earth's surface. Luke's Jesus continues his talk about signs by saying that "on the earth (there will be) distress among nations confused by the roaring of the sea and the waves." Back in the mid-nineties, I got a taste of what the mighty Mississippi can do when its banks can no longer contain the water. As terrifying as floods are today, imagine how helpless people felt about river floods and rising ocean tides in the ancient world. I'm sure only one thought would enter our minds in that day: "What is God trying to tell us?" Or worse, "Is this the end of the world?" Actually, their lives sucked so bad they hoped the end was near.

Verse 26 reflects this ancient response to natural disasters. Jesus said, "People will faint from fear and foreboding of what is coming upon the world, for the powers of the heavens will be shaken." The early Christians were as fearful as anyone else about nature's wrath. Yet unlike other people they had hope. And that hope came in the form of the cosmic Christ, the Christ who had become Lord over the entire cosmos, or world. Luke's Jesus describes the cosmic Christ: "Then they (the people) will see 'the Son of Man coming in a cloud' with power and great glory." The notion that the Son of Man would be coming in a cloud was significant because this meant that he was coming from the heavens, the place where God dwells. So when the sky begins to offer signs, and natural disasters are occurring, "stand up and raise your heads, because your redemption is drawing near," Jesus says in verse 28.

Like many other passages in the Bible, Luke 21 teaches us how reliant the ancient mind was on signs or omens. They had no other way to make predictions. They didn't have the *Farmer's Almanac* or Doppler radar. Yes, the *Farmer's Almanac* is my go-to mag for weather predictions. That, and my knee joints. The only thing they could predict were the seasons, which explains the parable of the fig tree Jesus tells in verses 29–30. And yet even the seasons can play tricks on a person. Weather can change drastically from one day to the next. Weather patterns are unpredictable in a lot of places around the world. So try to put yourself in the world of the ancients. Try to imagine having no idea if the world would last another day, month, or year. Life in the ancient world was fraught with fear of the unknown, and the only way they could possibly overcome their fear was to find a way to hope. Jesus became the hope of the early Christians. He became the cosmic Christ, the Lord of nature, and Ruler of the world.

Now let us leave the first century and bring our minds back to the twenty-first century. Theologically, we can hold on to the notion of the cosmic Christ and perhaps even his reappearance in history, yet we no longer have to look for signs of his appearance. We no longer have to look for shooting stars and planetary alignments to tell us that God is up to something. We no longer need to look up into the heavens for signs that Jesus is coming back or the world is coming to an end, or the rapture is about to take place, or whatever the doomsday theologians are teaching these days. We have simply outgrown the need to watch for signs of the times or listen to redneck comedians.

IT'S THE END OF THE WORLD AS WE KNOW IT

I have never understood the fascination with end-of-the-world predictions, mainly because I'm not all that interested in the world coming to an end. I know that billions of years from now the sun is going to burn out and life as we know it will cease to exist on this planet if it hasn't already been destroyed by then, yet I don't see how anyone thinks they can make an accurate prediction about the earth's or humanity's demise. December 21, 2012 has come and gone. Since you are reading this book after 2012, the world did not end as the Mayans allegedly predicted. Although they really didn't. They just ran out of calendar space. In truth, there were limited numbers of quality pin-up Mayan women and men so the village calendar maker decided to sell life insurance and design grass skirts instead.

Is the world as we know it going to end soon? Or, to put a Christian spin on this: is Jesus going to come back in *our* generation, although the New Testament claimed he was going to come back in *their* generation? (Scholars have long wondered why the early Christians wanted him to come back. I think I know the answer. He left them hanging with too many open-ended parables.) The answer to both questions is "no," although I guess a lot of things could happen to destroy or nearly destroy the earth or humanity in the near future: A nuclear holocaust, a disease pandemic, an asteroid or comet colliding with the earth, global climate change, or my favorite, an alien invasion. We could also run out of toilet paper, an event that would surely lead to mass extinction. The funny thing about alien invasions, however, is that if we are ever visited (and I doubt even the possibility of such a thing), I don't see why they would necessarily want to destroy us. What would be the purpose of that? Truly, if we are ever visited by aliens I suspect they will only be interested in our toilet paper.

There must be some psychological reason why human beings have always tinkered with end-time scenarios and prophecies. Even the biblical writers thought they would try their hand at it. Luke 21 is borrowing directly from Mark's Gospel, a section called "The Little Apocalypse." Apocalyptic writings in the ancient world usually include descriptions of future cataclysms. In this section in Luke, Jesus "predicts" the destruction of the temple in Jerusalem, which occurred about forty years after his death. This suggests to most scholars that the Gospel writers, putting pen to paper after the destruction of the temple, have merely gone back in history to attribute a prediction of the temple's destruction to Jesus. Whether this is true or not, the apocalyptic theme of destruction in this section in Luke seems to include more than just the destruction of the temple. "Heaven and earth will pass away," says Luke's Jesus, "but my words will not pass away." The Jewish and Christian traditions have always dabbled with apocalyptic scenarios such as the day of the Lord, the day of judgment, the Second Coming, the rapture, the tribulation, and the war of Armageddon. And after two-thousand years the interest in doomsday scenarios continues to interest and perhaps even delight some Christians. One thinks of the popularity of the *Left Behind* series[1] about the rapture. In those books, the return of Jesus is not exactly good news for most people. The fact that *Left Behind* is so popular tells me that humanity probably needs to hit the reset button.

I may be going out on a limb here, but I think it's safe to assume that all of this is utter hogwash. End-of-the-world predictions have been common throughout Christianity and other religions for almost 2,000 years. Thus, the public has little to fear from prophets who predict a particular date for the world's end. Failed predictions of the end of the world are as common as Chinese restaurants in American cities. Some of the predictions have been linked to the actions of Israel, earthquakes, comet or asteroid activities, the date June 6, 2006 (06/06/06, the "mark of the beast"), the return of the Hidden Imam in Islamic belief, Bible Code hysteria, and even a prediction that the Second Coming will occur in Puerto Rico. (After Hurricane Maria, I can't think of a better place for a returning Messiah.) There will always be people who look for and expect a literal end-of-the-world scenario as if this is part of God's master plan. And like the Y2K scare, the year 2012 produced its share of crazies who sold all their belongings and headed to the mountains in Colorado for a better chance of survival. (Do you think they're still there? I bet their weed is primo.) I frankly don't know how to respond to end-of-the-world predictions, even the ones that are found in our sacred Scriptures. I just chalk it all up to the ancient mindset which was extremely credulous about such things. In fact, life was often so miserable in the ancient world that they couldn't wait for the end, or at least a major shaking up of the natural order.

---

1. By Tim LaHaye and Jerry B. Jenkins, published by Tyndale House, 1995–2007.

I say that I'm not all that interested in such things, and yet once upon a time my cellphone's ringtone was from the band R.E.M. singing, "It's the end of the world as we know it." The song is actually poking fun at end-time scenarios, yet in a world of war, economic instability, and climate change, the song does a good job of exploiting our fears. I still claim that I'm not interested in end-time scenarios, yet I am interested in ending the world as we know it. That is, I am interested in producing a better world, if at all possible. This is the difference, in my mind, between bad religion and good religion. Bad religion focuses on the literal destruction of the world, or at least a significant portion of the human population. Good religion focuses on changing the world for the better. Bad Christianity focuses on the Second Coming, the rapture, and the tribulation period, all of which is terrible news for the "non-believer." Good Christianity focuses on the Kingdom of God in the here and now, which is good news for believers and non-believers alike.

THE GOSPEL GENERATION

One of the more fascinating fields of inquiry is the study of generations. Generational studies reveal noticeable differences between each generation (a generation is measured by eighteen-year increments). The term "generation gap" arose to describe the wide differences in cultural norms between members of a younger generation and their elders; they do not understand each other because of their different experiences, opinions, habits and behaviors. The dirty little secret of generational studies, however, is that each generation has their own hairstyles. That's pretty much it. The term "generation gap" first came into prominence in our culture in the 1960s. It described the seemingly vast cultural differences between the baby boomers (born between 1946 and 1964, of which I am a part) and their parents. Most experts agree that the gap between the Boomers and their predecessors is larger than all previous and subsequent gaps in the history of Western culture. Think of rock music, long hair on males, mini-skirts on females, large scale protests against the Vietnam War, the loosening of sexual mores, and increased drug usage, and the baby boomer generation quickly comes to mind.

This gap was also noticeable because of the large numbers of baby boomers, giving it unprecedented power and influence. The influence of the baby boomers was so significant that the entire generation was named "Man of the Year" by *TIME* magazine in 1966, which reveals how utterly sexist we were in 1966. The youth today (including my millennial children) may think they are more rebellious and less understood than all other previous generations in the history of the human race, but we baby boomers know better.

And yet as much as I might want to brag about my generation, I would be remiss not to mention the "G.I. Generation," what Tom Brokaw dubbed "The Greatest Generation," those rapidly disappearing folks who came of age during the Great Depression and World War II. Next was the "Silent Generation," the group that served as a buffer between the Greatest Generation and the baby boomers. My own parents are members of the Silent Generation and I'm pretty sure they wish there had been a buffer between them and me. In fact, one of the things you learn in generational studies is how every other generation is a dominant generation, while the generations in between are almost non-descript, contributing very little to the culture. After the baby boomers came the baby busters or Generation X (1964–1982, "X" denoting their perceived lack of a distinct identity), Generation Y or the Millennial Generation (1982–2000), and now Generation Z or the Internet Generation. Does anyone not realize that by naming the last three generations "X," "Y," and "Z," we have painted ourselves into an apocalyptic corner? Other names attributed to some of these recent generations include "the MTV Generation," "the Me Generation," and my favorite, "The Pepsi Generation," which causes obesity and diabetes.

Do generational studies have any relevance in the life of the church? You bet they do. The main dilemma in church life today is how to find a way to connect people who live on either side of the generation gap of the 1960s. The worship wars refer to those who prefer traditional worship in contrast to those who prefer contemporary worship. Generally speaking, pre-Boomers (people who came of age before the 1960s) prefer traditional worship, Boomers (people who came of age during the 1960s and 1970s) prefer a mix of traditional and contemporary, and post-Boomers (people who came of age after the 1970s) prefer contemporary worship (although not everyone fits neatly into these categories). All of this would seem to imply that we don't have enough in common to be a harmonious community. There is now some indication that young adults prefer more traditional and liturgical worship, leading to the odd scenario where the parents want "Entertainment Church" even as their offspring prefer "Authentic Church."

As a humorous side note, however, I've found one thing that seems to characterize Christians from all generations: our lack of evangelism. As one writer said, "The church today is raising a whole generation of mules. They know how to sweat and to work hard but they don't know how to reproduce themselves."[2]

2. Landis, *Cowboy Steward*, 117.

All this talk of generations makes me curious about how to understand Jesus' statement recorded in Luke 21:32: "Truly I tell you, this generation will not pass away until all things have taken place." What's he talking about? As noted above, in the ancient world people were constantly making predictions about the end of the world. In fact, almost every generation in human history has believed that their generation might be the last. Today, because of global warming and nuclear weaponry, we actually have more justification in predicting the end of the world, yet in the ancient world they were just as fearful (if not more so) about things happening in nature that were beyond their control.

Listen to the fear in the words put on the lips of Jesus in Luke 21:25f: "There will be signs in the sun, the moon [solar and lunar eclipses?], and the stars [shooting stars?], and on the earth distress among nations confused by the roaring of the sea and the waves [tsunamis?]. People will faint from fear and foreboding of what is coming upon the world, for the powers of the heavens will be shaken [earthquakes?]." If the writer, Luke, had stopped right there we would assume he is making a standard end-of-the-world prediction. People in the ancient world were naturally scared out of their wits when they experienced natural phenomenon of these sorts because they couldn't explain them scientifically. In verse 27, he adds a little twist: "Then they will see 'the Son of Man coming in a cloud' with power and great glory." This is a reference to Daniel 7:13, which gives a messianic explanation for the end of the world. In other words, the power of the coming messiah will cause these natural disasters to occur, creating fear and panic among the world's people. Not a pretty sight, for sure.

Now, let me reiterate what I noted earlier. I don't believe this is Jesus talking at this point, but rather the Gospel writer, Luke, who bought into the popular notion that the Messiah would appear someday "in a cloud with power and great glory." If you remember, Jesus didn't enter the world in such a manner the first time around, so many of the early Christians believed the second time he arrives on this planet he will make a much bigger splash. And in case the reader would be fearful of such a grand appearance, Luke writes the following comforting words in verse 28: "Now when these things begin to take place, stand up and raise your heads, because your redemption is drawing near." In other words, yes, the world is about to be shaken to its core, but don't worry because the Messiah, presumably Jesus, is on your side. Again, I believe these are the words of the evangelist, Luke, who really, really, really wants Jesus to come back. In fact, he wants him to come back with a big bang. Some scholars agree with me that this is the voice of the early church speaking, yet others claim Jesus himself believed he would come back in such a grand fashion. If I really thought Jesus wanted to come back in a kick-ass mood, I'm pretty sure I would give up preaching and start a dairy farm.

Verse 29, however, is the part where I believe the authentic voice of Jesus first appears in this passage. Jesus shares a brief parable with his listeners. He says, "Look at the fig tree and all the trees; as soon as they sprout leaves you can see for yourselves and know that summer is already near. So also, when you see these things taking place, you know that the kingdom of God is near." Doesn't that have a different tone than the dire warnings of signs in the heavens and natural disasters and such? Isn't it much kinder and gentler? That's right. George H.W. Bush was a messianic figure. Here, Jesus isn't talking about the end of the world, the coming of the Son of Man in a cloud, or anything quite so loud. Instead, he's talking about discerning the nearness of the kingdom of God in something as simple, quiet, and peaceful as sprouting leaves.

And when will this occur? "Truly I tell you, this generation will not pass away until all things have taken place." Here's where it gets tricky. If Jesus is saying that the current generation of people he is speaking to would still be around when the sun, moon, stars, and oceans go crazy and he shows up riding on a cloud with power and great glory, then he was wrong and we might as well label him a first-century crackpot. Because none of that happened. Yet if he meant that the current generation of people he is speaking to would still be around when the leaves on the trees sprout—an annual occurrence—then it all makes beautiful sense. Every generation, he is saying, is witness to the kingdom of God because it is as near and subtle and beautiful and non-threatening as the sprouting of the leaves on a tree. This is why we recently planted a tree in our front yard. We're the only neighbors who took advantage of our neighborhood's "free tree" program for theological reasons. This is what makes us such interesting neighbors.

If Jesus is right the people he ministered to became what I call "the Gospel Generation." Unlike all other generations in the history of humanity, however, the Gospel Generation didn't last a mere eighteen years. The Gospel Generation reveals itself again and again, anytime a generation of people are able to look at the simple and subtle signs around them and understand that the kingdom of God is as near to them as the leaves on the trees. This means my folks and I have a chance to bridge the generational gap, link arms, and forget about our hair differences.

The Greatest Generation is great not just because it survived poverty and destitution and saved the world from the Axis powers. They are great because they continue to reveal the nearness of the kingdom of God in their acts of civic responsibility and their unconditional love for their rebellious children and grandchildren. They are the Gospel Generation when they are at their best. The baby boomers are great not just because there are so many of them. They are great because they taught the world how the kingdom of God could come near in the struggle for justice and peace like no other generation before or since. They are the Gospel Generation when they are at their best. Generation X may complain that they have no identity, hence the "X," yet they become the Gospel Generation every time they remind us that compassion for the lonely and depressed is the heart of what it means to be human, and that people are not defined by how much money they have or how many possessions they own. They are the Gospel Generation when they are at their best. (I also like to tell my Generation X friends that I write "Merry X-mas" on my Christmas cards so they will know they are loved and appreciated by their more dominant baby boomer elders.) This is true for every generation. The gospel—"the kingdom of God is near"—is at the heart of every generation that remembers it.

Luke 23:33–43

When they came to the place that is called The Skull, they crucified Jesus there with the criminals, one on his right and one on his left. Then Jesus said, "Father, forgive them; for they do not know what they are doing." And they cast lots to divide his clothing. And the people stood by, watching; but the leaders scoffed at him, saying, "He saved others; let him save himself if he is the Messiah of God, his chosen one!" The Soldiers also mocked him, coming up and offering him sour wine, and saying, "If you are the King of the Jews, save yourself!" There was also an inscription over him, "This is the King of the Jews." One of the criminals who were hanged there kept deriding him and saying, "Are you not the Messiah? Save yourself and us!" But the other rebuked him, saying, "Do you not fear God, since you are under the same sentence of condemnation? And we indeed have been condemned justly, for we are getting what we deserve for our deeds, but this man has done nothing wrong." Then he said, "Jesus, remember me when you come into your kingdom." He replied, "Truly I tell you, today you will be with me in Paradise."

JESUS DOESN'T MEET OUR EXPECTATIONS

IF YOU ARE A Christian, your allegiance should lie ultimately with Jesus. He is, in a metaphorical sense, our king. Jesus was never a king in any literal sense. When we think of a king we have certain expectations about kingship. A king is someone who rules over a country and a people. In most cases in the pre-modern world, a man became king either through battle or inheritance. Sex change operations were not available. Perhaps we could argue that Jesus inherited his particular kingdom through inheritance, being the Son of God and all, whatever that means. At the same time, Jesus never sat on a throne and ruled over anyone. He certainly never went to battle against his enemies. Most scholars even doubt that he was literally a descendent of a king, namely David. Jesus, in other words, never met our expectations of what it means to be a king.

Let's look at the expectations people had for a messiah-king in Jesus' day, but first a word about the phrase "messiah-king." The word "messiah" is the Hebrew word that was translated into the Greek as *christos* or "Christ." Both words mean the "anointed one." The kings of Israel were often thought of as anointed by God. They were literally messiahs. So when we refer to Jesus as the Messiah or Christ we are claiming that he is the anointed king. And yet in what sense was or is he a king? Jesus' contemporaries were all familiar with the Old Testament prophecies of a future messiah-king, a descendent of David, who would one day assume the mantle of kingship and lead God's people into a time of peace and prosperity. A good example is found in Jeremiah 23:5-6: "The days are surely coming, says the LORD, when I will raise up for David a righteous Branch, and he shall reign as king and deal wisely, and shall execute justice and righteousness in the land. In his days Judah will be saved and Israel will live in safety. And this is the name by which he will be called: 'The Lord is our righteousness.'"

Jeremiah wrote these words shortly after the nation of Judah lost their king and their kingdom. In 587 BCE, the Babylonians sacked Jerusalem and removed Zedekiah from the throne, taking all possible future kings into exile. Understandably, Jeremiah's oracles reflect a very somber tone. At the same time he expresses genuine hope that someday a descendent of David will once again reign over Judah. Unfortunately, this never happened. There were other kings reigning over the Jews in subsequent years, yet none from the lineage of David. King Herod is a good example of this. He was half-human, half-turd.

Christians have always had a tendency to read this prophecy in Jeremiah 23—and many others like it—as referring to Jesus of Nazareth. Jesus is the king who inherited the throne of David. Again, that's not what literally happened. Jesus was rejected by many of his contemporaries precisely because he did not meet the expectations of a king born in the line of David. This disappointment in Jesus is clearly reflected in Luke 23:33-43. Jesus is nailed to a cross by the Roman government, with the support of many of the Jewish religious leaders. The Romans saw Jesus as a political agitator. The Jewish leaders saw him as a false messiah-king. Ironically, the Romans probably viewed Jesus as more of a potential threat to become a Jewish king than Jesus' own people did.

In Luke's recording of the crucifixion, Jesus is scoffed at three times. First, by the Jewish religious leaders who said, "He saved others; let him save himself if he is the Messiah of God, his chosen one!" This clearly indicates that the Jewish religious leaders, who were most familiar with the Old Testament prophecies, did not believe Jesus met the expectations of a Jewish messiah-king. Plus, they didn't appreciate a young upstart stealing their thunder. The Roman soldiers were the next ones to scoff at him, saying, "If you are the king of the Jews, save yourself!" According to Luke, the soldiers even put a mock inscription over Jesus' head, which read, "This is the King of the Jews." They wrote it in multiple languages so that their commanding officers would think they deserved a promotion. Didn't happen. Nevertheless, clearly they were ridiculing a man they viewed as unqualified to be a king, even a king of the lowly Jews. And yet, he must have been a threat to them or they would not have executed him. Finally, one of the two criminals who were hanging on either side of Jesus mocked him by saying, "Are you not the Messiah? Save yourself and us!" Even a man with nails in his wrists and feet has enough energy to ridicule Jesus. Or he was hoping Jesus was the real deal so that he could climb down from the cross and pick up the groceries he had promised his wife earlier in the day.

In the minds of most of his contemporaries, Jesus did not meet the expectations or requirements of a messiah-king as expressed in their prophetic hopes and dreams. And to be honest Jesus doesn't quite meet the expectations we modern folks have of a king, although he compares rather favorably to Donald Trump. He doesn't even meet the expectations we have of people we honor, or people we consider heroic. On our proverbial thrones, we prefer warriors, those who can wield the sword against real-life enemies. Jesus wasn't a warrior. We prefer the wealthy, the kings and queens of capitalism. Jesus distrusted wealth. We prefer the powerful, those who control the hearts and minds of the masses. Jesus rejected coercive power. We prefer to have on our thrones those with common sense, people who reflect the common wisdom of our day. Jesus' wisdom was not common. He expressed an alternative wisdom. For these reasons and more Jesus does not meet our modern expectations of someone worthy to be honored and respected as royalty.

Our country, of course, is not a monarchy, but a democracy. We elect people to our thrones, especially if they suck as human beings. And yet Jesus doesn't even meet the expectations of a good political candidate. Was Jesus a failure? By our modern American standards he was. He never sat on a throne or was elected to an office. He never had a successful business, made a lot of money in the stock market, or was named to the Fortune 500. He only had influence and power over a few uneducated peasants. He never won a Nobel Prize. He never made it on the New York Times best-seller list, or even published a book. In fact, he probably couldn't even read or write. I realize that statement startles those who harbor a high Christology; however, it's very possible that Jesus wrote "X" whenever he signed his name, just as we do when we want to shorten the word "Christmas." Oh, and by the way, he was executed as a common criminal. That will never qualify as a characteristic of success.

Nevertheless, does Jesus deserve to be our king? Yes, precisely because he does not meet our expectations he deserves to be our king. He didn't meet the expectations of his contemporaries who were looking for a messiah-king; he went beyond those expectations. He went beyond our expectations as well, not short of them. If there is one thing we ought to know by now it is this: our expectations fall short. We should know by now that our warring madness, our greedy ways, our lust for power, and our common sense will never be good enough. The world isn't getting any better with us in charge. Maybe we need a new king, one who doesn't conform to our shortsighted expectations. And yet look at what humanity has done to Jesus the king. We have failed to acknowledge him as our king and we have abused him, even to the point of crucifixion, because our expectations about him are warped by our views of success, honor, and heroism. We are like the criminal hanging next to Jesus who scoffed at him because we believe a true messiah-king would never be so unsuccessful.

On the other hand, the one person who didn't scoff at Jesus for failing to meet the expectations of a messiah-king was that other criminal hanging on the cross. After he scolded the first criminal for being so shortsighted, he said to Jesus, "Remember me when you come into your kingdom." In other words, "Jesus, when people finally come to their senses and realize you deserve to be king, I would love to serve in your Cabinet." Jesus' response to the criminal gives us all hope, especially those who have elected Jesus to be our king, sans hanging chads or Russian hacking: "Truly I tell you, today you will be with me in Paradise." Prepare the ballots. Let's drain the swamp.

Luke 24:13–35

Now on that same day two of them were going to a village called Emmaus, about seven miles from Jerusalem, and talking with each other about all these things that had happened. While they were talking and discussing, Jesus himself came near and went with them, but their eyes were kept from recognizing him. And he said to them, 'What are you discussing with each other while you walk along?' They stood still, looking sad. Then one of them, whose name was Cleopas, answered him, 'Are you the only stranger in Jerusalem who does not know the things that have taken place there in these days?' He asked them, 'What things?' They replied, 'The things about Jesus of Nazareth, who was a prophet mighty in deed and word before God and all the people, and how our chief priests and leaders handed him over to be condemned to death and crucified him. But we had hoped that he was the one to redeem Israel. Yes, and besides all this, it is now the third day since these things took place. Moreover, some women of our group astounded us. They were at the tomb early this morning, and when they did not find his body there, they came back and told us that they had indeed seen a vision of angels who said that he was alive. Some of those who were with us went to the tomb and found it just as the women had said; but they did not see him.' Then he said to them, 'Oh, how foolish you are, and how slow of heart to believe all that the prophets have declared! Was it not necessary that the Messiah should suffer these things and then enter into his glory?' Then beginning with Moses and all the prophets, he interpreted to them the things about himself in all the scriptures. As they came near the village to which they were going, he walked ahead as if he were going on. But they urged him strongly, saying, 'Stay with us, because it is almost evening and the day is now nearly over.' So he went in to stay with them. When he was at the table with them, he took bread, blessed and broke it, and gave it to them. Then their eyes were opened, and they recognized him; and he vanished from their sight. They said to each other, 'Were not our hearts burning within us while he was talking to us on the road, while he was opening the scriptures to us?' That same hour they got up and returned to Jerusalem; and they found the eleven and their companions gathered together. They were saying, 'The Lord has risen indeed, and he has appeared to Simon!' Then they told what had happened on the road, and how he had been made known to them in the breaking of the bread.

RECOGNITIONALLY CHALLENGED

HAVE YOU EVER HAD trouble recognizing someone? Everyone has trouble recognizing faces or remembering names on occasion. Some people even suffer from a serious recognition impairment called prosopagnosia, or face blindness. Prosopagnosia is much more severe than the ordinary occurrence of forgetting a face. On more than one occasion I have had the experience of walking into a local restaurant and hearing someone say to me, "Hi, how are you doing Dr. Watson?" I answer, "Fine, how are you?" I usually know I have met this person before, yet for the life of me I cannot place a name to their face or remember where I met them. This sort of thing happens to me quite frequently because in my profession more people recognize me than vice versa. To state this more arrogantly (and falsely), I am a "public figure."

The medical ailment called prosopagnosia is very rare. Prosopagnosics often find it difficult to recognize people they have encountered many times. In extreme cases, they have trouble recognizing even those people they spend the most time with, such as their spouses and their children. (Admittedly, this comes in handy from time to time.) One of the most common complaints of prosopagnosics is that they have trouble following the plot of television shows and movies because they cannot keep track of the identity of the characters.

I don't believe for a minute that the two men who walked with Jesus to a village called Emmaus were prosopagnosics, and yet they certainly had a difficult time recognizing him. To be politically correct, I'll refer to these two men as "recognitionally challenged." They didn't know, at first, that they were walking and talking with Jesus. According to Luke, this event occurred on the day of Jesus' resurrection. As they are walking to Emmaus (a small village about seven miles from Jerusalem) the two men are engaged in a passionate discussion about the day's events. We can only imagine how the conversation went back and forth about whether or not Jesus actually rose from the dead. I may sound a little anachronistic here, yet I suspect the phrase "horse crap" was used.

But then, out of the blue, Jesus enters the picture (although they didn't recognize him), engaging them in their conversation. At first Jesus acts ignorant about what has happened, forever proving that "telling the truth" is not an absolute moral necessity. One of the men (unless he is a woman), Cleopas, says to him, "Are you the only stranger in Jerusalem who does not know the things that have taken place there in these days?" He was referring, of course, to the crucifixion and the story they had heard about Jesus' tomb being empty. Jesus then launches into a long explanation about how the resurrection was "supposed" to happen, according to Scripture, which is odd because there isn't, as far as I know, a direct prophecy of a messianic resurrection. Even so, they do not recognize him. It was only when they make it to Emmaus, enters one of their homes, and shares a simple meal of bread with them, that they finally recognized Jesus.

Why did it take them so long to recognize him? I mean, after all, if he were a snake, he would have bitten them.[1] Were they looking for the European Jesus, yet saw a brown-skinned man in front of them? Whatever they knew about his racial profile, here he is, right in front of them, talking to them presumably for several hours. Why do they not recognize him for so long? They weren't the only ones who had this problem, by the way. The New Testament gives us other post-resurrection stories in which people fail to recognize the risen Lord (at first). The Apostle Paul did not immediately recognize Jesus in his vision on the Damascus road, which makes sense because he had never personally met Jesus, and Jesus seems to be fairly ghost-like in the Pauline account. Nevertheless, how do we explain the fact that some of Jesus' closest friends did not recognize him at first? According to John 20:14, Mary Magdalene did not immediately recognize Jesus at the tomb, and seven disciples did not immediately recognize him when

---

1. I don't mean to frighten people unnecessarily about snakes. One of my uncles was a rattlesnake roundup world champion (until he was bitten and nearly died). I also used to babysit a college friend's five-and-a-half-feet long black snake back in the day and I never got bit, although my sister nearly bit my head off when I let the snake loose in her bedroom.

he appeared on the shore of the sea, a story related in John 21:4. Why did so many people fail to recognize the risen Lord (assuming, of course, that these stories represent actual events)? Did he grow a David Letterman-like beard so quickly?

One reason may have been that they didn't expect to see him. When a loved one dies we may want to see them alive, yet we certainly don't expect to see them alive. Our emotions at a time like this can lead to contradictory experiences. On the one hand, the desire to see the newly-deceased person is so strong that we imagine seeing them alive in various places. In my pastoral role, people have told me things like, "I kept thinking he was going to start breathing in his coffin," or "I saw someone in the mall who looked just like her, and for a moment I thought it might have been her," or even, "I was driving the other day and my dad (recently deceased) was sitting in the passenger's seat, talking to me." I know; creepy, right? We have a very difficult time letting go of our deceased loved ones, so much so, in fact, that we often imagine seeing them alive in some form or another.[2]

Surely the disciples must have had the same sort of feelings, a strong desire to see Jesus alive. Some scholars believe this is why there are post-resurrection stories in the first place. The point is, as much as we want to see our deceased loved ones pull up in our driveway or appear in line at the ice cream stand, we know it's not going to happen. It could be, therefore, that the two disciples walking toward Emmaus do not recognize Jesus because, as much as they want him to be alive, they simply do not expect him to be alive. They aren't looking for him. This could account for the delayed recognition, especially if he appeared differently than they remembered him, what with a five o'clock shadow and all.

This leads to a second possible explanation for the disciples being recognitionally challenged: Jesus' appearance may have been altered. Have you ever run into someone you have known for a long time, yet did not recognize that person because he or she had changed a lot in appearance? (As I write these words, I'm hanging out on the beach with my wife and decided to shave my goatee and mustache earlier in the week. I'm trying to grow it back, yet I'm afraid my parishioners will mistake me for a younger Jeff Bridges when I return.) Perhaps they had added a few extra pounds or shed a few. Maybe their hair was grayer or disappearing altogether. Is it possible that the appearance of Jesus to the disciples on the road to Emmaus was something like that? Is it possible that they do not recognize him because he

---

2. I have learned to never question people's accounts of these experiences because, well, I believe in zombies; therefore, I have no reason to be critical. If you don't believe in zombies, then I encourage you to shop in Walmart after midnight.

is somehow different? We can speculate about how he was different, yet we just don't have enough information.

Willi Marxsen, in his book, *The Resurrection of Jesus of Nazareth*, points out how difficult it is to determine what the post-resurrection stories are trying to tell us about Jesus' appearance. He writes,

> The 'body' of Jesus is conceived of in different terms at the different appearances. On the one hand we have the 'material' features (the tomb was empty; Jesus eats; he can be touched), on the other, Jesus can pass through closed doors. The two are not easily reconcilable.[3]

We can only guess why the post-resurrection stories are so vague in telling us what Jesus was like. So answering the question, "Why are the two disciples on the road to Emmaus recognitionally challenged?" is not easy to answer. Were they just not expecting Jesus to be alive? Were they not very familiar with what he looked like in the first place, given the fact that they were not part of his inner circle? Or, had Jesus' appearance been altered beyond recognition? Why did it take them so long to recognize who this man was? This is assuming that the story itself is not horse crap.

Instead of focusing on how they are recognitionally challenged we should focus on the moment when they do finally recognize him: in the breaking of the bread. We can speculate until the cows come home about why the early disciples had trouble recognizing the risen Jesus, yet there is one thing we know for certain: the early church experienced the risen Jesus primarily in the breaking of the bread.[4] Matthew quotes Jesus as saying, "Where two or three are gathered in my name, I am there among them." What happened when two or three (or more) of the early Christians gathered in his name? They broke bread. They may have played Frisbee golf as well, although there is no record of that. Luke tells us that at the moment Jesus took bread, blessed, and broke it, the disciples' "eyes were opened and they recognized him." No longer were they recognitionally challenged.

Marxsen suggests that Jesus' manifestation of himself to the two disciples at supper is the center of the story. He writes, "I . . . think it very probable that this story was originally designed to exemplify the presence of Jesus at the common meal of the early church—a presence which had been constantly experienced as reality."[5] The Lord's Supper, both then and now, is an eye-opening event. For millions of Christians throughout history, the

---

3. Marxsen, *Resurrection of Jesus of Nazareth*, 67.
4. Can anyone tell me exactly when the cows are coming home?
5. Marxsen, *Resurrection of Jesus of Nazareth*, 160.

observance of communion with the breaking of the bread and the pouring of the wine has been the ultimate object lesson. I have no idea why. Perhaps we just like to eat.

A CONVERSATION PIECE

I love a good conversation. I love to engage in good old-fashioned chit-chat. Of course, good conversation is an art form. Some people are better at it than others. One of the best pieces of advice I've ever heard says that a gossiper talks about others, a bore talks about herself, and a brilliant conversationalist talks about you. Sometimes this is rather tricky. When I go home to Texas to see family, I often get stuck visiting relatives with whom I have very little in common, except for a few ounces of DNA. It's often very tricky just finding something to talk about that won't lead to a red-faced argument, especially with the ubiquitous presence of FOX News on every television screen.

At the annual White House Correspondent's Dinner a few years ago, comedian and *Saturday Night Live* star Seth Meyers told members of Congress that he wasn't all that impressed when Democrats and Republicans sat together at that year's State of the Union Address. He said that the sight of people with radically different views and opinions sitting together is not all that different than what happens every Thanksgiving in most American homes. Have any of you have ever had to endure a family gathering where a Dallas Cowboy fan has to sup with a rabid (irrational) Washington Redskins fan? Not a pretty sight. So what is often needed in these situations is safe conversational territory. If you are not exactly a brilliant conversationalist, then you need a safe, neutral conversation piece.

Originally, a conversation piece was a portrait depicting a group of people united in conversation about something. The observers would look at the portrait and speculate about what the people in the portrait were talking about. (That seems rather stupid, but I'll go with it here.) Later on, the phrase "conversation piece" acquired a broader meaning. It came to refer to any objects or topics that were perceived to be interesting enough to spark conversation. Nowadays a conversation piece might just be something that is happening in the world or in one's own neighborhood. By the way, has anyone ever invented a better conversation starter than the weather? Whoever came up with the idea of the Weather Channel should win a Nobel Peace Prize for, well, peace.

Speaking of the weather, I had a terrifying weather experience not too long ago. I was traveling back home to Texas to visit family and friends. I flew in to DFW airport and was already enduring a three-hour layover when I learned that my short flight to West Texas had been delayed because of inclement weather. The word "inclement" means "no mercy." Perfect word. After waiting about forty-five minutes for my delay, the flight was canceled due to lightning. Along with a couple dozen other irate customers, I lined up at the service desk to reschedule my flight. After about thirty minutes we were told that there were no flights available for two days. We were then told that our luggage would be available in terminal "B-8," so I scurried down the escalator in that direction.

I waited in B-8 for about thirty minutes, yet to no avail. No luggage was coming. They told us the luggage was outside on a cart and the workers were not allowed to retrieve the luggage because of lightning. Then I went to get a rental car, which required about a 15-minute van drive to the car rental agencies. It wasn't until my fourth stop at a rental agency that I found one that would rent one-way to West Texas. I left DFW airport at about midnight and began a four-and-a-half hour drive. Along the way I saw a funnel cloud, was belted by marble-sized hail, and experienced torrential rain and wind that would blow over an SUV. At one point the National Weather Service interrupted the radio and said that I was heading for tennis ball-sized hail and 60 mph winds, so I immediately took cover under a bridge. Eventually I made it safely to my destination.

That story may not be as dramatic as some weather events you may have experienced, and yet I got a lot of mileage out of it with my family. It was a lot safer than talking politics with my family in ultra-red Texas.

This compels me to wonder about the conversational experiences of the two men who were walking to Emmaus. We know only the name of one of them, Cleopas, and we know that they were disciples, or followers of Jesus. We don't know how long they had been disciples of Jesus because they weren't part of the original Twelve, so maybe they had been following Jesus for only a short time. Chances are they had traveled the seven miles from Emmaus to Jerusalem for the festival of Passover and while there they became part of the drama of Jesus' final week. We also know that they witnessed some of the events that led to Jesus' death. Maybe they had actually witnessed his crucifixion and were privy to the knowledge that Jesus' tomb was found empty that very morning. Whether or not they had anything to do with the Jesus movement before that final week of Jesus' life, they were certainly a part of it now.

So here are these two men, Cleopas and his friend, walking home to their village, and I seriously doubt that they were talking about the weather. Luke tells us that while they are walking to Emmaus, the risen Jesus suddenly accompanies them, but they don't know it is him. To continue with my speculation started in the previous section, maybe they didn't recognize Jesus because they really didn't know him that well. Maybe the only time they saw him he was a battered and bloodied figure hanging on a cross. Maybe they didn't recognize him because they assumed he was dead and they were so traumatized they wouldn't have even recognized their own mothers. Maybe they didn't recognize him because his resurrected "body" was not exactly the same as they had known before. There are probably other explanations for this, including the possibility that this story is just part of Luke's overactive imagination (i.e. horse crap).

Regardless, Jesus asks them, "What are you discussing with each other while you walk along?" He knew they weren't talking about politics, the weather, or sports. The Jerusalem Jaguars were playing out of town that weekend. There was only one thing to discuss, and Luke tells us they were sad while discussing it. By asking them what they were discussing, Jesus is feigning ignorance. He knows very well what they are talking about. He knows what the topic of the day is. He was there. But again, they don't know this is Jesus. Even in this era before telephones, television, email, the internet, and CB radios, the two men are astounded that anyone who had been in Jerusalem the past week did not know what had happened. Can you imagine the Facebook frenzy or Twitter tsunami today if someone had walked out of their tomb?

Have you ever been surprised to learn that someone has no clue about the big news of the day? A few days after Osama bin Laden was killed by the Navy Seals, a friend told me that a friend called her and asked, "What is this about Osama being killed? Who is he?" Really? How could someone not know about Osama bin Laden or his death? Can a person put their head in the sand that deeply? That's a rhetorical question in an age when we all get to live in our own customized and personalized bubbles.

That's sort of the response of Cleopas and his friend to Jesus' question. Mister, where have *you* been? What were you doing in Jerusalem all week? Have you been hitting the hash pipe a little too much? Cleopas asks, "Are you the only stranger in Jerusalem who does not know the things that have taken place there in these days?" And then he proceeds to talk about all that had happened to Jesus in terms of his death and subsequent empty tomb. All they knew was that Jesus was executed and now his body is missing. And they are sad.

Like all of Jesus' followers they must have thought Jesus was going to take them to new heights. They must have thought that their lives were going to be all blue skies and calm waters from now on. Instead, their flight is canceled, their luggage is lost, and now they have to drive home amidst dark funnel clouds, pelting hail and rain, and fierce winds. Their journey just got difficult. They have a "conversation piece" that will, unfortunately, last a long, long time . . . or so they assume.

But suddenly there is a change in weather. (You know what everyone says everywhere I have ever lived? If you don't like the weather here, just wait until tomorrow because it will change. The only thing that doesn't change is the fact that everyone thinks their neck of the woods experiences the most unpredictable weather on the planet.) Suddenly the clouds break apart, the rain and hail ceases, the wind calms down, and the tornadoes choose another path. This happens as suddenly and as surprisingly as a tornado, yet as calmly and serenely as a faint breeze. Cleopas and his friend invite Jesus to stay with them for the night. He obliges. As their guest he breaks bread with them, they recognize who he is, and then he vanishes from their sight.

This is a magnificent and mysterious story. All we know at the end of the day is that these two obscure followers of Jesus are witnesses to the most important and mind-boggling conversation piece you and I will ever discuss: the Resurrection. Is it a safe topic to discuss among those who have very different views and opinions about domestic and foreign policy? Who knows? The good thing about discussing the Resurrection story is that it is not just a conversation piece. It is also a *conversion* piece. (Yes, you may applaud now.) It can change our hearts and our lives as quickly as a West Texas grassfire and as ferociously as an Alabama tornado. And at least it gives us something to talk about.

Luke 24:36–48

While they were talking about this, Jesus himself stood among them and said to them, "Peace be with you." They were startled and terrified, and thought that they were seeing a ghost. He said to them, "Why are you frightened, and why do doubts arise in your hearts? Look at my hands and my feet; see that it is I myself. Touch me and see; for a ghost does not have flesh and bones as you see that I have." And when he had said this, he showed them his hands and his feet. While in their joy they were disbelieving and still wondering, he said to them, "Have you anything here to eat?" They gave him a piece of broiled fish, and he took it and ate in their presence. Then he said to them, "These are my words that I spoke to you while I was still with you—that everything written about me in the law of Moses, the prophets, and the psalms must be fulfilled." Then he opened their minds to understand the scriptures, and he said to them, "Thus it is written, that the Messiah is to suffer and to rise from the dead on the third day, and that repentance and forgiveness of sins is to be proclaimed in his name to all nations, beginning from Jerusalem. You are witnesses of these things.

EPIC LOG: THE ELEPHANT IN THE ROOM

A sermon preached on the day St. Andrew United Church of Christ, Louisville, Kentucky, voted to become an "Open and Affirming" Congregation

ONE OF MY FAVORITE types of humor is the elephant joke. Believe it or not, there is a history to the elephant joke genre. According to Wikipedia, they first appeared in the United States in 1962 in Texas (of all places, because as you know, there are a lot of elephants there) and gradually spread across the United States. By July 1963, elephant jokes were ubiquitous and millions of people tried to construct more and more jokes according to the same formula. Here's a sample:

> Q: How can you tell that an elephant is in the bathtub with you?
> A: By the smell of peanuts on its breath.
>
> Q: How can you tell that an elephant has been in your refrigerator?
> A: By the footprints in the butter.

Obviously, elephant jokes have a certain kind of flair about them. According to the website, they "rely upon absurdity and incongruity for their humor, and a contrast with the normal presumptions of knowledge about elephants."

Isaac Asimov did some writing about humor years ago, and he discusses one particular elephant joke that is more sophisticated in its humor than others. A joke was told in the aftermath of the murder of Lee Harvey Oswald by Jack Ruby, who had walked into Dallas police headquarters carrying a gun:

> Q: What did the Dallas chief of police say when the elephant walked into the police station?
> A: Nothing! He didn't notice.

In other words, to not notice Jack Ruby walking into the police station is about as absurd as not noticing an elephant walking into the police station.

Even before the elephant joke began making its appearance in the early 1960s, the notion of an "elephant in the *room*" was born, which, of course, was used in telling the joke about Jack Ruby and the Dallas chief of police. According to the *Oxford English Dictionary*, the *New York Times* first used the phrase in an article on June 20, 1959: "Financing schools has become a problem about equal to having an elephant in the living room. It's so big you just can't ignore it." The phrase, "elephant in the room" is an idiom for an obvious truth that is being ignored or goes unaddressed.

In some weird way, probably as a result of my overactive imagination, this reminds me of the story in Luke 24. Jesus appears to the disciples after his execution and says, "Peace be with you." To ignore Jesus in that situation would be like ignoring an elephant in the room. A man who had been executed a few days earlier and is now standing in your room asking you to look at his hands and feet, to touch his wounds, and asking for something to eat is obviously something too big to ignore.

Today, at this time and place in history, there is an elephant standing right in the middle of our sanctuary. We can no longer ignore it. We have to address it. This elephant, which I will name in a moment, relates to our congregational meeting following worship today, a meeting which will decide whether St. Andrew will officially become Open and Affirming or not (or not yet). In case you are somehow out of the loop, "Open and Affirming" is an official designation given to congregations in the United Church of Christ which "publicly welcome gay, lesbian, bisexual, and transgender people (LGBT) into their full life and ministry." You may say we already do this, so why the official designation? Well, my response to that is that we do welcome folks from the LGBT community into the full life and ministry of our church, yet the question is whether we have done so publicly.

If we choose to do so, becoming Open and Affirming (ONA) will accomplish two things. First, it will help us send a public welcome to the LGBT community. By putting our name on the ONA list through our national office in Cleveland, members of the community and those who are sympathetic to the community can find us more easily. In that sense, an ONA designation serves as an evangelism tool. It helps us to reach out to a community that is often ignored by other churches (as if they are an elephant in the room). Second, an official ONA designation affirms what our church constitution says in Article V, #3: "We believe that all who desire to journey with us in faith are welcome to become full members and participants in the life of the church, regardless of, but not limited to, membership in another church, gender, race, age, sexual orientation, socio-economic status, marital circumstance, ethnic origin, theological perspective or physical/mental challenges." To be frank, if we vote down an official ONA designation for our church, we are in essence contradicting our constitution.

I want us to be very clear about this because I know there are a lot of concerns, doubts, and confusion about what we are going to be voting on in a little while. An official ONA designation means that our name will go on a list in Cleveland so that LGBT people and their supporters can find us, and it will affirm our already existing constitution. But we can't just say it, we have to be it. I have heard many people in the past few weeks make the comment, "We already *are* Open and Affirming, so why do we need to vote on it?" My response to that is that, no, we are not open and affirming; we are *closeted* and affirming. Until our welcome to the LGBT community becomes public, we are not "open," we are "closeted" as a congregation. At most, we are limited in our openness.

I realize that we have talked about this issue so much in the last couple of months that it feels a bit like beating a dead horse. But beating a dead horse means that we have resolved an issue and any more discussion about it is futile. This may apply when we wake up tomorrow morning, yet for now we still have an issue to resolve. And besides, today we are talking about elephants, not horses. (That comes next week when the Kentucky Derby comes to town.)

So, what is the elephant in the room? The answer, already alluded to, is that members of the LGBT community are already here in this room with us. They are part of our church family as well as our biological families. Most, if not all of you, already know this, but the reason I refer to this as "the elephant in the room" is because we often talk about the Open and Affirming issue as if it really doesn't apply to us, as if it is an academic issue. We assume we can talk about it calmly and rationally because "it's not personal." We assume it's a moral quandary that we just need to discuss and pray about. Well, to the contrary, this is personal for a lot of people, gay and straight. It is not just an academic issue. It is not just a moral quandary. It is certainly not just a "matter of biblical interpretation." When I spent several years in graduate school researching and responding to the research of others about the issue of homosexuality, I never thought it was a dry, intellectual endeavor. I always knew that we were talking about living and breathing human beings with feelings.

According to Luke's Gospel, when the disciples of Jesus first saw him after the resurrection, they thought they were seeing a ghost. He couldn't be real flesh and bones, could he? So to prove that he was real, he asked them, "Have you anything here to eat?" (I guess being dead for several days would make one a little hungry.) They gave him some fish and he ate it.

Lesbians, gays, bisexuals, and transgender folks are real flesh and bones. They eat, sleep, work, and play just like straight people. We all share the same DNA. We're all created from the same star dust. We're all children of God.

Members of the LGBT community are not only in *our* room. They are present in virtually every faith community in every corner of the world. As they stand in our midst they want nothing more than to say to the rest of us, "Peace be with you." And yet like those original disciples who experienced the risen Christ many Christians are startled, terrified, and frightened by their "sudden" presence (or what many perceive as sudden). This is what we call "homophobia." The heterosexual majority may not be treating them as ghosts per se, yet they often treat them as if they are invisible. The church does its best to keep them hidden from view, closeted from their fellow parishioners. Or, in congregations like our own, congregations that allow people to be visible and un-closeted within the protective womb of our church family, there yet remains the issue of visibility to the wider community that is at stake.

Becoming an officially ONA church begins a process whereby the visible in here becomes the visible out there. It begins a process whereby we move from being "Closeted and Affirming" to "Open and Affirming." Our personal preference might be that our openness toward and affirmation of gay and lesbian people be limited to this room on Sunday morning. Yet I suspect we all realize deep down inside that this issue isn't about personal preferences. God gave us a conscience so that we can overcome our personal preferences and prejudices. That's one of the things that separate us from the rest of the animals (even elephants). We don't have to make all of our decisions based on self-interest. We can be altruistic and consider the interests of others, even if it makes us uncomfortable. So maybe we should treat today's congregational meeting as a moral quandary rather than an exercise of personal preference. And our moral quandary is this: Do we wish for members of the LGBT community to be treated as invisible ghosts or do we wish for them to be treated as flesh-and-bone people? If the latter is what we think we are called to do, then we have an opportunity in a few minutes to take a step in that direction.

Well, that's the elephant in the room. No need to be one any longer. In fact, by tomorrow morning it can be the dead horse. All I ask of each one of you is that you do what I had to do years ago when I left the narrow confines of a small West Texas town—not exactly a gay-friendly environment—to go back to college. I had to really grow in my thinking. My educational journey eventually led me to graduate from two Southern Baptist universities where I majored in the field of ethics, the study of standards of conduct and moral judgment. (I figured I would study something that I didn't know much about.)

I still remember the first time I researched the topic of homosexuality. It was the late 1980s and the first author I read on the subject suggested that this issue will define the direction of Christianity for the next generation. I read and I read. I learned, as many of you have, that the Scriptures are not as clear about this topic as many Christians would have us believe. Just as Luke tells us that Jesus opened the minds of his disciples "to understand the Scriptures," so have many contemporary Christians opened their minds to the possibility that "God is still speaking" on this topic just as God spoke to previous generations about slavery and the rights of women in a way that seemingly contradicted the clear teaching of Scripture. In fact, if I may be bold and provocative for a moment, let me suggest that voting against an official Open and Affirming designation today in the presence of gay and lesbian brothers and sisters would be similar to voting against the abolition of slavery or civil rights legislation in the presence of African-Americans, or the voting rights of women in the presence of women.

I'll conclude by saying that I completely understand the anguish some of you are feeling. As your pastor I want you to know that no matter what happens today or how you vote I will continue to be your pastor. I realize that even if we disagree about this issue we have more commonalities than differences. We are all flawed human beings, just trying to understand our world and our place in it. However, God's grace is bigger than all our flaws, shortcomings, and sins. God will blanket us with unconditional love whether we have the letters "ONA" on a list in Cleveland or not. I just hope that regardless of the outcome today, each and every one of you will continue to take your faith seriously, that you will seek God's guidance in all your pursuits, and that you will find the face of Christ in everyone you meet. May God bless and protect us as we venture into uncharted territory, a land where elephants dwell and humans dare to tread.

Bibliography

Borg, Marcus J. *Conflict, Holiness and Politics in the Teachings of Jesus.* Harrisburg: Trinity Press International, 1984.

———. *Meeting Jesus Again for the First Time: The Historical Jesus and the Heart of Contemporary Faith.* New York: HarperCollins, 1995.

———. *The Heart of Christianity: Rediscovering a Life of Faith.* New York: HarperCollins, 2003.

Borg, Marcus J. and John Dominic Crossan. *The First Christmas: What the Gospels Really Teach About Jesus's Birth.* New York: HarperOne, 2007.

Cobb, John B., Jr. *Can Christ Become Good News Again?* St. Louis: Chalice, 1991.

Commager, Henry Steele. "Religion and Politics in American History." In *Religion and Politics*, edited by James E. Wood Jr., 37–57. Waco, TX: Baylor University Press, 1983.

Crossan, John Dominic. *God & Empire: Jesus Against Rome, Then and Now.* New York: HarperCollins, 2007.

———. *Jesus: A Revolutionary Biography.* New York: HarperCollins, 1994.

Eck, Diana L. *A New Religious America: How a "Christian Country" has Become the World's Most Religiously Diverse Nation.* New York: HarperCollins, 2002.

Ehrman, Bart D. *Jesus: Apocalyptic Prophet of the New Millennium.* New York: Oxford University Press, 1999.

Eliot, George. *Adam Bede.* London: John Blackwood, 1859.

Fromm, Erick. *Escape from Freedom.* New York: Holt McDougal, 1941.

Kraybill, Donald B. *The Upside-Down Kingdom.* Scottsdale, PA: Herald, 1990.

Landis, Kevin. *The Cowboy Steward: The Cowboy Way to the Christian Life.* New York: iUniverse, 2006.

Marxsen, Willi. *The Resurrection of Jesus of Nazareth.* Philadelphia: Fortress, 1970.

Patterson, Stephen J. "Dirt, Shame, and Sin in the Expendable Company of Jesus." In *Profiles of Jesus*, edited by Roy W. Hoover, 195–222. Santa Rosa: Polebridge, 2002.

Pinker, Steven. *The Better Angels of Our Nature: Why Violence has Declined.* New York: Penguin, 2011.

Rawls, John. "A Theory of Justice." In *Ethics: History, Theory, and Contemporary Issues*, edited by Steven M. Cahn and Peter Markie, 621–40. New York: Oxford University Press, 1998.

Wink, Walter. *The Powers that Be: Theology for a New Millennium.* New York: Doubleday, 1998.

www.ingramcontent.com/pod-product-compliance
Lightning Source LLC
Chambersburg PA
CBHW071243230426
43668CB00011B/1569